THE HANDBOOK OF INVESTMENT TECHNOLOGY

THE HANDBOOK OF INVESTMENT TECHNOLOGY

A State-of-the-Art
Guide to Selection,
Implementation
& Utilization

KEVIN J. MERZ
AND
JOSEPH ROSEN
Editors

McGraw-Hill
New York   San Francisco   Washington, D.C.   Auckland   Bogotá
Caracas   Lisbon   London   Madrid   Mexico City   Milan
Montreal   New Delhi   San Juan   Singapore
Sydney   Tokyo   Toronto

McGraw-Hill

A Division of The McGraw-Hill Companies

© Richard D. Irwin, a Times Mirror Higher Education Group, Inc. company, 1997

Library of Congress Cataloging-in-Publication Data

Rosen, Joseph.
  The handbook of investment technology : a state-of-the-art guide to selection, implementation & utilization / Joseph Rosen, Kevin J. Merz.
    p.   cm.
  Includes index.
  ISBN 0-7863-0996-2
  1. Financial services industry—Data processing—Planning.
  2. Information technology—Planning. 3. Client-server computing.
  4. Information resources management.   I. Merz, Kevin J.   II. Title.
  HG4515.5.R67   1997
  332.6'0285—dc20   96-8790

Printed in the United States of America
2 3 4 5 6 7 8 9 0   DO   3 2 1 0 9 8

To our wives and best friends, Anne Merz and Rachel Rosen

ABOUT THE AUTHORS

Mike Abbaei (Chapter 3)
Mr. Abbaei is senior vice president and chief information officer for Legg Mason Wood Walker, Incorporated. His expertise is in client/server technology, with an emphasis on financial and brokerage applications specifically in equity and fixed-income trading systems. Previously, he worked at Kidder Peabody & Co. as a senior vice president in charge of the distributed technology department. Mr. Abbaei has also held positions at Lehman Brothers, First Boston Corporation, and Western Electric/Bell Laboratories. He received a BA in computer science from Kean College and an MS in management from the New Jersey Institute of Technology.

C. Warren Axelrod (Chapter 5)
Dr. Axelrod is president of the information systems and technology consulting firm of C.W. Axelrod Associates, Inc., in Great Neck, New York. He has had extensive experience in evaluating and implementing sophisticated new technologies and developing state-of-the-art systems.

At HSBC Securities, where he was senior vice president of corporate information systems, Dr. Axelrod introduced relational-database technology for the analysis of marketing information, advanced digital data distribution systems, computer- to-computer interfaces with customers and business partners, and touch-screen customer workstations for real-time pricing and order entry.

He has also implemented for an advanced high-speed computer printing environment has pioneered the use of simulation for computer performance measurement and evaluation, and has obtained a patent for mark-sense card technology used on the floors of the New York and American Stock Exchanges. Dr. Axelrod's consulting clients in financial services include several internationally-based brokerages and firms. He has published two books on computer management and more than 60 articles and papers on a variety of computer-related topics.

Dr. Axelrod holds a B.Sc. in electrical engineering and an M.A. in economics and statistics, both with honors, from the University of Glasgow, and a Ph.D. in managerial economics from the Samuel Curtis Johnson Graduate School of Management at Cornell University.

Dean S. Barr (Chapter 16)

Mr. Barr is chief investment officer for Advanced Investment Technology. His background includes institutional block and computerized trading with Goldman, Sachs. Mr. Barr has worked with some of the country's largest and most sophisticated institutional investors and is an authority and expert in the development of advanced computational systems for market and security analysis. He is a former adjunct professor of international finance at Eckard College and the author of several technical papers on artificial intelligence. Mr. Barr received his BA from Cornell University and his MBA from New York University Graduate School of Business.

Don Berliner (Chapter 17)

Mr. Berliner is head of the management information and analysis department at Kenmar Advisory Corporation. He has been involved with computer systems since the early 1960s and has worked for a variety of firms, including both Fortune 500 companies and smaller businesses, as well as his own consulting firm. He has published a number of articles and books, both in the general business and microcomputer fields. Mr. Berliner graduated from the Massachusetts Institute of Technology with a B.S. in applied mathematics, and from the University of Pennsylvania, where he received masters degrees in electrical engineering and operations research.

Elizabeth C. Church (Chapter 9)

Ms. Church is vice president, new business development, for Advent Software, Inc., responsible for the strategic development of new markets and business lines. A principal in the firm, her focus is on identifying new products for existing target markets, new markets for existing products, and new ancillary business opportunities. Ms. Church also has responsibility for cultivating enterprisewide, strategic relationships in the investment industry, and contract negotiation. Prior to joining Advent, Ms. Church spent six years in the investment industry as a securities analyst and portfolio manager. She received her MBA in finance from the University of North Carolina at Chapel Hill.

Michael Frank (Chapter 14)

Mr. Frank is managing director of information systems at ESI Securities Co. He is responsible for the planning, design, and operation of data systems, voice communications, and data communications. Among the systems he has helped ESI deploy is TEAM, a proprietary technology platform for order routing and trade order management.

Mr. Frank's achievements at ESI are the culmination of 20 years of experience in implementing and managing computer technologies. Prior to joining ESI, he held the position of vice president with the technology strategic planning organization at Bankers Trust. Prior to Bankers Trust, he held the position of vice president at First Boston, where he was responsible for developing and implementing the technical infrastructure for that firm's new trade-processing architecture, including CASE tool development, communications architecture, system security, and workstation support.

Mr. Frank holds a bachelor of engineering degree from the City University of New York, with graduate work at Fordham University.

Claire L. Frankel (Chapter 11)

Ms. Frankel, as vice president of the National Securities Clearing Corporation, is a hands-on data/object designer and a large-scale project manager. She designed minicomputer hardware configurations as an engineer in the late 1970s to early 1980s, when she switched to designing and delivering software applications for power and process control plants, satellite television, and banking applications. For the past seven years, Ms. Frankel has worked in the securities industry, delivering mission critical applications and relational databases. She is one of the three U.S. delegates to the International Standards Organization's Working Group 7 on the data field dictionary.

Ralph Frankel (Chapter 15)

Mr. Frankel is a principal consultant at CSC Consulting, where he is spearheading a large object-oriented and three-tier system for a major broadcast firm. Previously, he served as a director of object technology for SHL Systemhouse, a major systems integrator. Mr. Frankel has extensive experience with systems architecture and design and development, particularly with client/server technology. As a recognized expert in distributed computing, object technology, and database design, he is frequently quoted in industry periodicals. He has consulted at some of Wall Street's major investment firms working on trading and market data systems.

Robert F. Gartland (Chapter 12)

Mr. Gartland is a managing director of Morgan Stanley & Co., Incorporated, and head of Morgan Stanley Services, a business unit that provides global custody and clearing services to corporations and institutions.

Mr. Gartland joined Morgan Stanley in 1979 as manager of financial planning and analysis, serving as an internal consultant to the head of information services and operations. In addition, he has held the positions of vice president of money cashiering operations; head of finance, administration, and operations for Morgan Stanley International in Europe; and chief information officer of Morgan Stanley Group. He was appointed as a managing director of the firm in 1987 and assumed his current role as head of Morgan Stanley Services in January 1991. Mr. Gartland is a member of the board of directors of the National Securities Clearing Corporation, chairs its international committee, and is a member of the board of Comprehensive Software Systems.

Mr. Gartland has an M.S. in industrial engineering from Columbia University and an undergraduate degree from Hofstra University.

Esther Eckerling Goodman (Chapter 10)

Ms. Goodman is the chief operating officer and senior executive vice president of Kenmar Asset Allocation Inc., an asset management firm resonsible for the design and active management of managed futures investments for large institutional and private clients throughout the world. Ms. Goodman is responsible for the day-to-day management of the firm and is actively involved in the research on and analysis of traders as well as ongoing risk management activities. She has held positions with leading firms in the futures industry since 1974. Ms. Goodman has served as director of the

Managed Futures Trade Association and the Managed Futures Association. She graduated from Stanford University with a BA degree.

Armand Keim (Chapter 2)

Mr. Keim is the president of Keim Consulting Associates, a firm that specializes in the automation of the securities business. Previously, he was the chief information officer of Cowen and Co., a full-service brokerage firm. He has been involved in the securities business with brokerage firms, exchanges, clearing corporations, and service companies for more than 30 years. His expertise spans from mainframes to the latest LAN/WAN/client/server technology. He is the coauthor of *Fundamentals of Digital Computers* and has taught computer science and management at Fordham University.

Mr. Keim holds a B.S.E.E. from the Polytechnic University of New York and an M.B.A. from Baruch University.

James T. Leman (Chapter 7)

Mr. Leman is manager and vice president, equity support group, equity trading and sales at Salomon Brothers, Inc., where his responsibilities include supporting the domestic and international program trading desks, the options/futures desk and the block equity desk.

Additional responsibilities include the development of proposed proprietary trading and customer sales systems in both domestic and international markets, program trading support of New York and branch sales activities, and participation on the Equity Systems Review Committee which will oversee all technological application enhancements and equipment acquisition by the equity area.

Mr. Leman holds a BS in accounting from St. Petter's College and an MBA in financial management from Fordham University.

Russell D. Lewis (Chapter 4)

Mr. Lewis is the chief information officer at Jefferies & Co., responsible for global technology strategy. He has worked in the financial industry in technology for 15 years and has had extensive experience in designing, implementing, and managing technology for both back-office and front-office functions. Previously, Mr. Lewis was vice president responsible for the automation of equity and derivative products for Salomon Brothers Inc. His expertise is in developing time critical equity trading techologies that interface with exchanges and customers globally. Mr. Lewis, a frequent speaker at conferences worldwide, graduated from Drew University in 1981 with a BA in political science. He has received a master of science degree from Pace University in investment management.

Kevin J. Merz (Introduction)

Mr. Merz is managing director and chief executive officer of Enterprise Technology Corporation. He serves as a senior industry consultant specializing in the application of modern computer software technology in the financial community. Mr. Merz has spent two decades in the computer and information sciences field. He has been the project manager and/or lead developer on over 40 significant information systems projects during his career, assisting pension funds, broker/dealers, life insurance companies, venture capital firms, and many others. A well-known author and lecturer, he is also the executive editor and a regular contributor to *Technology Trends*, an industry newsletter.

Before founding Enterprise Technology Corporation, Mr. Merz was a senior project manager with Index Systems, a large technology consultant firm, and served as a systems analyst/programmer at St. Olaf College.

Jeff Monassebian (Chapter 6)

Mr. Monassebian is a practicing attorney in New York City with more than 10 years of specialized experience in computer technology transactions. Between 1985 and 1995, Mr. Monassebian was a principal in and general counsel to TCAM Systems, an international software development and licensing company where he was responsible for the negotation of software development and licensing agreements with securities trading firms, investment banks, stock exchanges, and central banks in the United States, Europe, Asia, and Australia.

Mr. Monassebian is a partner in the law firm of Lieberman & Nowak and is the founder and president of CADRE, Inc., a forum dedicated to the resolution of technology related disputes by means other than litigation. He is the author of *A Survival Guide to Computer Contracts* and has been interviewed on CBS News where his companies were featured. Mr. Monassebian is a graduate of Georgetown University Law Center.

Lance J. Naber (Chapter 13)
Naber is a vice president with Enterprise Technology Corporation. He serves as a consultant in the strategic application of information technology to improve business productivity and as a bridge to more technical issues of modern system architecture, network design, database architecture and design and implementation of multi-tier distributed client/server systems. Mr. Naber speaks frequently at international conferences and has published articles in both academic and technical journals.

Previously, Mr. Naber was chief information officer and managing director of Rogers, Casey and Associates, a major pension fund consulting and diversified financial services vendor in Darien, CT. His accomplishments include application of strategic technology to improve overall productivity and efficiency, which result in higher margins. The strategic technology included a state-of-the-art telephone system, voice mail, corporate wide E-mail and scheduling, Internet access, strategic propriety systems innovations, higher quality client presentations, more timely and accurate client reporting and support for new products and services.

For nearly twelve years prior, Mr. Naber operated L. J. Naber & Associates, Ltd., a technology consulting and software development firm whose clients were, among others, the Bonds Buyer, Securities Industry Automation Corporation and Rogers, Casey.

Mr. Nabers attended the Wharton School of the University of Pennsylvania. He holds a B.S. in economics from the University of Pennsylvania with majors in finance and decision sciences.

Caroline Poplawski (Chapter 10)
Ms. Poplawski is a senior research analyst with Kenmar Asset Allocation, Inc., where her responsibilities include the evaluation of commodity trading advisors, the markets they trade, as well as the risk monitoring and management of managed futures investments. One of her focuses has been in researching and developing tools for risk analysis. Previously, she held positions with Mocatta Futures Corporation, a futures commission merchant, Shearson Lehman

Hutton, and Prudential Bache Securities. Ms. Poplawski graduated from New York University with honors, with degrees in both economics and finance.

Joseph Rosen (Introduction; Chapter 10)
Mr. Rosen is a managing director of Enterprise Technology Corporation and an authority on the strategic use of information technology for competitive advantage in financial services. A frequent lecturer, he chaired the seventh annual Computers in the City conference in London, and has published numerous articles in industry journals. Mr. Rosen is also technology editor for *Investment Operations: The Quarterly Journal of Securities Custody, Clearance and Settlement.*

Prior to joining Enterprise, Mr. Rosen was chief information officer of Dubin & Swieca Capital Management, a leading money management firm specializing in managed futures, multiasset, and derivatives fund management. He has worked with the U.S. Congress Office of Technology Assessment on studies of technology in the securities markets and has served in senior management positions with a leading Japanese securities dealer and a pioneering software company providing on-line trading systems to Wall Street firms.

Mr. Rosen holds M.A. and A.B.D. degrees in international politics and quantitative methods from the State University of New York at Stony Brook, and received his M.B.A. in finance, international business, and marketing from Columbia University.

Janet L. Rovenpor (Chapter 1)
Ms. Rovenpor is an assistant professor of management at Manhattan College in Riverdale, New York. She has taught courses in strategic management, organizational theory, managerial decision making, and organizational change and development at both the undergraduate and graduate levels. Ms. Rovenpor has written numerous articles for academic and professional journals. She has extensive consulting experience as senior consultant for Mobley, Luciani and Associates, New York, where she developed service quality programs, seminars on innovative thinking for technology professionals, customized performance appraisal systems, and strategic planning procedures for universities. Ms. Rovenpor

received her Ph.D. in organization and policy studies from the City University of New York.

Vincent A. Walsh (Chapter 8)
Mr. Walsh is vice president, trading support, for the Pershing division of Donaldson, Lufkin & Jenrette Securities Corp., and is responsible for the day-to-day block desk operations and technology support. He has helped Pershing's special handling desk design and implement a state-of-the-art order management system. It is the premier neutral, agency, block desk offering institutions liquidity in size while crediting commissions to any of hundreds of brokers.

Prior to joining Pershing, Mr. Walsh was product manager for the Intermarket trading network of Merrin Financial, the leading vendor of buy-side order management systems. He has 18 years of financial industry experience primarily in operations and technology development roles, at leading firms including Morgan Stanley, Instinet Corporation, and Fidelity Investments. He has an M.B.A. from Columbia University and a B.B.A. from the University of Notre Dame.

PREFACE

The *Handbook of Investment Technology* focuses on how information technology (IT) is and can be used in securities and investments firms. It aims to be more practical than academic in its coverage, with an emphasis on how readers themselves can actually utilize and deploy investment technology for their firms' competitive advantage. The chapter contributors comprise a wide range of industry professionals with diverse areas of expertise. These include representatives from the buy and sell sides as well as from the custodian, vendor, industry utility, and academic communities. Among the authors are eight current or former chief information officers.

The critically important role that technology plays in the financial services industry and markets increases by the day as the IT spending continues to accelerate. Few in fact would dispute the notion that as we head toward the millennium, investment technology is one of the key forces that is changing the very nature of competition in the global capital markets. The *Handbook of Investment Technology* is intended for any securities and investments professional who must deal with technology. Because of the very pervasiveness of IT, this can include almost any professional working in the industry.

This book will be especially useful for executives who must set their organizations' strategic direction as well as for IT management responsible for integrating and deploying the IT strategy chosen to support the business. The three parts of the book each come at investment technology from a slightly different perspective, but none of the chapters is on a bits-and-bytes level, nor are any chapters filled with technical jargon that would be difficult for any industry professional to comprehend.

Part I, *Selection, Implementation, and Management of Technology*, contains six chapters on management issues that cut across both technologies and business areas.

The six chapters in Part II, *Investment Technology Applications*, present case studies of business-segment-specific applications of technology, including portfolio management, trading, order routing and electronic markets, risk management, and global custody/ back-office processing.

Part III, *New Technologies and Their Applications*, presents from a technology perspective and angle, overviews of specific technologies. Among the topics included in the five chapters are object-oriented technology, groupware, expert systems, neural networks, and data security.

We both wish to thank the 20 authors, industry friends, and clients, who were so giving of both their time and expertise to make this volume such a valuable resource to all our colleagues in the securities and investments industry.

Last but not least, many thanks to Bob Klein and Jess Lederman for their invaluable assistance, as well as to the staff at Irwin Professional Publishing for helping to turn this idea into reality.

Kevin J. Merz
Joseph Rosen

MAKING INVESTMENT TECHNOLOGY SPENDING PAY: KEY SUCCESS FACTORS

Kevin J. Merz, CEO and Managing Director
Joseph Rosen, Managing Director
Enterprise Technology Corporation

This introduction presents our view of the key factors for success and failure—gleaned from nearly four decades of combined financial technology experience—in exploiting information technology (IT) for competitive advantage in the securities and investments industry. We address the fundamental question of why some firms consistently "do their systems right" while others time and again fail, quite often endangering their firms' very existence in the process. The most vital element—on which all others depend—is senior management commitment and support. Management issues addressed also include organizational culture and structure, the bells-and-whistles syndrome, the proper integration of business and IT planning, and the critical importance of having the right people.

The introduction is organized into two major parts. First, we review the environment: spending, return on investment, and strategic importance. Second, we discuss a number of brief case studies to illustrate our key lessons. We conclude with a summary and checklist of the key success factors for exploiting investment technology.

INVESTMENT TECHNOLOGY ENVIRONMENT

Spending

To say that the securities and investments industries are information technology intensive is an understatement. Billions of dollars are spent annually by financial institutions worldwide in support of their IT needs. Several billion dollars is estimated to be spent each year on market data alone. In addition, some firms already exceed $1 billion each in total spending on IT.

How unfortunate then, that so many firms have so little to show after spending so much money (and let us not forget time—an equally scarce and valuable resource). Exactly how much effort is wasted is quite difficult to estimate—even though we all know stories of nightmare projects that have been particularly awful failures.

Black Holes and Blunders

Suffice it to say, for various reasons an unacceptably large percentage of the resources expended on information systems by buy-side and sell-side firms alike seems to disappear into a veritable black hole. Some ill-conceived systems thankfully are canceled in the middle, or sooner, and never see the light of day.

Worse still are completed systems that are never used, either because they do the wrong things right or visa versa. Most distressing of all are those defective systems that somehow sneak through testing by the firm's quality assurance staff and then proceed to show off their pernicious bugs at the most inopportune moments.

At best, these programming and/or design flaws are annoying or embarrassing. For example, the market data service that ran out of digits for the Nikkei Index and was forced to truncate its display.

In some instances the costs are quite a bit dearer, both in dollars and tenure. Consider the cases of two U.S. investment banks that were prominent in the mortgage-backed securities market. Design flaws in their allocation and deal-capture systems, respectively, led to hundreds of millions of dollars in losses and redundancies at both firms.

Why do these sorts of annoying and sometimes costly glitches occur so frequently, and so often to the same firms? And conversely, how do others time and again manage to do their systems right? What can the unlucky majority do to emulate the fortunate few?

EXHIBIT I-1

U.S. Government Software Projects: Are We This Bad, Too?

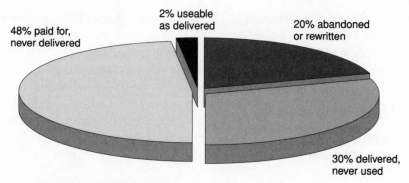

48% paid for,
never delivered

2% useable
as delivered

20% abandoned
or rewritten

30% delivered,
never used

Sources: *Financial Times, Sloan Management Review*

On a more fundamental level, why do so many IT projects fail, and among financial institutions in particular? The answer may have less to do with technology per se and more to do with management, or a lack thereof. In fact, even the business press appears to be catching on to this phenomenon. "Management Attitudes Are More Important Than Technology" read the headline of a *Financial Times Survey*[1] on computers in finance. The subtitle of the main article pointed out the major issue even more clearly, "While the fiercely competitive financial services industry is increasing its spending on information technology, it frequently fails to achieve the full benefits."

Another recent article, in the weekly *ComputerWorld*,[2] noted widespread communication gaps between CEOs and CIOs and suggested a new approach to deployment of IT. The findings of a study on U.S. government software projects conducted a few years back by the General Accounting Office (GAO) arm of Congress are especially illuminating and relevant here. The study underscores the need to reexamine how we manage IT. Exhibit I-1 illustrates the survey results.

---

1. Alan Cane, "Computers in Finance: Management Attitudes Are More Important than Technology," *Financial Times Survey*, November 15, 1994, p. 1.
2. Thomas Hoffman, "Bank Execs, IS Not Talking: Studies Say Communication Gaps Call for New Approach," *ComputerWorld*, November 14, 1994, p. 4.

According to the GAO, 48 percent of government software projects are paid for but never delivered; 30 percent are delivered, but never used *(hmm, perhaps because they did not meet the needs of users?)*; 20 percent are completely abandoned or rewritten; *and all of 2 percent are usable as delivered.*

Sections that follow address these questions about IT success and failure by example in primer fashion, offering a recipe for success but not a cookbook, which would require considerably more space. We present our view of the key factors for success and failure, based on our financial technology experience with financial organizations of all sizes and shapes: public and private, retail and institutional, American and foreign, and dealing in most types of securities products.

Strategic Importance

Let us be clear that this is no mere academic exercise. On the contrary, IT is growing in strategic importance as well as in costs. Furthermore, one would expect this to continue, if not accelerate, because of increasing global competition and the nascent integration of markets, both electronically and via regulation. Financial institutions are also increasingly dependent on IT because of the growing complexity of investment products and the need to manage their associated risks.

As industry observers with a sense of history understand very well, firms that fall too far behind in the IT race stand to lose much more than their competitive advantage. One need only recall the demise of many distinguished and old-line Wall Street firms during the back-office crunch of the 70s, mostly because their trade processing systems—read IT—were not up to snuff.

The short answer to the questions we posed above (i.e. how to make the technology spending pay off) is almost too simple. We submit that the proper level of senior management support, adequate planning, and a suitable organizational structure, mixed with a dose of common sense, will together forestall major system mishaps.

The most vital element on which all others depend is senior management, with which we deal next. Following this we discuss key issues in planning, organization, and culture, the bells-and-whistles syndrome; and staffing. We conclude with a summary and checklist of the key success factors for exploiting investment technology.

LESSONS

Management: The Buck Stops Here

There is no substitute for active senior management support and involvement. Throwing money at and abdicating all responsibility to "Jones, to fix up the back office-mess," just will not do.

Consider the example of a large U.S. wire house—let us call them House A—known for its aloof and somewhat erratic senior management. This firm spent some seven calendar years (how many person-years?) attempting without success and with untold millions of dollars down the tubes, to automate its capital markets area with an integrated deal capture, order processing, and risk management system.

In addition to the uncertainty and turmoil engendered by management vacillation at the top, House A also suffered the consequences of violating some cardinal rules of systems in the trenches. To wit: too many chiefs, little cooperation between business and IT units, and little or no sense of the need to integrate information systems (IS) developments with corporate business strategies.

As the saying goes, when everyone is in charge *nobody* is in charge. Rather than having one senior-level businessperson with overall responsibility, three different consulting organizations were working with and under the nominal authority of House A's IT unit. In reality, as one can easily imagine, responsibility was so diffuse as to be virtually nonexistent.

No great surprise, when a full year after project inception, the team proudly presented its six-volume functional specifications report only to have it unceremoniously and flatly rejected by the capital markets management. Oh well, we'll just start all over again.

A stark study in contrasts is presented by IT developments at Dealer B, a privately held market maker in New York and London. Under the strong leadership of the head trader, a director and number two at the firm, the development group benefited from active support and participation of senior management at the highest level. No doubt the business side was in firm control of the project; no tail wagging the dog here.

Of equal importance was the involvement of the entire community of ultimate users from beginning to end. Neither senior management nor the systems group were interested in IT for the bells and whistles, but rather wanted a system that would support their business plan for achieving a competitive edge over others using technology.

The head trader put the lie to the cliché that traders are too busy to be bothered by systems analysts and designers, who often have a fresh and rather democratic approach. Premarket open, and often postmarket close IT design meetings were obligatory for all potential users, as were the homework assignments.

The rationale, as the head trader put it was, "You are the ones for whom the system is being built, so you better speak up (with your suggestions and criticisms) now, or shut up later." Clearly management's prerogative and vision.

The unsurprising result was a state-of-the-art analytic, deal capture, order processing, and risk management system that is an integral part of their business, actually used as intended by those for whom it was developed, and most important, it has enabled the firm to more than triple its volume with negligible cost and staff increases.

Management support and leadership are also crucial for proper planning, both at the strategic/corporate level and at the personal level between business unit and IT staffers. A healthy organizational structure and culture must be fostered; one that encourages communication and understanding, in other words, a common language between the business and technical people.

Planning: It Will Be More Costly Later

As with senior management support, there is no substitute for proper planning. Thorough analysis and design will more than pay for itself by detecting serious flaws when it is still relatively cheap (and easy) to correct them. The costs of correcting IT errors grow increasingly dearer the farther along that the project has advanced. Most expensive to fix, of course, are bugs in live systems.

Shearson was one firm that epitomized the effectiveness and efficiencies of careful and meticulous planning, particularly during its many acquisitions over some three decades, until it was ultimately bought by Smith Barney. A case in point was its seemingly effortless conversion of E.F. Hutton's systems—with hundreds of branches, millions of accounts, and billions of dollars in assets—to those of Shearson, in just a few short weeks.

Sadly for the Street, this was the exception that underscores the rule. Closer to the norm was the agony endured by House A as its takeover of a fellow investment bank proved very costly in both time and money. The problems associated with merging of the two back offices took countless hours to solve and kept legions of New York car service drivers busy ferrying House A staff through the night at all hours.

Examples of inadequate up-front planning are not limited to the United States or Wall Street. Global fiascoes include London Clear, and especially the Taurus debacle in the City of London.

At the simplest and highest level, planning should ensure that IT is in tune and integrated with the firm's business strategy. In other words, let's be certain that we have the right system. For some this is easier said than done. Take for example the U.S. investment bank that withdrew from a major line of business soon after bringing on-line a multimillion dollar trade-support system.

The proper meshing of business and technology planning can pay off for vendors as well. For example, an American purveyor of portfolio management software rose from nowhere to become the market share leader as it shrewdly caught the wave of the PC revolution and—just as important—listened carefully to the market, anticipating evolving user needs with timely enhancements year after year. Unfortunately, this firm later missed the boat on the Windows revolution and is now trying to quickly recover. It is fascinating how rapidly market positions can change in this industry.

Organization and Culture

Equally important as choosing the right system is that the system actually works right. A prerequisite for ensuring the synchronization of business and IT strategies is for IT staff to be knowledgeable about the firm's business.

Often this cardinal rule is observed in the breach. Consider another large American securities firm—let us call them House B—with a well-regarded over-the-counter equity trading department and system. Prior success apparently went to their heads, as they tried to clone the OTC equity system into a fixed-income system using the same equity IT specialists. No surprise when the initial attempt failed, as the staff even had trouble with the concept of yield to maturity.

Of course, there must be a two-way street of mutual respect and understanding between the business and IT sides for both to work together, planning and implementing attainable IT objectives for the firm. For this reason the attitude that continues to this day at otherwise first-class firms—that systems people are somehow less than the other parts of the firm—is doubly disappointing and counterproductive to their continued success. How much easier things would be if both types could somehow think alike.

Morgan Stanley was a pioneer of the trend to develop business and IT staff in similar fashion and to draw them from the same pool of high-caliber applicants. Liberal arts graduates were recruited and offered both the technical and business training necessary. In addition, career paths leading to business operating units were also opened to them. No wonder that Morgan Stanley is widely regarded as a leader in exploiting IT to its competitive advantage, for example through its internally developed integrated trade processing system (TAPS), which is still proving valuable despite its age. By contrast, one would expect difficulty attracting the best people into IT at firms where they are barely considered human.

An increasing number of firms is trying to instill a corporate culture of cooperation among IT and business units. (In contrast to the us-versus-them attitudes in the IT departments of many other firms.) One way to facilitate this is to reorganize the IT department into separate units, one for each business line, and physically locate them with their respective business units.

Bells-and-Whistles Syndrome

Firms that are duly diligent in their own IT analysis and design should be far less susceptible to the sin of hubris or what we like to call the bells-and-whistles syndrome. Those afflicted will choose a system or design less for how closely it meets business requirements or how feasible it is than for how sexy or state-of-the-art it is, à la buying the hot box du jour without a real business need.

An example from the recent past was the costly and time-consuming attempt by several large institutions to transplant the highly regarded TAPS system from Morgan Stanley.

Careful analysis and planning by these firms—not to mention common sense—should have suggested to them that their chances for achieving timely and successful installations were slim, because of a combination of highly unfavorable factors:

- Morgan Stanley was no longer directly involved.
- The new owner of the system (renamed TRADEPRO) was not known for its brokerage industry expertise.
- The system was several *thousand* programs in scope.
- There was little in the way of usable documentation.

The strategic implications of dependence on a competitor's system are another, not inconsequential, issue, discussion of which we limit here to one simple question: What would Machiavelli have said?

One should not misconstrue this as an argument for, or for that matter against, custom-built systems. Rather, we believe that requirements must be determined on a case-by-case basis. Quite often a strategy of buy and build, or systems integration with some customization offers the best of both worlds; that is, meeting core business requirements, while at the same time facilitating faster and less-expensive development.

Cooperative planning should become easier and therefore more widespread as the use of GUI (graphical user interfaces), RAD (rapid application deployment), and other development tools and environments become more accepted.

These tools must be used with care and not become an end to themselves. Balance is the key here. We recall the large foreign bank whose IT managers became quite fixated with their new project management software. They soon ended up spinning their wheels, creating page after page of often meaningless GANTT charts. Tools are certainly no substitute for careful thought.

People Are the Most Important Resource

A prime example of the difference that can be made by having the right people—quality as opposed to quantity—is presented by the vastly contrasting experiences of two major insurance companies just about a decade ago. The investment management organizations of the two companies both wanted to automate their operations via building fully customized systems from scratch.

Firm A met with complete success, going live with a fully integrated trading, portfolio management/accounting, and general ledger system, on time and on budget, in under two years, and for less than $1 million.

Unfortunately, Firm B went through a systems nightmare while attempting to build only a subset of the functions of Firm A. After spending somewhere north of $30 million over the course of three years, they mercifully decided to pull the plug on their runaway project.

So what accounts for one sweet success and another ignominious failure? The first company assigned the project to a small, select team of highly experienced superprogrammers well-versed in the intricacies of the securities and investments business, and drawn from a financial technology consulting boutique that specialized in developing such applications. By contrast, the second insurance company outsourced their development project to the consulting arm of a large public accounting firm, which proceeded to build a virtual army for its team.

Two related lessons are most evident here. First, it is really hard to overestimate the magnitude of differences in both quality and productivity between average and superprogrammers. Second, it is equally easy to underestimate how quickly—and exponentially—communications costs can escalate among the programmers of a development team that has grown too large and bloated. This is one of the key principles of *The Mythical Man-Month*[3] made famous by Fred Brooks.

In summary, the key elements associated with successful IT developments on Wall Street are strong management support and leadership at the top, meticulous and careful planning, a culture of cooperation between business units and IT staff, hiring and keeping the best people, and of course, common sense.

Technological developments will amplify the importance of these attributes, in particular the level of cooperation (or friction) between IT staff and the end-users. As PC power grows to where we all have desktop supercomputers, so too will the power and independence of the end-users vis-à-vis IT staff, especially as user

---

3. Frederick P. Brooks, Jr. *The Mythical Man-Month: Essays on Software Engineering*. Reading, MA: Addison-Wesley Publishing Company, 1982.

interfaces and all manner of development tools become increasingly friendly and easy.

This distributed, as opposed to IT controlled, centralized processing, can be a double-edged sword. For those firms with the culture of mutual respect and understanding that we have discussed, the new technology could well usher in an era of unparalleled cooperation, to their competitive advantage. Other firms may see an increasingly destructive battle for control with attendant consequences for their competitive positions.

There is a growing realization about and among senior management that the key to successfully deploying IT for competitive advantage has relatively little to do with the technology itself. Rather, the primary factors in reaping decent, let alone good returns on investment technology spending are simple: quality management and people. Indeed, the technology itself is at best a secondary, or perhaps, even a tertiary element.

We conclude with a checklist of key success factors that we consider the most important guidelines to follow for successful deployment of IT within a securities and investment firm. The interaction among these 16 factors is illustrated in Exhibit I–2.

- Active senior management support and participation.
- Appreciation of IT's criticality for competitive position.
- One strong business unit executive leads project team.
- Corporate culture of teamwork, benefits system rewards it.
- IT & business staff have similar background, training.
- IT staff understands the business.
- IT staff are not second-class citizens.
- IT and business units do not conflict.
- Adequate up-front planning is conducted.
- CASE tools are employed, but not as toys.
- Business and IT strategies are synchronized.
- Avoid bells-and-whistles syndrome.
- Trainers know the business (in addition to the system).
- Postinstallation appraisal/audit performed on system.
- Common sense and balance are employed throughout.
- Always remember that IT is only a tool, and never a substitute for human thought and judgment.

EXHIBIT I–2

Key Success Factors—Mutually Reinforcing

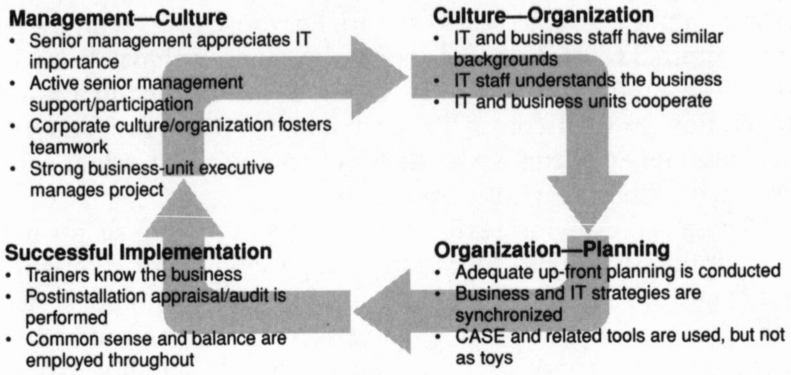

Management—Culture
- Senior management appreciates IT importance
- Active senior management support/participation
- Corporate culture/organization fosters teamwork
- Strong business-unit executive manages project

Culture—Organization
- IT and business staff have similar backgrounds
- IT staff understands the business
- IT and business units cooperate

Successful Implementation
- Trainers know the business
- Postinstallation appraisal/audit is performed
- Common sense and balance are employed throughout

Organization—Planning
- Adequate up-front planning is conducted
- Business and IT strategies are synchronized
- CASE and related tools are used, but not as toys

C O N T E N T S

About the Authors   vii
Preface   xvii
Introduction   xix

PART I

SELECTION, IMPLEMENTATION, AND MANAGEMENT OF TECHNOLOGY

Chapter 1

Business Process Reengineering in the Financial Services Industry   3

An Introduction to the BPR Concept   4
A Business Executive's Quandary   6
Approaches to Managing Business Processes   8
A Closer Look at BPR   11
    Definition and Key Characteristics of BPR   11
    Successes and Failures of BPR Programs   13
The Role of Organizational Culture in BPR   18
The Role of Information Technology in BPR   20
BPR in Financial Services Companies   22
BPR in Action: The Case of EQ Financial Consultants, Inc.   26
    The Forces of Change   26
    The Decision Alternatives   27
    The New Work Processes   28
Lessons Learned from the Experiences of EQ Financial Consultants, Inc.   29
    Lesson One: Reengineer Work Processes First; Redesign Systems Second   29
    Lesson Two: Involve All Employees in Reengineering from Start to Finish   30
    Lesson Three: Develop a Partnership with Vendors, Consultants, and Programmers   31

*Lesson Four: Set Up Multiple Opportunities for
Learning the New Processes   31*
Lesson Five: Reengineering Requires Top Management Support   32
Lesson Six: It Pays to Share Information Internally   33
Toward the Restructuring of an Entire Industry   33

Chapter 2

Rightsizing: Client/Server versus Mainframe Platforms   41

How Client/Server and Mainframe Platforms Differ   43
   Hardware   43
   Operating Systems   46
   Networks   48
   Support   48
Applications Best Performed on Client/Server   50
   Batch Processing   51
   Transaction Processing   52
   Database Services   55
   Office Automation   56
Downsizing from a Mainframe to Client/Server   57
The Internet and Intranets   59
Conclusion   59

Chapter 3

Evaluating and Contracting with Vendors   61

Buy versus Build Analysis   62
   Resources   63
   Costs   64
   Management   65
   Business Knowledge   65
RFP Process   66
   RFP Steps   66
   Potential Benefits of the RFP Process   67
Vendor Evaluation and Selection   67
   Evaluate the Package (Service)   68
   Review the Technology   68
   Evaluate the Vendor   69

Evaluate the Costs   70
Comparison Process   71
Contract Negotiations   72
Preimplementation   73
Implementation   74
Postimplementation   75
Summary   75

Chapter 4

Global Technology Management   77

Business Drivers   78
Globalization   78
Technology as an Asset   79
Moving from Service Provider to Partner   81
How to Build a Technology Team   81
Staffing a Technology Team   81
Interview Process   83
Assessment Centers and Team Building   83
Product Management   84
Project Management   84
Buy, Build, or Outsource Decision   85
Outsourcing Issues   86
Financial Management   87
Organizational Development   91

Chapter 5

Financial Evaluation of Transition Technologies   95

The Transition Factors   96
Underestimated Time and Staff   97
Change in Corporate Strategic Direction   97
Shift in Technology Management   98
Unstable Technology   99
Overrated Project Benefits   100
Too Expensive to Implement   100
Determination of Costs and Benefits   101
Measurement of Costs and Benefits   104

Cost and Benefits Relationships   104
  Trends and Cycles   104
  Compression of Work Plans   107
Evaluation of Projects   107

Chapter 6

Legal Considerations   109

Deliverables   109
  Prepackaged Software and Hardware   110
  Custom Software Development   110
  Customized Software Development   110
  Third-Party Software   111
Software License   111
  Common Licensing Provisions   111
  Site and Corporate Licenses   114
  Shrink-Wrap Licenses   114
Documentation   115
  Examples   116
  Prepackaged Software and Hardware   117
  Custom Software Development   118
  Customized Software Development   118
Pricing and Payment Terms   118
Price Protection   119
Ownership   120
Confidentiality   120
  Purpose   121
  Oral Disclosure   121
  Exclusions   121
  Independent Development   121
  Procedures   122
Site Preparation   122
Delivery   122
Installation   123
  Computer Hardware   123
  Software   123
Acceptance   124

Computer Hardware 124
Documentation 125
Software 125
Training 126
Training the Trainers 126
User Training 126
Warranty and Maintenance 127
Commencement 128
Warranty Term 128
Response Time 129
Location 129
Updates 130
Year 2000 130
Virus Protection 130
Intellectual Property Rights Indemnity 131
Defense 131
Indemnity 131
Continued Use 132
Replacement 132
Assistance 132
Counsel 133
Remedies 133
Termination 134
Confidentiality 134
IPR Indemnity 134
Injury 134
Liquidated Damages 134
Change in Scope 135
Termination 135
Wind-Down Period 136
Cause of Default 136
Vendor Default 136
Ownership 136
General Provisions 137
Amendments 137
Assignment 137
Escrow 138

Project Personnel   138
Notice   138
Injunctive Relief   138
Nonwaiver   139
Force Majeure   139
Integration Clause   139

PART II

INVESTMENT TECHNOLOGY APPLICATIONS

Chapter 7

Electronic Market Mechanisms   143

Research   144
Liquidity Indicators   145
Electronic Order Delivery   147
Integration of Trade Management   151
Post-Trade Processes   154

Chapter 8

Integrated Order Management Systems   159

Overview of Integrated Order Management   160
  Investment Decision Stage   162
  Trading Stage   163
  Post-Trade Stage   164
Benefits of Integrated Order Management   164
Portfolio Modeling   166
  What-if Modeling   166
  Rebalancing   167
  Compliance   168
Trade Blotter   169
Broker Links   171
Post-Trade Linkages   172
  Allocation Process/ Vendor Links (OASYS/DTC-II)   172
  Bookkeeping Link/Portfolio Management Systems   173
Reflections on the Implementation Process   173
  Get Management Buy-in   173

Prepare a Business Case and Needs Analysis   173
Identify a Focal Point Liaison Group or Individual   174
Decide on a Build or Buy Approach   175
Identify and Screen the Potential Alternative Vendor Solutions   175
Arrange a Test of Leading Vendors   177
Choose Your First Implementation Strategically   177
Build Versus Buy?—The In-House Versus Vendor Decision   178
Looking to the Future   179

Chapter 9

Portfolio Management and Accounting   181

Dynamics of the Investment Industry   182
Change in Technology   184
The Needs of the Business   185
Operations   186
Marketing   189
Future Business Needs   189
    Your Firm's Future   191
    Your Firm's Options   191
    References   191
    Look for an Evolving Product   192
    Corporate Infrastructure   193
    Corporate Politics   194

Chapter 10

Measuring Trading/Investment Performance & Risk   195

Risk Management   196
    Themes   196
    Managed Futures as a Case Study   197
    Organization of the Chapter   197
Lies, Damn Lies, and Statistics   198
    One-Dimensional Views and the Herd Mentality   199

Graphical and Other Views of Risk/Return in Tandem   203
    Windows Analysis   203
    A Picture Is Worth a Thousand Words   204

Drawdown Analysis   209
Replacing Standard Deviation   211
Analyzing the Trades   213
Ongoing Monitoring of Traders   213
Portfolio Monitoring   215
Qualitative Side   217
Managing the Risks in a Portfolio of Traders   219
MPT in Theory   220
MPT for Real   222
Additional Readings   223

Chapter 11

Electronic Messaging Standards and Standards Development Organizations   227

Industry Standards Groups and Their Functions   228
The Trading Cycle and Its Associated Standards   232
Trade Routing and Trade Execution   232
Trade Settlement and Confirmation (Post-Trade)   232
The Near Future   233
ISO 15022—The Data Field Dictionary   233
The Internet   234
Appendix A: Securities Industry Swift Message Types   235
Appendix B: Swift Message Layout Sample   237
Appendix C: Internet Addresses of Interest to the Brokerage Standards Community   238

Chapter 12

Payment, Clearance, and Settlement Systems   239

The Role of Technology   240
The Players   241
Setting Standards   245
Risk Reduction   245
New Risks   248
The Future   248
Standardization and Reduction in the Trade-Date/Settlement-Date Time Lag   249

Growing Role of Clearing Corporations, Depositories, and Utilities 250
Outsourcing to Reduce Costs 250
Alliances, Joint Ventures, and Cost Sharing 250
Other Challenges 251
Appendix: The Process: Payment, Clearance, and Settlement 253

PART III

NEW TECHNOLOGIES AND THEIR APPLICATIONS

Chapter 13

Strategic Systems Technology: Ignore at Your Own Risk 257

Strategic Technology Risks 258
Other Factors 260
Strategic Technologies 261
Electronic Mail 261
Groupware 262
Intranets 265
Desktop Publishing 266
Internet 268
Videoconferencing 270
Voice Synthesis 272
Voice Recognition 272
Data Warehouses/Enterprisewide Databases 274
Document Imaging 276
Telephony 278
Multimedia 280
ISDN 281

Chapter 14

Telecommunications and Competitive Advantage 285

Telecommunications and the Strategic Plan 286
From the Boardroom to the Back Room—Implementation Issues 289
From the Boardroom to the Back Room—Management Issues 291
The Internet 293
Some Technical Background 295
Standards 295

OSI: The Mother of All Standards 296
A Sampling of Standards and Where to Apply Them 296

Chapter 15

Object Technology in Finance   299

A Brief Introduction to Object-Oriented Technology—Key Concepts   299
  Class versus Object   300
  Inheritance   300
  Encapsulation   302
  Polymorphism   303
  Object-Based versus Object-Oriented   305
  Messaging   305
The Business Case   307
  Time to Market   307
  Quality   308
  Cost Reduction   309
Object-Oriented Analysis and Design   309
  The Importance of Analysis and Design   311
  The Object-Oriented Methodologies   311
  Object Modeling Technique Highlighted   312
  Use Cases   313
Key Success Factors   314
  Management Support   314
  The Paradigm Shift   314
  Project Staffing   315
  The Project Scope   315
  Project Management for Object-Oriented Technology   316
  Organizational Issues   316
Preparing for Reuse   318
Planning toward a Software Development Process   319
  The Object-Oriented Project Life Cycle   319
  Object-Oriented Architecture   321
  Object-Oriented Testing   322
Risk Factors   322
  Lack of Analysis and Design   323
  Lack of System Design and Architecture   323
  Lack of Software Development Process   323

Building a Design and Architecture around a Tool   324
Know Thy Vendor   324
Parting Words   324

Chapter 16

Financial Computational Intelligence   327

The Tools for Financial Time-Series Forecasting   328
Nonlinear Complex Systems   330
Neural Networks and Genetic Algorithms   332

Chapter 17

Data/Computer Security   337

Hardware: Physical Security—*Don't Let 'em Touch It!*   337
Software: Intellectual Security—*Don't Let 'em Touch It*   340
    Don't Let 'em See It   345
    Did They Touch It or See It?   346
Remote Access—*Can They See It from Jersey City?*   349
Backup—*If They Did Touch It, Did They Steal It or Break It and Can I Get It Back?*   351

Index   355

THE HANDBOOK OF INVESTMENT TECHNOLOGY

SELECTION, IMPLEMENTATION, AND MANAGEMENT OF TECHNOLOGY

⑥ BUSINESS PROCESS REENGINEERING IN THE FINANCIAL SERVICES INDUSTRY

Janet L. Rovenpor
Assistant Professor of Management
Manhattan College

This chapter explains what is meant by the term *business process reengineering* (BPR), and describes how the method's techniques are currently being applied within the financial services industry.* It also demonstrates the similarities and differences between BPR and other popular methods used by companies to improve performance (e.g., total quality management); discusses the relationships among BPR, organizational culture, and information technology (IT); relates the experiences of a company that has successfully implemented a major BPR project; and describes the challenges facing financial services companies when they begin to explore BPR strategies.

---

*I gratefully acknowledge the expert advice on technology and securities trading issues provided to me by Joseph Rosen, managing director of Enterprise Technology Corporation (ETC). I would also like to thank the following individuals: Kevin Merz, managing director and chief executive officer of ETC for opening up the company's library to me; Michael Norwich, formerly head of a business reengineering group at Merrill Lynch, for his helpful comments on a draft of the manuscript; and Peter B. Madoff, senior managing director, for providing a description of Bernard L. Madoff Investment Securities and its operations. The case study appearing in the chapter would not have been written if it had not been for the generous time and thoughtful insights provided by Theresa Nurge-Alws, senior vice president and chief operations officer of EQ Financial Consultants, Inc., and Karen Curtis, division manager of information services of The Equitable Life Assurance Society of the United States.

AN INTRODUCTION TO THE BPR CONCEPT

Business process reengineering (BPR) has been promoted in the business community as an effective technique for achieving a wide range of highly desirable outcomes including lower costs, higher profits, better quality, faster product development, and improved customer service. First popularized by Michael Hammer in 1990, BPR encourages executives to adopt a new set of principles regarding how businesses should be organized and managed.[1] Traditionally, work is subdivided into smaller parts and assigned to different employees. Employees are placed into functional departments, such as marketing, production, research and development, and human resources. Organizational charts are drawn to show who reports to whom. Job descriptions are written to delineate the specific tasks and responsibilities of every employee. Proponents of BPR believe that this approach is wrong; they prefer to organize work according to processes, not according to functions or tasks. Processes, defined as sequences and combinations of activities that deliver value to a customer, cut across hierarchy. Inefficiencies result when work is handed from one specialist to the next, from one department to the next. It becomes necessary, therefore, to eliminate barriers, delays, and obstacles encountered as work makes its way through the organization.

When companies are organized according to processes, results are dramatic. Consider, for example, the success of the IBM Credit Corporation, a wholly owned subsidiary of IBM, offering loans to customers who purchase IBM computers, software, and services.[2] Due to cumbersome paperwork, the hand-off of responsibility from one department to the next, and the existence of separate computer systems, sometimes it took a week to handle a request for financing from the time a call was received from an IBM salesperson in the field to the time a quote letter was delivered to that person by Federal Express. By examining how the credit issuance process could be improved, managers realized that one person,

---

1. M. Hammer, "Reengineering Work: Don't Automate, Obliterate," *Harvard Business Review* 90, no. 4 (July–August, 1990), pp. 104–12.
2. M. Hammer and J. Champy, *Reengineering the Corporation: A Manifesto for Business Revolution* (New York: Harper Collins Publishers, 1993), pp. 36–39.

called a deal structurer, supported by a user friendly computer system with access to data and specialized tools, could handle the entire request from start to finish. The time it took to process the request was reduced from an average of six days to four hours. It was not necessary to increase staff size; in fact, the redesign made it possible for the number of requests being handled to increase a hundredfold. Other companies that used BPR successfully were Ford Motor Company, Hallmark Cards, Eastman Kodak, and Xerox Corporation.

Financial services companies have jumped on the reengineering bandwagon for a number of reasons. Since the stock market crash of 1987, managers have tried to cut costs by laying off employees and investing heavily in information technology. In many cases, however, they have not been able to significantly reduce operating costs.[3] Financial services companies are searching for ways to bring better data to traders, to comply with new regulations, to provide better service to customers, and to integrate the deal-making activities of traders in the front office with the accounting and record-keeping activities of employees in the back office. The solution to these pressures is to reengineer business processes. Merrill Lynch & Company, Wall Street's largest brokerage firm, plans to spend $1 billion over the next five years to reengineer its retail brokerage business. It has already installed its advanced order entry (AOE) workstation that has eliminated the need for 500 wire-room data-entry jobs and has made it possible for 75 percent of its market orders to get executed and returned to the broker's workstation within 45 seconds.[4] Smith Barney has recently moved to a modern five-floor, 1,900-desktop, trading facility. The firm will invest $100 million in a client/server system to provide customer account activity data to 11,000 financial consultants and 500 branches. It is offering on-line services with Quicken personal financial software in a joint venture with the Intuit Corporation.[5]

---

3. "The Wiring of Wall Street," *The Economist* 322, February 22, 1992, pp. 69-70.
4. I. Schmerken, "Reengineering Wall Street's Systems," *Wall Street Computer Review* 9, no. 4 (January 1992), pp. 14-22.
5. R. Sales, "Five Decisions: Smith Barney's Trading Room Relocation Project," *Waters*, Summer 1995, pp. 65-67, 98-100.

A BUSINESS EXECUTIVE'S QUANDARY

Jack Borstin, CEO of a moderate-size manufacturer of seat belts, air bags, and antilock brakes for the automotive industry, settles into his seat on the commuter train taking him to his suburban home outside of Detroit. He is perplexed. He has just spent the last few days listening to well-polished, high-powered presentations from three of the top management consulting firms in the country. He had contacted them because he had a number of concerns about his company that currently operates eight production facilities, employs 6,500 workers, and is worth approximately $600 million. Despite his company's rapid growth, profits are down 10 percent from the previous year. The company's current problems can be attributed to increased competition from a large diversified German manufacturer of automotive and electronic products; a decision made by U.S. automobile companies not to offer antilock brakes and other features as standard equipment in their vehicles; pressures from buyers who are demanding lower prices, better quality, and faster delivery times for automotive components.

In the first presentation, the consultant spoke of the need to study the entire organization. Continuous improvement systems would be set up to focus on cost structures, quality goals, delivery times, product development cycles and, most important, customer satisfaction. Tools that would be used included a Pert chart to map out the sequence of events necessary to complete a project; a matrix diagram to show relationships among objectives, strategies, and potential problems that might arise during a project; and a check sheet to record the number of defects found during quality-control inspections. A training program would help employees see themselves as having two jobs—one that they perform every day when they fulfill the tasks appearing in their formal job descriptions and one that requires them to stand back and reflect on how they can improve what they are doing and how they are relating to others.

Borstin prides himself on being up-to-date on his business. He regularly reads the trade journals and attends conferences. He even sits on the board of directors of a company that is smaller than his own. He was surprised, therefore, when the second consultant used terms, such as *nodes, prosumerism,* and *holonic networks,* that he had never heard of before. The thrust of the presentation focused on the need for companies to go beyond the confines of their traditional boundaries. To compete in today's global marketplace, a company must join a set of organizations that act together. Each company is chosen to become a node in the holonic network because of its process excellence. The core competencies held by each individual member enables the network to respond to any customer requirement. Financial success occurs when information is shared among all members and when the network is committed to constantly improving its coordination and communication. Customers become prosumers because they get actively involved in product design.

How does holonic networking operate in reality? It makes it possible for a Japanese company, Sikisui, to build houses within nine days. A customer enters a sales office. Computer terminals linked to the company's design office enable the customer to select the home's layout and add personalized features. A sales agent is available to discuss different options. Once the exact specifications are drawn up, a quotation is prepared. The customer signs a contract. Within minutes, the company sends orders to all of its suppliers to prepare materials for the customized home. If a supplier is unable to fulfill its order within three days, it must find another supplier in the network who can. Two days before the home is to be built, Sikisui assembles the components into modules in its factory.[6] The consultant offered to help Borstin's company identify its core competencies and to search for other business partners with whom to form a holonic network.

The third and last presentation had a dramatic opening. Pointing to a blank sheet of paper on her flip chart, the consultant asked Borstin what he saw. When Borstin said the obvious, "Nothing," she replied, "Precisely . . . that is what you must do. Start over. Start from scratch. Throw out the old and bring in the new. Competitive times demand nothing less than revolutionary change." She proceeded to draw a business system diamond, formed by arrows, on the blank flip-chart sheet to show how four key aspects of a company—business processes, jobs and structures, values and beliefs, management and measurement systems—are linked together.

---

6. P. McHugh, G. Merli, and W. A. Wheeler III. *Beyond Business Process Reengineering: Towards the Holonic Enterprise* (Chichester, England: John Wiley & Sons, 1995), pp. 16–17.

First, a company starts by identifying a number of core business processes (e.g., product development, order fulfillment, sales generation) that are crucial to success. Second, qualified employees are pulled from their functional departments and put into case teams with one team responsible for an entire process (jobs and structures). Third, managers create measures by which performance is evaluated; compensation systems are built to reward teams based on their abilities to create value for the customer (management and measurement systems). Fourth, employee values and beliefs must be shaped to be consistent with the new requirements of speed, quality, and accuracy. The consultant's approach to change would include identifying processes important to Borstin's company, redesigning who does what, and giving employees new tools to get more done.

Borstin was confused by everything he had heard. At one level, the presentations were unique—each consultant used different terminology and recommended different tools. At another level, however, there was a familiar ring resounding throughout all the presentations. What should Borstin do? Which, if any, of the consultants should be hired?

APPROACHES TO MANAGING BUSINESS PROCESSES

Jack Borstin's dilemma, as just described, is fictional. The content of the consultants' proposals, however, was based on actual descriptions appearing in their how-to books. Readers may have guessed that the first presentation embodied some of the key principles inherent in total quality management (TQM). TQM had its origins 40 years ago in a series of lectures on product quality given by Dr. W. Edwards Deming and Joseph M. Juran. The Pert chart, matrix diagram, and check sheet are some of the tools used in statistical control. The second presentation, discussing the holonic network concept, was based on ideas found in *Beyond Business Process Reengineering*. It was written by Patrick McHugh and William Wheeler III (from Coopers & Lybrand Management Consultants), and Giorgio Merli (from an Italian consulting firm, Galgano &

---

7. Ibid.

Associati).[7] The third presentation described important features of BPR as originally expressed by Michael Hammer and James Champy.[8] Hammer is a former MIT computer science professor and Champy is chair of a management consulting firm, CSC Index. Their book has been translated into 14 languages; its hardcover version has sold more than 1 million copies worldwide.

Ever since the reengineering craze began, consultants have scrambled to differentiate their offerings. As one might expect, BPR is a profitable business. Fees for reengineering advice can go as high as $1 million a month.[9] A year after Hammer and Champy published their book, CSC Index's revenues grew 30 percent to $150 million.[10] Another consultancy specializing in reengineering, Symmetrix, has seen its revenues rise to $20 million.[11] Nonetheless, it has become difficult to distinguish between a totally new approach to the structuring of organizations and between an old approach repackaged with a new name. The proliferation of terms—*process reengineering, process improvement,* and *process innovation*—adds to the confusion.

As Exhibit 1–1 shows, there are at least five distinct approaches to the management of business processes. They are similar because they all speak to the current need for corporations to identify their core processes, improve customer service, use information technology, and empower employees. They all believe that teams, should be created—be they called case teams, cross-functional teams or even quality circles—to assist in managing the business processes. They differ, however, regarding whether or not a firm's core processes should be contained within one company or owned by several different companies linked together via a network of experts.

Suggestions regarding the role played by top management in the reengineering process differ as well. Some consultants believe it should be a top-down approach; others believe it should be a bottom-up approach. The type of organizational change required—incremental or radical—has also been the subject of heated debate.

---

8. Hammer and Champy, *Reengineering the Corporation.*
9. P. Hemp, "Preaching the Gospel," *The Boston Globe,* June 30, 1992, p. 35.
10. "Call My Agent," A special background report on trends in industry and finance, *The Wall Street Journal,* May 19, 1994, p. 1.
11. Hemp, "Preaching."

E X H I B I T 1-1

A Comparison of Different Approaches to Managing Business Processes

	Total Quality Management	Business Process Reengineering	The Holonic Enterprise	The Horizontal Organization	Process Innovation
Consultants	J. McHugh (American Supplier Institute)*	Hammer & Champy (CSC Index)	P. McHugh, Merli & Wheeler (Coopers & Lybrand; Galgano)	Ostroff & Smith (McKinsey)	Davenport (Ernst & Young)
Key Principles	Quality gives meaning to what everyone does. Create products and services tailored to customer requirements. Use statistical controls.	Start with a clean slate. Define 5 or 6 core processes. Assign a case manager. Use IT as an enabler. Empower employees.	Core business processes extend far beyond the boundaries of a single company. Need to reengineer cross-company core processes.	Eliminate hierarchy and functional/departmental boundaries. Teams are used to manage everything.	Apply innovation to key processes. Consider new work strategies, actual process design, and the implementation of change in all its complex technological, human, and organizational dimensions.
Unit of Analysis	A single company	A single company	Many companies forming a holonic network.	A single company	A single company
Type of Change	Evolutionary	Revolutionary	Evolutionary	Revolutionary	Revolutionary
Participation	Bottom-up	Top-down	Between top managers of different firms	Top-down	Top-down
Scope	Encompasses the whole organization	Focuses on core business processes	Focuses on networks of organizations	Usually occurs at lower levels in organizations	Innovation can occur in single or multiple processes of a firm

*For a list of other TQM consultants, please see J. A. Edosomwan, *Organizational Transformation and Process Reengineering* (Delray Beach, FL: St. Lucie Press, 1996), pp. 175–77.

Hammer insists that the only way to get senior managers committed to BPR is if it calls for discontinuous and revolutionary change. This attitude, however, seems to ignore the human factor affecting the success of BPR programs. Ranganath Nayak, a senior vice president at Arthur D. Little, said, "Redesigning complex processes from scratch on a clean sheet of paper can be incredibly traumatic for an organization."[12]

I believe that companies should take a hard look at themselves and their capabilities before deciding which process approach to use. If, for example, a company is relatively successful, operates in a protective niche, and benefits from efficient operations, the continuous improvement techniques of TQM might be most appropriate. If, on the other hand, a company faces intense competition to the extent that its very survival is threatened, then the more comprehensive and radical approach to change associated with BPR would be necessary. If a company's employees are likely to resist change and to be reluctant to embrace new technologies, it might be better to follow an incremental program that is less intimidating to them. Here the approach would be to improve communication and coordination before attempting to change work flow or install advanced computer systems to automate processes. Yet another possibility would be to use BPR and TQM in combination: One division of a company might need a radical approach to change while the other might require incremental change.

A CLOSER LOOK AT BPR

Definition and Key Characteristics of BPR

The focus of the rest of this chapter is on the BPR approach to change. The people widely credited for inventing the term are Michael Hammer and James Champy. Their ideas are not grounded in theory but were derived from their empirical observations of companies. They studied the experiences of companies that 10 years ago were able to dramatically improve performance and radically change the way of work. BPR, therefore, is defined as, "The

---

12. Ibid.

fundamental rethinking and radical redesign of business processes to achieve dramatic improvements in critical contemporary measures of performance such as cost, quality, service, and speed."[13] The authors are careful to explain each phrase in their definition:

a. Fundamental thinking requires managers to ask the most basic questions about their companies and how they operate (e.g., Why do we do what we do? Why do we do it in the way we do?).

b. Radical redesign demands that companies invent completely new ways of managing their operations. Superficial changes, or activities intended to fine-tune existing structures, systems, and procedures, are not sufficient.

c. Dramatic improvements in performance occur through quantum leaps. Reengineering helps companies achieve a 100 percent improvement in quality, not a 10 percent improvement.

d. A process consists of a set of activities that enable a company to transform needed inputs into outputs of value to customers.

Several characteristics typify reengineered processes; as a result of BPR:

- Several jobs that were formerly considered distinct are combined into one.
- Workers make decisions by themselves and do not have to ask their superiors for solutions to problems.
- Many steps in a process that were once performed in a linear sequence can now be completed simultaneously.
- Multiple versions of processes are created so that special, complex, or large orders are handled separately from simple, routine, and small orders.
- Work is performed where it makes the most sense via outsourcing certain functions or allowing functional managers to bypass formal authority to get what they need.
- Checks and controls are conducted periodically when needed and not as every single activity is completed.
- The need to reconcile purchase orders and invoices or incoming goods and outgoing goods, is reduced because there are fewer handoffs.

---

13. Hammer and Champy, *Reengineering the Corporation,* p. 32

- Customer service representatives have all the information they need at their fingertips to handle customer requests, orders, or complaints.
- Information technology enables the home office to define acceptable parameters that allow it to remain competitive (e.g., the lowest price, the fastest delivery time) while giving the field representative greater autonomy to complete the sale without calling in for a quote or waiting for approval.

Questionnaires, such as the one developed by Coopers & Lybrand (see Exhibit 1–2) were developed so that managers could assess their company's readiness for reengineering. To these items, I would add the following questions particularly relevant for financial services companies:

1. Do you receive complaints from your traders that they are spending too much time processing transactions and too little time talking to clients? Y/N
2. Have you updated your computer system in the last three years with hardware enhancements and/or new software packages? Y/N
3. Are your brokers able to handle 90 percent of a client's buy or sell order by themselves, without handing it off to assistants or data input clerks? Y/N
4. Can your brokers handle routine orders placed by retail customers within one minute? Y/N
5. Has your firm been losing customers because they have taken their business to competitors or have begun using alternative market mechanisms, such as electronic trading, for their transactions? Y/N
6. Do your brokers spend most of their time handling the accounts of large institutional investors and thinking of ways to add value to the firm? Y/N

Successes and Failures of BPR Programs

A recent survey of 1,200 U.S. corporations conducted by Computer Economics Inc. of Carlsbad, California, estimated that spending on business reengineering will grow by 20 percent a year for the next

E X H I B I T 1–2

Questionnaire

Instructions:

The following self-assessment questions devised by consultants Coopers & Lybrand detect whether a company is ready to make a success of business process reengineering. Each requires a simple yes or no (Y/N) answer.

1. Do you review customer perception of your products and services monthly? Y/N
2. Does the team's reward depend specifically on achieving some measure of customer satisfaction? Y/N
3. Can you define your company's basis of competition as a process based on core competence? Y/N
4. Have you benchmarked your company's core business processes against those of your major competitors? Y/N
5. Does your business use process costing? Y/N
6. Could you write down more than three nonfinancial quantified targets for your company? Y/N
7. Has a new technology caused a major shift in your company's activity during the past three years? Y/N
8. Do you have a unique technical competitive advantage in any of your core business processes? Y/N
9. Is your company vulnerable to a takeover? Y/N
10. For new investments in core business processes, do you have a return-on-capital expenditure hurdle of at least 20 percent? Y/N
11. For new investments in noncore business processes, do you have a return-on-capital expenditure hurdle of at least 50 percent? Y/N
12. Does the head of your company pursue personal recognition ahead of recognition of your business? Y/N
13. Does the head of your company emphasize how people are expected to act? Y/N
14. Is there a commonly held view of the likely market share that will be held by your company in five years' time?
15. Have you any business-process or cross-functionally-oriented teams? Y/N
16. Do you consider that teams are less successful at achieving their goals than individuals? Y/N
17. Was the last major reorganization in your company more than one year ago? Y/N
18. Has your company ever launched a new product or service that if it failed would destroy the company? Y/N
19. Is it difficult for individuals to make career moves between different functions in the company? Y/N

EXHIBIT 1–2 *(CONCLUDED)*

---

20. Is everyone in the company required to undertake more than five days' training each year? Y/N

21. Are you achieving a 20 percent or more annual effectiveness improvement in your core business processes? Y/N

Assessment

Score 1 for each answer that tallies with the following: 1Y; 2Y; 3Y; 4Y; 5Y; 6Y; 7Y; 8Y; 9N; 10N; 11Y; 12Y; 13Y; 14Y; 15Y; 16N; 17N; 18Y; 19N; 20Y; 21Y.

Interpretation

Score 0–7

You have a long way to go. So many conditions for success are absent that the scale of the change needed will be beyond your current capability. Instead, you should undertake targeted improvement programs in a few areas such as customer research, market share projections, and cross-functional teams.

Score 8–14

You have got some conditions—begin to think about how a reengineering program could make a significant difference.

Score 15–21

You have great potential as a holonic node. You need to reorient your strategic thinking around participation in holonic networks.

Source: Patrick McHugh, Giorgio Merli, and William A. Wheeler III, *Beyond Business Process Reengineering: Toward the Holonic Network* (Chichester, England: John Wiley & Sons Ltd., 1995), pp.70–71. Reprinted with permission from Patrick McHugh, EDS Management Consulting Services, London, England.

three years. In 1997, U.S. companies will spend $52 billion on reengineering, with $40 billion of that going toward information systems.[14] Are these investments warranted? Does BPR deliver on its promises? What are the challenges and obstacles facing companies when they reengineer their businesses?

Many people believe that BPR is just the latest fad of the hour. Even though Hammer claims that BPR is a rejection of the old industrial model of division of labor, economies of scale, and hierarchical control, the approach nevertheless shares points of similarity with Frederick Taylor's time and motion studies from the 1920s. Taylor examined processes such as the sequence of activities required to lay bricks or shovel coal. He believed that by watching

---

14. B. Caldwell, "Missteps, Miscues," *Information Week,* June 20, 1994, pp. 50-52, 56-57.

films, observing workers, and redesigning tools, certain steps could be eliminated, combined, or moved to different parts of the body. When jobs were made more efficient, results were rather dramatic. Using scientific management techniques, Frank and Lillian Gilbreth, for example, reduced the number of motions used in bricklaying from 18 to 5 and increased average productivity from 120 to 350 bricks laid per hour.[15] Sounds like reengineering, albeit at a construction site or on the factory floor. Hammer and Champy's major contribution, therefore, becomes introducing reengineering into the workplace on a much broader scale and helping companies focus on core processes that affect the jobs of all employees—clerks, manual laborers and middle managers—whose activities are part of that process. The tools of the trade are no longer shovels and wrenches but Unix workstations and workflow software.

BPR also seems to have borrowed heavily from TQM, with the only main difference being BPR's emphasis on radical top-down change as opposed to incremental bottom-up change. It encompasses many of the seven criteria established by the Malcolm Baldridge National Quality Award in 1987 to promote quality excellence among U.S. companies. Award-winning companies must demonstrate a strong customer focus; effective, hands-on leadership; good systems for acquiring, analyzing, and using information; a strategic, long-range outlook toward quality; a focus on human resources development and excellence; effective process management; and a focus on a variety of measurements and results indicators.[16]

Similarly, BPR reiterates a few of the characteristics of successful companies; for example, close to the customer, simple form, lean staff, and simultaneous loose-tight properties identified by Peters and Waterman.[17] As David Lord, managing editor of *Consultant News*, has said, BPR is "a hot word. But you have to come at it with a fair amount of skepticism as to whether there's really anything new under the sun."[18]

---

15. S. J. Carroll and H. L. Tosi, *Organizational Behavior* (Chicago: St. Clair Press, 1977), p. 13.
16. G. M. Bounds, G. H. Dobbins, and O. S. Fowler, *Management: A Total Quality Perspective* (Cincinnati: South-Western College Publishing, 1995).
17. T. J. Peters and R. H. Waterman, *In Search of Excellence: Lessons from America's Best-Run Companies* (New York: Warner Books, 1982).
18. Hemp, "Preaching," p. 35.

There are some signs that reengineering programs do not always achieve their objectives. Survey after survey has revealed that many executives are not completely satisfied with the results. A recent Arthur D. Little survey of 350 executives in 14 industries reported that 68 percent of the executives polled felt that their companies experienced unanticipated problems from reengineering while 31 percent said their companies did not experience unanticipated problems (1 percent replied that they did not know).[19] Only 16 percent were fully satisfied with the reengineering efforts; 45 percent were partially satisfied, and 39 percent were dissatisfied.[20] A Price Waterhouse survey reported that 63 percent of executives from Fortune 500 and large British companies said reengineering did not help their firms expand market growth or increase the speed with which new products and services are introduced into the market.[21] Hammer, himself, was widely quoted as saying that between 50 and 70 percent of reengineering efforts do not achieve the desired breakthrough performance.

Another survey of 47 companies conducted by Dataquest, a subsidiary of Dun and Bradstreet, had favorable results to report. Of the 47, 34 percent were totally satisfied, 50 percent were highly satisfied, 10 percent were modestly dissatisfied, and 5 percent were somewhat dissatisfied with the results of BPR programs.[22] The consultants believe that some of the variance in satisfaction levels across surveys can be attributed to different definitions of BPR and different data collection methods. Although this may be true, companies should still undertake careful planning before embarking on a reengineering program. BPR may not be for everyone. Managers should take steps to ensure that failure does not characterize their company's BPR efforts.

As a starting point, companies should try to learn from the successes and failures of others. A Deloitte and Touche survey may be helpful in this regard. Sixty percent out of a sample of 400 U.S. and Canadian chief information officers said that "resistance to change" was an obstacle to business reengineering success. Forty

---

19. J. King, "Reengineering Slammed," *ComputerWorld* 28, no. 4 (June 13, 1994), pp. 1, 14.

20. Caldwell, "Missteps."

21. S. Berman, "Strategic Direction: Don't Reengineer without It," *Planning Review* 22, no. 6 (November-December 1994), pp. 18-23.

22. D. K. Carr and H. J. Johansson, *Best Practices in Reengineering: What Works and What Doesn't in the Reengineering Process* (New York: McGraw-Hill, 1995).

percent said that "limitations of existing systems" was an obstacle; thirty-eight percent said that "lack of executive consensus" was an obstacle.[23] Says Phillips Andrews of EDS Management Consulting Services, "There are a thousand reengineering trapdoors, and companies typically fall through at least one."[24] Reengineering requires hard work and persistence. According to Lynne Markus, a professor of information science at Claremont Graduate School, BPR is driven by lots of blood, sweat, and tears.[25]

Michael Norwich, formerly head of a business reengineering group at Merrill Lynch, identified the following factors as crucial to BPR success: sponsorship by top management; access to the right and the best people; a flexible but formal methodology; alliances formed between employees in business units, operations, technology, human resources, and finance; the inclusion of technology-related objectives in a company's formal strategic planning; the linking of BPR with other company initiatives (e.g., TQM; cost cutting); the development of customer-based measures; a recognition that BPR is a long-term initiative requiring three to seven years of work; and careful alignment of process, technology, and people.[26] A similar but less complete list of success factors were identified in a recent KPMG Peat Marwick study of 20 leading financial services companies. Strong senior management commitment, a long-term orientation, customer input, and quality were found to be important.[27]

THE ROLE OF ORGANIZATIONAL CULTURE IN BPR

According to many reengineering experts, management must formally assess a company's culture before embarking on a major change program. Employees are notoriously resistant to change, possess a fear of the unknown, and prefer habitual ways of performing tasks. An understanding of organizational culture is necessary so that a manager can more accurately determine which direction the company should take, when to introduce the change,

---

23. Caldwell, "Missteps."
24. Ibid., p. 50.
25. Ibid., p. 56.
26. Personal communication, March 29, 1996.
27. V. Elliott, "Quality Initiatives in Finance Services: What's Working and What's Not," *Bankers Magazine* 177, no. 6 (November-December 1994), pp. 49-52.

and how to educate and train employees who must embrace the change. Daniel Denison has proposed that organizations can be classified into one of four categories of culture based on (1) the extent to which the competitive environment requires change or stability and (2) the extent to which a company's strategic focus is internal or external.[28] I add to Denison's work by suggesting that managers should choose a change initiative based on the culture category that best reflects their organization's basic character.

Dension has suggested that companies with an adaptability culture focus on the external environment and are able to adapt to changing customer needs. Such companies can easily translate signals from the environment into new behavioral responses; they can quickly prepare a bid for a major new project and adopt a new set of processes for a task. Because employees are accustomed to change, are highly flexible, and are strongly committed to customers, BPR and process innovation methods might work best. I would also expect these companies to be quite willing to link with other companies in a holonic network to improve service to customers even further.

Companies with a mission culture place importance on a shared vision of organizational purpose. Managers shape behavior by envisioning a desired future state that is accepted by everyone. Such companies have an external focus but do not perceive the need for rapid change. TQM, with its emphasis on the overall organization, coordination of efforts among employees, and long-term improvements in quality, might be most appropriate for these types of organizations. The clean slate approach endorsed by BPR might be seen as too threatening for a company that imparts a sense of unity, purpose, and stability to employees.

Companies with an involvement culture recognize that flexibility is important in a changing environment. They encourage extensive participation from organizational members in decision making; employees are viewed as the key to a company's success. Employees feel a sense of ownership and responsibility. They become extremely committed to the organization and its achievement of goals. Here, I would think that those methods that empower

---

28. D. Denison, *Corporate Culture and Organizational Effectiveness*, (New York: John Wiley & Sons, 1990).

employees, use cross-functional teams, and eliminate levels of managerial hierarchy (e.g., the horizontal organization) would be most appropriate. Any method associated with a major workforce reduction program, however, would be devastating. Layoffs would be seen as a breach of trust that existed between managers and employees; they would deliver a severe blow to employee morale.

Finally, companies with a consistency culture have an internal focus and perceive the environment as being stable. Conformity, reliability, and efficiency are valued by managers. Employees are encouraged to follow established policies and practices as a way to achieving goals. Clearly, process innovation, would not be recommended in this case. Employees are not taught to question existing norms and operating policies. On the other hand, the emphasis on continual measurement, as well as the use of statistical controls, available in the TQM approach to change, would probably be appreciated by managers of such companies.

THE ROLE OF INFORMATION TECHNOLOGY IN BPR

Someone once complained that "If the automobile industry had progressed as fast as the computer industry, we'd all be driving Rolls-Royces that go a million miles an hour and cost 25 cents."[29] These advances in computer technology, bringing with them the capacity to process more and more information in less time, are revolutionizing the ways companies conduct business. T. H. Davenport has developed nine categories to describe the ways in which IT can support process innovation.

a. Automation: IT eliminates human labor from a process. In manufacturing companies, this occurs through robotics and cell controllers. In service companies, document imaging systems remove paper from the process while work-flow software defines the paths the images take through a process.

b. Information: IT allows data to reach employees; data are shared among the people who need them the most.

29. C. Currid, *Computing Strategies for Reengineering Your Organization,* (Rocklin, CA: Prima Publishing, 1996).

c. Sequentiality: IT makes it possible to switch from sequential processing to parallel processing. Work does not have to get passed from one person to the next in a cafeteria style. Instead, some activities within the process can be done simultaneously.

d. Tracking: IT helps employees track and monitor the status of a customer's order. It can show where the package, transaction, or order is located in the process. The goal is to avoid bottlenecks (e.g., too many client checks waiting to be scanned into the system).

e. Analysis: IT assists in the analysis of information needed for decision making. Through such tools as expert systems, companies can process more data in a shorter time. When reports are generated and distributed to key managers, they gain a better understanding of the business and can spend less time in routine meetings.

f. Geographical coordination: Computer-aided tools, electronic mail, and videoconferencing can bring together experts who may be dispersed geographically in different parts of the world. They can work on design or manufacturing issues while viewing the same images on their workstations.

g. Integration: IT provides database systems that enable members of a cross-functional team to share information. They can better manage all aspects of a product or service delivery process.

h. Distribution of intellectual assets: IT permits widespread distribution of knowledge so that successful practices and procedures that worked well in one unit of a company can be passed on to other units of the company.

i. Elimination of intermediaries: People serving as intermediaries—real estate agents, retail stores, stock brokers—are becoming scarce due to the rise of web pages showing images of houses, home shopping networks that display products on television, and electronic trading systems that enable investors to execute transactions via the telephone.[30]

Essinger and Rosen have compiled a checklist of the 10 most important guidelines for successful deployment of IT within an investment management firm. The checklist contains the following items:

---

30. T. H. Davenport, *Process Innovation: Reengineering Work through Information Technology,* (Boston: Harvard Business School Press, 1993).

- Recognize the need for active senior management support and participation.
- Appreciate the importance of IT in maintaining a firm's competitive position.
- Appoint one strong business unit executive to lead the project team.
- Make sure that IT staff understand the business side of the firm and are not treated as second-class citizens.
- Understand that IT and business units do not conflict but can work together in cooperation.
- Conduct adequate up-front planning.
- Synchronize business and IT strategies.
- Make sure that IT trainers have a first-class understanding of the business and the system deployed.
- Conduct post-installment appraisals and audits.
- Use common sense throughout; new technology should be seen as a tool, not as a substitute for human input.[31]

BPR IN FINANCIAL SERVICES COMPANIES

BPR, accompanied by IT, has the potential to significantly change the ways in which financial services companies conduct business in both their front and back offices. Exhibit 1–3 lists some of the core processes of financial services companies that might be appropriate for reengineering. Greater efficiency in managing these processes can result in a reduction of staff, increased capacity to handle large volumes of transactions, better service to customers, increased control, and error reduction. Traders can benefit when routine chores and cumbersome paperwork are eliminated; they will be free to concentrate their efforts on handling large customer transactions and adding value to the firm. Securities firms are especially interested in satisfying their customers since there is a growing tendency for customers seeking greater speed and accuracy to bypass brokers and complete their transactions by themselves through electronic off-exchange networks. As far back as 1971,

---

31. J. Essinger and J. Rosen, *Advanced Computer Applications for Investment Managers* (Oxford, England: Elsevier Science Publishers, 1989).

EXHIBIT 1–3

Processes in the Financial Services Industry

Opening and maintaining customer accounts: Setting up an account for a customer, recording investment objectives, keeping track of transactions, updating the account with new information.

Execution of orders: A client's buy or sell order is routed to the stock exchange, over-the-counter dealer, or alternative trading mechanism. The exact route depends on whether the order is an odd lot, a round lot, a large transaction, and so on.

Confirmation of transactions: After a transaction, the customer is informed of the terms and is billed for monies or securities due the brokerage firm.

Clearance and settlement of transactions: Transactions are compared to make sure buyers and sellers agree on price and quantity. Funds or securities must be transferred to the appropriate parties. As of spring 1995, the Securities and Exchange Commission has required that all stock transactions be settled in three days instead of five.

Compliance management: Brokers must establish the suitability of transactions and activities in the account ("know the customer" rule). Stockbrokers must make trades for customers based on investment objectives (e.g., growth, income, speculation) stated in writing.

Risk management: Monitoring individual traders to make sure that they do not overexpose the company to risky situations or engage in illegal behaviors.

Cashiering: Moving all securities and funds within the firm. Checking to determine that securities are properly endorsed, have been reregistered into a negotiable name, and so forth. Undeliverable securities are returned.

Margin lending: Some customers purchase securities on margin; that is, they pay for part of the purchase and the firm lends the rest to them.

Selecting the company's product mix: Determining the combination of types of securities (e.g., common stock, bonds) the firm wants to offer customers.

Investment research: Preparing and issuing research reports.

Providing financial planning and investment advice: Determining and satisfying customer needs for financial investments.

Stanley Ross, a London banker, made the following prediction: "What we shall eventually see is one vast over-the-counter market, embracing all forms of intangibles, bonds, equities, commodities, etc., where the major stock exchanges of the world—New York, London, Paris, Tokyo—will be all bypassed by the over-the-counter trader."[32]

---

32. M. E. Blume, J. J. Siegel, and D. Rottenberg, *Revolution on Wall Street: The Rise and Fall of the New York Stock Exchange*, (New York: W.W. Norton, 1993), p. 241.

To explore the benefits of BPR, let us take as an example the retail-client trade-execution process. First, I will explain the basics of how transactions are handled in firms with nonautomated processes. Then, I will describe what happens in firms using advanced computer technology. In the first scenario, a client calls a broker in one of the security firm's branches to purchase 100 shares of Apple Computer, an over-the-counter security, at market price. The broker (or the broker's assistant) writes a paper ticket with the customer's name, account number, Apple's ticker symbol, the amount of shares, whether the order is a buy or sell order, and any special instructions. The broker stamps the time he took the order on the ticket and forwards a carbon copy, on a conveyor belt, to the wireroom. In the wireroom, the order is keypunched into the central computer system. If the firm makes a market in this security, the order goes to the trading desk of the brokerage house. Since the trading desk is not located in the same branch in which the order was placed, a copy of the ticket must be printed out. The trader executes the market order against his inventory. He prepares a paper confirmation slip with all the details of the transaction that goes to the keypunch operator at the trading desk. A copy gets printed out at the branch, it gets passed to the broker, the broker calls the client to inform her that the transaction was completed.

The second scenario demonstrates how technologically advanced securities firms can expedite this labor-intensive process. A call comes in from a client in Peoria who wants to purchase 100 shares of Apple at the market price. The broker at the local branch is connected to an Integrated Services Digital Network (ISDN) telephone line that transmits the telephone number to the brokerage house's integrated computer system. The computer is thus activated automatically and sends relevant customer account information back to the broker's computer screen—even before the telephone rings. The broker picks up the telephone and says, "Hi, Mrs. Jones. How are you today?" He can then use his mouse to click on his screen and type in Apple's ticker symbol, the number of shares, information on pricing, and whether this is a buy or sell order. (The customer's name and account number already appear on the screen.) The broker clicks on another box on his screen and the order gets sent electronically to the trading desk of the market maker for Apple at the brokerage firm.

Because the security firm's trading manager and the traders have set certain parameters in advance (e.g., for small trades under 1,000 shares, for a certain fixed spread between bid and ask prices, for low-volume versus high-volume trading days), this particular order can be executed automatically. The trader gets a message at the bottom of his screen that he just sold 100 shares of Apple at the market price of $20½. He also sees in his logs that he now has 900 shares left in his inventory. A message is sent back to the broker in Peoria. Only five seconds have passed and he is still on the phone with the client. He tells the client that she has just purchased 100 shares of Apple for $20½ per share. The entire trading process has been seamless for the customer.

In terms of some of the hardware and software required for the second scenario, the brokerage firm needs to supply its brokers with, for purposes of illustration, IBM-compatible Pentium personal computers. A client/server system is set up to handle transmissions of customer information to and from its database systems and the broker's personal computer. ISDN communications equipment must be linked to the firm's integrated computer system. Software is required so that the telephone number of an incoming call can be matched with the telephone number appearing in a customer's computerized account file. The trader also needs a personal computer connected to the integrated system. His software captures information from the branches electronically and executes certain transactions automatically. Using such a process, not a single paper ticket is written. The wire room has been bypassed. The trader does not get actively involved in the transaction and can devote his energies to handling the more profitable institutional investor accounts.

Transitions from manual trading processes to electronic trading processes are seldom smooth. One needs to consider how BPR is implemented in the real world with all of its complexities. One must anticipate the obstacles that might arise when companies change their technologies, and what companies can do to overcome these obstacles. The case study that follows is based on interviews with two key managers who oversaw a BPR project. It is intended to provide insights on those factors that contribute to successful reengineering. It demonstrates the requirement for highly involved and strong top management; for compatibility among the client, the vendors, and the programmers; and for consideration of the needs of the eventual users of the technology.

BPR IN ACTION: THE CASE OF EQ FINANCIAL CONSULTANTS, INC.

EQ Financial Consultants, Inc. (formerly known as Equico Securities, Inc.) is a wholly owned broker-dealer subsidiary of The Equitable Life Assurance Society of the United States. EQ Financial offers mutual funds from more than 25 fund companies, as well as discount brokerage services to individual clients and businesses. Equitable agents can provide these investment opportunities to clients, along with life insurance products and annuities. I had the opportunity to meet with Theresa Nurge-Alws, senior vice president and chief operations officer of EQ Financial, and Karen Curtis, division manager of information services with Equitable, in EQ Financial's Manhattan offices. What follows is a description of a major reengineering project undertaken by EQ Financial that began in 1992. Fine-tuning of the reengineered processes is still being done today in an ongoing effort to seek additional improvements.

The Forces of Change

In the early 1990s, pressures to reengineer EQ Financial's processes came from a number of sources:

1. Due to the tremendous growth in the mutual funds business, the volume of transactions and related activity greatly taxed the capabilities of the existing computer system. Consultants were often being called in to make enhancements to the system to accommodate increased volumes of work.

2. EQ Financial's operations were paper intensive. Completed customer documentation was kept in paper folders in a file room. If an agent called to find out the status of a client's transaction in process, or with a general problem regarding the transaction, it was cumbersome to retrieve documentation in a timely fashion. Yet, employees needed to have customer information at their fingertips.

3. Each transaction involved unnecessary costs because of the amount of manual processing and potential for human error.

The Decision Alternatives

EQ Financial began its reengineering project with a comprehensive business review in which supervisors from all functional areas were involved. They were asked to map out the steps encountered in the work process and identify ways to streamline the processes and eliminate unnecessary steps. The firm developed three different decision alternatives in an effort to eliminate the inefficiencies stemming from its paper intensive processes and to implement new technologies that would support the redesigned work-processes. The first alternative was to install an entirely new computer system, along with vendor-developed imaging and work-flow software. The second alternative was to enhance the existing mainframe system by upgrading the hardware and by purchasing new vendor-developed imaging and work-flow software that would be customized to meet EQ Financial's needs. The third alternative was to create new imaging and work-flow software in-house according to specific EQ Financial requirements and to integrate it with the existing mainframe computer system.

A decision was made to pursue the first alternative. An entirely new system was to be built. An outside consulting firm was brought in to develop the new system that would use the latest technology, including software programming using C++ object-oriented programming language. The goal was to have the new system up and running within nine months. Several months into the project, however, the project team realized that they had set overly ambitious goals. The technology was too new and too sophisticated for the firm's needs. The outside consulting group did not have a clear enough understanding of the complexities of the business to totally reinvent an accounting system and a trading system in such a short time. Work on the new system could not possibly be completed before the deadline and within the budget. The difficult decision was made to abandon the initiative. Fortunately, senior management at The Equitable remained committed to the project.

EQ Financial, with the support of Equitable's top management, decided to pursue the second alternative, that is, to enhance the existing mainframe computer system, purchase new vendor-developed imaging and work-flow software, and customize it to meet EQ Financial's needs. Enterprise Technology Corporation (ETC), a New York-based financial technology consultancy, was hired to work alongside Equitable's programmers and enhance the mainframe systems. ETC's consultants had installed EQ Financial's original mainframe computer system and had been maintaining it up to the present. They were, therefore, intimately knowledgeable about EQ Financial's businesses and systems requirements. This time, progress was much smoother. The first phase of the enhanced system was up and running within eight months. The third and last phase was installed two months later.

The New Work Processes

Before reengineering, every transaction passed through 10 desks before being completed and filed away. Much time was spent opening, sorting, and distributing the mail. Handwritten logs of checks were kept because checks could not be removed from the cash control room. Many documents had to be photocopied and sent to the various processing groups. The work came out in batches and was routed to supervisors who manually assigned the work to employees. Supervisors had to check the in boxes of every employee to determine the progress made toward completing the work.

In the new system, the mail is opened, sorted, scanned into the computer system, indexed, and placed into electronic folders. The electronic folders are automatically routed to a number of work baskets. Usually, four or five employees are responsible for completing the work in each main work basket. They select work from the work basket and process it. Items in the basket are prioritized by of what must be done first (e.g., large dollar trades; individual retirement accounts during tax season). Work is then automatically routed to the next work basket in the process.

The supervisor can monitor the status of work in process by logging directly into the work-flow system. He or she can also obtain productivity statistics by function and by individual employee. An on-line tracking system enables supervisors to locate a work item in process, to identify who has worked on it so far, and what action was taken. They can determine when a delay occurred and why. Summarizing the impact that these changes have had on EQ Financial, Theresa Nurge-Alws said, "What we have been able to do essentially, by streamlining the process and the system, is allow our employees to focus on the more important aspects of their work by eliminating the time-consuming clerical functions. For example, order takers can now devote their attention to a suitability check and review of each transaction, instead of spending a portion of their time matching and assembling the appropriate documents, creating a folder, and photocopying documents to be sent to the fund company."[33]

As a result of the reengineering project, EQ Financial employees have better control of documents. There is no longer the possibility of misplacing documents during the multiple steps in the processes. Every document reaches its endpoint in the process successfully. Supervisors have real-time access to information regarding the status of a trade. Problems that arise after a trade (e.g., the wrong fund is purchased or the registration is sent incorrectly) can be handled immediately, while the agent is still on the telephone. The firm is now approximately 85 percent paperless and has experienced roughly a 20–25 percent increase in productivity in the new business area and a 30–35 percent increase in productivity in other related areas. Whereas before it took five minutes to process a mail order (of which two minutes were spent logging the check, assembling the paper and photocopying various forms), it now takes under three minutes. Signs on the walls of EQ Financial's offices offer constant reminders to employees—Keep It Simple and Kill the Paper—Save a Tree.

LESSONS LEARNED FROM THE EXPERIENCES OF EQ FINANCIAL CONSULTANTS, INC.

The EQ Financial case brings to light a number of critical factors responsible for BPR success. The case is unique because one group of managers learned from two opposite experiences: one involved a failed initiative that had to be abandoned; the other involved a successful initiative that became a model for other Equitable business units to emulate. The specific lessons learned from the EQ Financial case follow.

Lesson One: Reengineer Work Processes First; Redesign Systems Second

The original outside consulting team hired by EQ Financial encouraged the firm to completely rethink its business. Employees

---

33. Personal communication, March 11, 1996.

at all levels—from managers to accountants to order takers—were gathered together in the same room. They were advised to eradicate from their minds all knowledge of the old operating processes. They were asked: "How would you *like* to conduct business, while keeping in mind what you need to do from a legal and regulatory perspective." This type of thinking helped EQ Financial avoid a common pitfall. Successful reengineering does not consist of merely transforming a company from a paper to a paperless one by keeping its existing processes, procedures, and policies intact. Managers who question all aspects of the business are freed of the old assumptions and can focus on genuine efforts to improve and update their current business processes.

Moreover, EQ Financial started using many parts of the newly designed work flows, policies, and procedures as soon as they were developed on paper. The functional areas did not wait for the on-line computerized system to be completed. Employees, therefore, had an opportunity to become comfortable with the revised format in which they were required to perform their jobs. It did not matter that they were still processing the work manually. People became comfortable with the new work flow. This phasing in helps to avoid the psychological shock employees sometimes encounter when they must adapt to both new processes and new technologies simultaneously.

Lesson Two: Involve All Employees in Reengineering from Start to Finish

EQ Financial employees, especially the end users who would handle the actual processing, were treated as customers. The programmers would map out a screen and ask the end users whether they liked it, if they thought it would work, and so on. During the entire project, programmers would give end users from each of EQ Financial's functional areas live demonstrations of the software. Their reactions were gauged; their suggestions were carefully considered. Because end users contributed to the design of the software, they embraced it enthusiastically once the new system became operational. Finally, throughout the project, a "One Team, One Goal" approach was adhered to. There was no us-versus-them mentality; this was an important factor in the smooth implementation of the project.

Lesson Three: Develop a Partnership with Vendors, Consultants, and Programmers

The days when technology-oriented companies purchase vendor hardware/software without a firm commitment from the vendors for after-sales support are numbered. It is important to establish clear communication among the company, the vendors, the consultants, and the developers. Each and every participant must view the company's success as a personal success. Everyone must have a stake in the outcome. EQ Financial managers also learned that it is often preferable to purchase a tool set, instead of a complete computer software package, so that programmers who know the business well can custom-design the new work flow themselves.

Theresa Nurge-Alws advises managers to ask vendors and consultants as many questions as they can think of, and as early as they can, to avoid surprises during the actual implementation of the system. She gives the example of one vendor-related problem that occurred early on in the EQ Financial project. Although the vendor had a solid foundation in the imaging business for 10 years—a long time considering how new imaging is—EQ Financial was unaware that this was one of the first times that the vendor was installing a new type of scanner software at a client site, and was therefore unprepared for the normal number of problems and bugs that can be encountered in a new release. More detailed research might have alerted EQ Financial to this potential problem.

Lesson Four: Set Up Multiple Opportunities for Learning the New Processes

Extensive training was critical to the success of the reengineering project. Formal classroom training was held twice a week for six weeks. Employees learned the meaning of new terminology and concepts; for example, what the words *imaging* and *work flow* meant. When the new computer equipment arrived on their desks, employees were trained in such generic applications as Microsoft Windows and learned how to use a mouse, along with a keyboard. All employees, including those in accounting, were trained on a generic work-flow process developed for the service function of the business. Even though many of the employees being trained would not be handling the actual processing, it was important for them to gain an appreciation of how imaging and work flow actually functioned. Employees were encouraged to practice using the new, stand-alone service-processing system during their free time. Finally, all EQ Financial employees were trained to use the new system specifically for their functions. On weekends, they participated in a simulation in which an entire day's work of transactions was recreated and reprocessed—this time, electronically.

EQ Financial managers were quick to realize that new technology can breed employee resistance and fear of change. Familiarity and practice with the new technology, however, raises employee comfort levels significantly. Because the employees knew in advance what was going to happen, the start-up of the new system went smoothly. Day one of the full implementation was quite successful. Aside from some minor problems preparing and scanning the documents, everything went well. No major changes had to be made to any of the programs once they were implemented.

Lesson Five: Reengineering Requires Top Management Support

EQ Financial benefited from the continual financial, technical, and management support provided by the parent company, Equitable Life. Top management demonstrated its commitment by assigning a full-time business manager (Theresa Nurge-Alws) to oversee the reengineering project. A steering committee that included Equitable's chief information officer and EQ Financial's president met on a regular basis. As Karen Curtis said, "I think another success factor was the support that we as middle managers received from upper management. Because the technology was new to the company, they were active and involved in its development. They were always there and were dedicated to the project; they took the time to meet with us whenever needed."[34]

Managers came out of the meetings with important decisions having been made and with the power to carry them out. To gain approval, decisions were niether deferred to different areas (e.g., to the business group or to the technology group) nor did they travel

---

34. Personal communication, March 11, 1996.

up and down the hierarchy (e.g., to Equitable managers or to EQ Financial managers); they were made at the work site. Senior managers were committed to the project because they wanted to implement the same technological innovations throughout the entire company. EQ Financial was an excellent candidate for experimentation. EQ Financial had a stake in the project because managers needed to gain control of the enormous increase in volume in the mutual funds business; they knew the answer was technology—not additional staff. Thus, a win-win situation existed for everyone.

Lesson Six: It Pays to Share Information Internally

EQ Financial's BPR project has become a training ground for other Equitable business units. Karen Curtis is now handling reengineering projects in the life insurance business. Many of the same programmers have moved there with her. The advice provided by Theresa Nurge-Alws has enabled other business areas to avoid some of EQ Financial's early obstacles. EQ Financial's major systems enhancements were finished two years ago. Since then, even more sophisticated technological tools have become available in the marketplace. Programmers involved in reengineering at Equitable's life insurance business have become knowledgeable about these tools and are sharing this information with EQ Financial. Because of this help, EQ Financial is now updating its systems to include these new tools.

TOWARD THE RESTRUCTURING
OF AN ENTIRE INDUSTRY

One of the more interesting ironies of today's marketplace is that information about securities transactions moves through our economy in an elaborate telecommunications network at blinding speed until it hits the point of trade—either in Chicago's futures pits or on the floor of the New York Stock Exchange. What happens at the point of trade? Information literally shifts gears from the speed of light to the speed of tennis shoes, as buy and sell orders pop out of computer networks into trading pits or specialist posts.

Former SEC commissioner, Joseph Grundfest[35]

---

35. Blume, Siegel, and Rottenberg, *Revolution*, pp. 203-04.

BPR in the financial services industry seems to have only just begun. It has the potential of changing forever the ways in which trades get placed and executed. It will affect all the major players in the industry, from the retail and institutional clients, to the brokerage firms, and to the major stock exchanges. Today, institutions can trade with other institutions directly through an electronic trading system known as Instinet owned by Reuters. Retail clients are able to place small orders electronically through such services as E-Schwab On-line Investing. E-Schwab's slogan is "helping investors help themselves." For a $39 commission, investors can use their personal computers and Schwab software to execute trades up to 1,000 shares. Another new service, provided by Lombard Institutional Brokerage, a division of Thomas F. White & Company, is accessible through the Internet. Free of charge, registered users can retrieve 15-minute delayed stock and option quotes as well as graphs that track changes in stock prices. Account holders can use the following services: order entry, portfolio management, and trade executions. Lombard charges $30 per trade regardless of whether the transaction is completed over the Internet or via more traditional routes. Interested in opening a Lombard account? Go to the firm's home page on the World Wide Web and request an application via E-mail, by clicking with your mouse. Lombard's CEO, Eric Roach, expects that 40 percent of its trades will be conducted over the Internet by 1999.[36]

According to a *Wall Street & Technology* report, electronic trading systems now handle only 10 percent of the volume traded by the New York Stock Exchange (NYSE).[37] Nonetheless, they are beginning to place competitive pressures on brokerage firms and traditional exchanges. Brokerage firms are likely to continue to cut staff and to eliminate branches. We will likely see further industry consolidation, with more brokerage firms merging with other brokerage firms. Technological developments in the industry may also signal the demise of some of the large stock-exchanges that have been slow to adopt electronic trading systems. Joseph Rosen, managing director of Enterprise Technology Corporation (ETC), a New

---

36. E. R. Chabrow, "Wall Street on the Desktop," *Information Week*, March 11, 1996, pp. 61-66.
37. C. Smith, "The Electronic Elite," *Wall Street & Technology* 12, no. 6 (October, 1994), pp. 22-24, 26-27.

York-based financial technology consultancy, said, "A lot of people see the New York Stock Exchange and its processes as woefully antiquated . . . specialists are always interjected in the middle."[38]

Up to a point, brokerage firms handling an order to buy or sell a listed security for a client can do it electronically. The broker transmits the order to the trader at the trading desk without having to write a paper ticket and without going through the wire room. The order can even be electronically sent to the brokerage firm's booth on the floor of the New York Stock Exchange (NYSE). For small orders placed by institutional clients (up to 30,999 shares), the order can continue an automated route to the specialist's post through SuperDOT, a computerized order routing system operated by the NYSE. For large orders placed by institutional clients, however, the floor trader has to pick up the order at the booth and walk it over to the specialist's post. Often the trader works the order by making small purchases (or sales) at a time to not drive the stock price up (or down) all at once. This time-consuming activity requires a good deal of finesse on the part of the trader. Confirmation of the order gets communicated back to the trader, to the institutional salesperson, and to the client. Many Wall Street observers would like to see traders connected with specialists through on-line computer systems that would allow them to negotiate the terms of a deal electronically instead of through a physical meeting held on the floor. This development is unlikely, however, due to the vested interests of the specialists who would like to keep their jobs.

There are, however, a number of alternatives to the NYSE. Bernard L. Madoff Investment Securities is, according to Joseph Rosen of ETC, "the archetypal trading firm of the future."[39] Madoff has provided trade execution services for banks, broker-dealers, and financial institutions for more than 35 years. Madoff is not a member of the NYSE but makes markets in at least 800 of the NYSE's most active stocks. Of the orders Madoff receives from its broker-dealer clients, 95 percent are for trades less than 5,000 shares. They are delivered electronically over the firm's proprietary network. Madoff's in-house automated system then executes the orders, usually within five seconds, at the best prevailing National

---

38. Personal communication, March 9, 1996.
39. Personal communication, March 16, 1996.

Market System prices after opportunities for price improvement have been explored in other markets. The trades are then simultaneously reported to the broker-dealer clients and the National Market System consolidated tape. All of this is accomplished through computer systems and networks linked to the National Association of Securities Dealers Automated Quotation (NASDAQ) service and the Cincinnati Stock Exchange as well as other primary and regional market centers. There is no trading floor.

Madoff makes its money by committing its capital as a market maker, not by charging commissions. The firm hopes to profit by purchasing stock at the lower bid price and selling it at the higher ask price. Typically, the spread between the bid and the ask price amounts to an eighth of a point. Madoff has made use of the practice of paying brokers a small fee, $.01 per share, for some of its order flow. The Securities and Exchange Commission and the National Association of Securities Dealers have reviewed and approved this practice and set guidelines for its use along with requirements for proper disclosure to the customer.

So far in this chapter, I have only discussed how electronic trading can improve processes in the execution of orders for listed and over-the-counter equity securities. Similar technological advances, however, are beginning to materialize in the trading of other financial instruments. Here are two examples. Futures trading firms in the United States are addressing issues of paperless trading, order routing, and system compatibility.[40] As a first step, the industry has developed a set of standards, with the help of a partnership formed between Tom Basso of Trendstat, the Managed Futures Association's standards committee, and the Futures Industry Association's technology committee, that will provide futures traders and brokers with a common language to electronically transmit trading instructions and reports. Says Robb Romaine, vice chair of RXR Group, "We're taking an industry that has operated at a cottage level and moving it into the 21st century."[41] The first fully automated anonymous trading system for odd-lot corporate bonds, BondNet Trading Systems, Inc., of Greenwich, Connecticut,

---

40. L. Barney, "Will the Futures Industry Live Up to Its Standards?" *Wall Street & Technology* 12, no. 15 (July 1995), pp. 28-32, 34.
41. Ibid, p. 31.

has just been introduced. Subscribers must trade a minimum of 2,000 bonds a month. According to BondNet's CEO, Gordon Henderson, "BondNet will do to the odd-lot corporate bond business what NASDAQ did to over-the-counter trading."[42]

Thus, we see that BPR in the financial services industry is enabling buyers to interact directly with sellers of stocks, bonds, futures, options, and mutual funds, without ever having to engage in face-to-face transactions and without having to go through stock brokers, specialists, or even traders. The possibilities are endless. Is there a downside to technological progress? The drive toward greater efficiency through automation in the financial services industry will mean that more and more employees will be laid off. BPR has become negatively associated with downsizing. Members of society are only beginning to address the emotional and financial impact that downsizing has on employees and their families.

To summarize, this chapter gave an overview of the different theoretical approaches to BPR. It discussed how BPR is not only changing processes within individual companies but also changing the structure of an entire industry. Based on a case study, I have identified some of the key factors that can lead to successful BPR. To those who argue that BPR is a fad, I would say, the debate is moot. It is impossible to reverse the far-reaching changes that it has already brought to the financial services industry.

REFERENCES

Barney, L. "Will the Futures Industry Live up to Its Standards?" *Wall Street & Technology* 12, no. 15 (July 1995), pp. 28–32, 34.

———. "Shedding Light and Liquidity on Corporate Bonds." *Wall Street & Technology* 12, no. 15 (July 1995), pp. 42–44.

Berman, S. "Strategic Direction: Don't Reengineer Without It." *Planning Review* 22, no. 6 (November-December 1994), pp. 18–23.

Blume, M. E.; J. J. Siegel; and D. Rottenberg. *Revolution on Wall Street: The Rise and Fall of the New York Stock Exchange.* New York: W. W. Norton, 1993.

---

42. L. Barney, "Shedding Light and Liquidity on Corporate Bonds," *Wall Street & Technology* 12, no. 15 (July 1995), pp. 42-44.

Bounda, G. M.; G. H. Dobbins; and O. S. Fowler. *Management: A Total Quality Perspective.* Cincinnati: South-Western College Publishing, 1995.

Byrne, J. A. "The Horizontal Corporation." *Business Week,* December 20, 1993, pp. 76–81.

Caldwell, B. "Missteps, Miscues." *InformationWeek,* June 20, 1994, pp. 50–52, 56–57.

"Call My Agent. A Special Background Report on Trends in Industry and Finance." *The Wall Street Journal,* May 19, 1994, p. 1.

Carr, D. K., and H. J. Johansson. *Best Practices in Reengineering: What Works and What Doesn't in the Reengineering Process.* New York: McGraw-Hill, 1995.

Carroll, S. J., and H. L. Tosi. *Organizational Behavior.* Chicago: St. Clair Press, 1977.

Chabrow, E. R. "Wall Street on the Desktop." *InformationWeek,* March 11, 1996, pp. 61–66.

———. "Information Week 500: A New Era Is Brokered In." *InformationWeek,* September 18, 1995, pp. 112, 114, 116.

Currid, C. *Computing Strategies for Reengineering Your Organization.* Rocklin, CA: Prima Publishing, 1996.

Davenport, T.H. *Process Innovation: Reengineering Work through Information Technology.* Boston: Harvard Business School Press, 1993.

Denison, D. *Corporate Culture and Organizational Effectiveness.* New York: John Wiley & Sons, 1990.

Edosomwan, J. A. *Organizational Transformation and Process Reengineering.* Delray Beach, FL: St. Lucie Press, 1996.

Elliott, V. "Quality Initiatives in Financial Services: What's Working and What's Not." *Bankers Magazine* 177, no. 6 (November-December 1994), pp. 49–52.

Essinger, J., and J. Rosen. *Advanced Computer Applications for Investment Managers.* Oxford, England: Elsevier Science Publishers, 1989.

Hammer, M. "Reengineering Work: Don't Automate, Obliterate." *Harvard Business Review* 90, no. 4 (July–August 1990), pp. 104–112.

Hammer, M., and J. Champy. *Reengineering the Corporation: A Manifesto for Business Revolution.* New York: Harper Collins Publishers, 1993.

Hemp, P. "Preaching the Gospel." *Boston Globe,* June 30, 1992, p. 35.

King, J. "Reengineering Slammed." *ComputerWorld* 28, no. 24 (June 13, 1994), pp. 1, 14.

McHugh, P.; G. Merli; and W. A. Wheeler. *Beyond Business Process Reengineering: Towards the Holonic Enterprise.* Chichester, England: John Wiley & Sons, 1995.

Peters, T. J., and R. H. Waterman. *In Search of Excellence: Lessons from America's Best-Run Companies.* New York: Warner Books, 1982.

Sales, R. "Five Decisions: Smith Barney's Trading Room Relocation Project." *Waters,* Summer 1995, pp. 65–67, 98–100.

Saunders, A., and L. J. White. *Technology and the Regulation of Financial Markets.* Lexington, MA: D. C. Heath and Company, 1986.

Schmerken, I. "Reengineering Wall Street's Systems." *Wall Street Computer Review* 9, no. 4 (January 1992), pp. 14–22.

Smith, C. "The Electronic Elite." *Wall Street & Technology* 12, no. 6 (October 1994), pp. 22–24, 26–27.

Stern, R. L. "Living off the Spread." *Forbes* 114, no. 1 (July 10, 1989), pp. 66–67.

"The Wiring of Wall Street." *The Economist* 322, no. 7747 (February 22, 1992), pp. 69–70.

Weiss, D. M. *After the Trade Is Made: Processing Securities Transactions.* 2nd ed. New York: New York Institute of Finance, 1993.

2

⑥ RIGHTSIZING: CLIENT/SERVER VERSUS MAINFRAME PLATFORMS

Armand Keim,
President
Keim Consulting Associates

The subject of rightsizing—the selection of the proper size and type of computer platform for an application set—could include consideration of a variety of alternatives. However, most discussions of rightsizing focus on whether to use a client/server or a mainframe platform. That is the primary focus of this chapter. When relevant, we discuss other platforms involved in rightsizing.

As noted later in this chapter, the whole question of client/server or mainframe derives from the evolution of a distributed model of computing based on the development of the PC, the client/server, and the networks that support their interconnection. In this model, processing and storage are distributed between the PC (the client) and the server. This model is in contrast to the centralized model where all processing is done on a central computer, usually a mainframe. The server in the distributed model provides processing, database services, and connectivity capabilities for the client computers in the network.

After describing the process of selecting the proper computer platform, we discuss some of the fundamentals involved in how and when to downsize from a mainframe to client/server. This is the activity most often performed in rightsizing. This chapter provides general guidelines and does not attempt to be a definitive text.

A simplification made in this chapter has to do with the nature of client/server platforms. There is a wide range of capabilities and structures within platforms commonly called servers. In addition to the fact that a single server unit can itself have a wide range of capabilities depending on the hardware and operating systems options selected, multiple server units can be combined to operate effectively together in several ways to greatly increase the overall capability. This chapter refers to the whole range of servers when it uses the term *client/server*.

Much has been said and written about rightsizing that a priori concludes that the right size for a system is always client/server with an open operating system. (Open operating systems are defined in detail later in this chapter.) Many have become so enamored with client/server and open operating systems that they lose perspective on what they should be trying to accomplish in rightsizing. Many factors must be considered in deciding how to select the right size hardware and appropriate operating system for a particular application set. This chapter will help you make these decisions rationally rather than based on religious fervor.

This chapter is written for both the technically sophisticated and for those who desire only a general understanding of the subject. The technically sophisticated are asked to bear with some of the explanations and definitions provided. This chapter is not intended to advance their technical knowledge but to give them a better understanding of the purpose and process of rightsizing from the management perspective.

The technically unsophisticated may find certain areas difficult to understand but should still gain much from the material. They too should gain an understanding of the alternatives involved and the basis for making rightsizing decisions from a management perspective.

This chapter will not help you make cookbook decisions; the subject is far too complex for that. Any attempt at a cookbook would be self-defeating. We are concerned with the concepts and principles involved in making these decisions. Hopefully the mainframe and the client/server zealots can both find reasons to think about the principles of rightsizing before plunging headlong into a potential disaster.

One of the important precepts of this chapter is that a computer is a computer, is a computer. That is to say that if you really consider the constituent parts and the architecture of servers and mainframes, they are more alike than they are different. Of course, the differences make one more suitable for a particular situation than another. Therefore an understanding of their differences is important in making the rightsizing decision. Later, this chapter describes the fundamentals of the alternative architectures. First, we discuss the four primary areas of difference:

Computer hardware—The actual physical parts of the computer such as the memory, central processing unit (CPU), disk memory, and communication devices.

Operating systems—The resident program that controls and directs the actions of the computer.

Networks—The communications mechanism that connects the various locations that interact to perform a processing function.

Support—The people required to create, maintain, and enhance the applications.

HOW CLIENT/SERVER AND MAINFRAME PLATFORMS DIFFER

Hardware

There is much that is very similar in the architecture and components of the server and the mainframe hardware. In the last several years the manufacturers of both have been incorporating one another's designs and using more and more of the same components. Their hardware has become more alike and will continue to do so.

Before going much further, it is necessary to review briefly the general nature of the server and the mainframe for the technically unsophisticated reader. The technologically sophisticated reader should at least scan this section to review its principles.

A mainframe is usually a very large computer with a design and operating system that is proprietary to its manufacturer. These designs generally date back 15 or 20 years. The manufacturers of these computers that commonly come to mind are IBM, Unisys, Amdahl, and Hitachi. These machines did the preponderance of computing until the emergence of client/server. Some readers might wonder why we have not mentioned the minicomputers that were so popular in the late 1970s and 1980s. For the purpose of the comparison, the minicomputers are included in the term *mainframes*. This simplification may be a difficult assumption for some readers.

Mainframes are still manufactured in large numbers and used for expanding existing applications and creating new ones, many of which are mission critical. They sometimes perform the functions of a server. To clarify this point, remember that the computers commonly called servers are not the only ones that can perform the function of a server. Any computer with proper capabilities can be programmed to perform the general functions of servicing client computers.

Mainframes continue to be used in situations where a large investment has been made in applications programs that are not readily transferable to a client/server platform. As we discuss more fully later in this chapter, such migration often does not make economic sense. Mainframes also are being used for new very large applications requiring high availability and security and having large databases.

One approach that many firms have taken to preserve their investment in mainframe applications is to download data from the mainframe to the server. This is often referred to as data warehousing. Once the data are on the server in an organized and rationalize way, they can be used in various ways. This provides features of the client/server environment while preserving the mainframe investment and minimizing the conversion risk. This is further discussed later in this chapter.

A client/server is commonly thought to be a computer of relatively new, efficient design that provides services to a client computer through a network. It is usually based on either a CISC (complex instruction set computer) or RISC (reduced instruction set computer) microprocessor. Intel-based machines are the primary users of CISC technology while Sun and Hewlett-Packard are examples of RISC-based machines. Previously RISC-based machines had a price/performance advantage, but now the latest Intel microprocessors are very competitive.

The function of a server is to provide client computers with significant processing power, a focal point for interclient communication and/or a central common database. Thus many client computers that have modest computational or storage capability use a common, relatively powerful server to perform the heavy-duty applications and database processing. The server can service a large number of client computers through their common network. When the nature and intensity of processing dictate, the server function can be separated into two parts: the processing part and the database handling part. This type of design decision is part of rightsizing a system.

Let's now take a general look at the constituent hardware parts of a computer and see where the differences are and what they may mean in rightsizing for a particular application set. The following describes the primary hardware components of any computer, the function of that component, and the differences between that component in a client/server and a mainframe:

• **Central processing unit (CPU)**—The central processing unit is the part of the computer that performs the actual calculations. Until recently, mainframes had more powerful CPUs than servers. Currently high-end servers approach mainframes in CPU power.

• **Memory**—Memory is the part of the computer that holds the programs and data the computer is working on at any point in time. As with CPUs, the high-end servers are approaching mainframes in memory capacity and speed.

• **Disk storage**—Disk storage is the part of the computer that holds the data and programs not being processed or that cannot all fit in main memory while being processed. It functions as an auxiliary memory. The programs or data can be transferred from disk storage to memory under the direction of the computer's operator or programs that are running on the computer. The gap between the disk storage capacities and speeds of servers and mainframes is also narrowing. In the last several years, array disks that combine multiple disk drives into a single unit have yielded economic, capacity, speed, and reliability improvement for both server and mainframes.

• **Tape drive (or cartridges)**—A tape drive or cartridge is also auxiliary memory to the computer. Its capabilities are different from a disk drive in that it can more economically hold large amounts of data or programs; however, the data or programs are relatively slow to access. Mainframes are using them less and less for processing, and servers and mainframes are using them primarily to back up data and programs. Servers are using Digital Audio Tape (DAT) to increase capacity.

• **Input/output transfer**—Input/output transfer refers to the speed of transferring data between the CPU and peripheral devices such as disk or tape drives. In this area mainframes have a distinct advantage over servers. This can represent a significant processing capability difference between a client/server and a mainframe for applications that require large amounts of transfer between the CPU and the peripherals. Client/server input/output transfer rates are being improved and may approach those of mainframes in the foreseeable future.

Other components to a computer hardware system are not discussed here because they tend to be relatively unimportant to rightsizing. Some of these are printers, modems, terminals, and controllers.

Obviously client/server and mainframe hardware requirements are for the most part similar in nature and becoming more so. The primary differences in the hardware are the greater input/output transfer capabilities and disk storage capacities of the mainframe; these of course lead to one basis for rightsizing.

Note that typical mainfame hardware may be built to more rigorous standards than some servers. In selecting hardware, the quality and reliability features of the hardware should be related to the needs of the application.

For the most part, no overwhelming arguments can be made about the differences in client/server and mainframe hardware. The differences lie elsewhere.

Operating Systems

An operating system is the master program that controls the internal operation of the computer. All of the processes of the computer are directed and coordinated by this program. It resides in memory and performs such functions as initiating start-up, handling input and output functions to the peripherals, interrelating the operations of the application programs, determining priorities when there is a contention for resources, and informing the operator of the system's status.

Operating systems can be considered to be open or closed. An open system (in its purest sense) is an operating system that is hardware manufacturer independent and can run on a large number of different hardware platforms without modification to the operating system. This independence has the advantage of allowing the operating system and application programs to be easily moved from hardware platform to hardware platform. Application programs usually require a significant amount of modification when moving to a new operating system. If an operating system is really open, it allows for uninhibited movement between many hardware platforms and removes the hold the manufacturer of closed software has on the user.

Unix is the original example of an open system though it does not meet the pure definition of an open system because there is not a single standard version of it. Moving from one version of Unix to another can require significant modifications. Windows NT also is considered an open system by a large and growing number of people. Windows NT does have a single version and works on a large number of hardware platforms. Only a few hold-out hardware manufacturers are not adopting Windows NT—often because they are strong advocates of their existing Unix capability. Windows NT is produced by a single manufacturer (Microsoft) whereas Unix is produced by a number of different manufacturers. There have been periodic unsuccessful attempts to unite Unix systems into a single system.

A closed operating system is the opposite of an open system. It is designed by a manufacturer to operate on a single type, or family, of hardware and is therefore called proprietary. The hardware and operating system manufacturer is usually one and the same. The operating system is optimized for the manufacturer's hardware. Examples of these are IBM's MVS and DEC's VMS. Note that other manufacturers sell hardware compatible with the IBM MVS operating system.

The origins of these proprietary operating systems are generally 15 or 20 years old but they are continually updated and improved by their manufacturers. They are very robust and have benefited from all the miles they have on them. But they are closed and tend to lock the user into the manufacturer because of the high cost of moving to another platform.

There are major differences in the operating systems used in client/server and mainframes. For most applications there is an obvious advantage to the open operating systems. There are some high-demand systems where the features of a proprietary operating system may be advantageous.

Networks

The classical mainframe architecture of the 1970s and 1980s was a highly centralized one in which all of the processing was done on the mainframe. The network connected the mainframe to dumb terminals that had little or no processing capability. Thus the network carried all of the terminal-user-generated inquiry or data input to and the responses from the mainframe. All editing processing and storage are done on the mainframe. An example of the inefficiency of this is that if the data entry operator made a simple entry error it would go all the way to the mainframe, be caught and then an error message would have to be sent all the way back to the terminal.

The advent of the PC suggested a more efficient model of computing. With the processing capability of the PC, processing and storage can be divided between a central computer and the user's terminal (now a PC). With this architecture, and the rapidly increasing power of the microprocessor, it was a short step to the creation of client/server as an alternative to the mainframe as the central computer. Thus new network designs and capabilities have been developed to accommodate the new, more efficient model of computing. The question of rightsizing derives from the existence of this powerful alternative architecture.

Mainframes have been enhanced to fit into the distributed computer environment. They can use the same communication protocols as the typical client/server networks (usually TCP/IP or IPX). Network capabilities are not a significant differentiator between client/server and mainframes. However, many mainframes are still using the old legacy communication networks that do not have the capabilities of the newer networks.

Support

To understand the nature of support requirements in client/server and mainframe environments, you must realize that:

1. In mainframe environments the hardware and operating systems are very integrated since they usually are supplied by one manufacturer. The application software is usually custom designed

for that well-defined environment. Sometimes a system such as a database management system or a security system from another manufacturer is used because it is deemed preferable. These foreign systems usually are designed for the particular mainframe environment and tend to integrate well and give the user few problems. These products are mature and have a moderate rate of change.

2. In client/server environments the situation is very different from the mainframe. The hardware and operating system vendors are often different. The supplier of the operating system has to make compromises in its design so that it runs on different manufacturer's computers. Likewise packaged applications are designed to operate in multiple environments and can come from a number of companies. The network operating system could be from still another manufacturer and must be designed to operate in varying environments. Further, the rate of change of software is very high and compatibility from manufacturer to manufacturer is weak.

In a client/server environment, therefore, the user must be (or hire) a systems integrator. Initial integration, subsequent maintenance, and enhancements can be more difficult and costly than in a mainframe environment. Troubleshooting these multivendor environments can be akin to communicating at the Tower of Babel. Compounding the problem is a shortage of skilled people to perform these functions. This shortage has caused salaries of qualified people to skyrocket. In making a downsizing decision, be sure to communicate with others who have done similar downsizing to get good estimates of support costs. There has been a tendency to underestimate significantly the support costs of the client/server environment.

Recent research has shown some interesting trends. Some firms have actually had to reduce the amount of outsourcing because their client/server problems are so complex that they believe they have to be handled internally. Also, more time is needed to test client/server systems because of the complexity of the multivendor environment. Help-desk calls were shown to go up by a factor of three or four.

Other differences between client/server and mainframes occur in the areas of systems management, network software, communication interfaces, security capabilities, environmental requirements, and availability of special software such as database and developmental tools. All of these are important; in the process of rightsizing, however, they tend not to be as important as the hardware, operating system, the network, and support required. There are situations where one or more of these other differences will be a major factor in rightsizing. For example, for certain applications security requirements may be of such a concern that the decision is pushed toward a mainframe.

Next, we discuss the various types of applications and how they relate to rightsizing. The application types discussed are batch processing, transaction processing, database services, and office automation.

APPLICATIONS BEST PERFORMED ON CLIENT/SERVER

Client/server systems and mainframes have different attributes that make them more or less suitable for the most common application programming, such as batch processing, transaction processing, database services, and office automation. As in most things, there are no simple answers. A particular application may seem to be rightsized to a client/server until consideration is given the scalability requirements that are so great that they could only be handled by a mainframe. Alternatively, a mainframe may seem the correct choice for an application until consideration is given to an organization's long-term plan to move into a more open environment.

Another significant consideration in rightsizing not previously mentioned is the availability of off-the-shelf application programs. For example, software vendors have built large numbers of business applications for the AS400. If a user finds a suitable application available only on an AS400, the rightsizing decision may be very easy. For example, some securities back-office packages run only on an AS400. (A number of AS400 application software developers have been rewriting their software for the client/server environment to expand their business base.)

Many customized mainframe application programs cost tens of millions of dollars to write and would cost large amounts of money to convert to a client/server environment. Thus when more capacity is required, there is a strong argument to upgrade to more powerful versions of the same mainframe manufacturer's hardware rather than make the enormous investment involved in converting to client/server. This decision is made somewhat easier by the fact that the mainframe prices have decreased significantly over the last several years both due to the adoption of some of the more cost effective technology of client/server and the business pressures created by the advent of client/server.

Batch Processing

Large-scale batch processing was the original meat and potatoes of the mainframe world. Back in the 1960s, when the concept and architecture of the mainframes were being developed, the primary consideration was batch systems. Then, and in the ensuing years, a large body of effective operating systems, management systems, file systems, and hardware capabilities were developed to support batch systems of various sizes and types. These are all in place today and very effective with two major caveats: The operating systems they use are proprietary and the hardware and operating systems are still relatively expensive.

A number of users with large batch processing jobs are understandably hesitant to invest in redeveloping applications programs costing tens of millions of dollars to fix something that "ain't broke." (Examples of these in the securities business are the batch overnight systems that handle the customer and street-side accounting of retail trades in brokerage firms and the clearing system run by the clearing corporation to settle these trades.) There is also an awareness that many who have converted to client/server have found that though hardware and operating system costs are lower, the overall costs may be higher due to the relative immaturity of client/server systems and their high support costs. Client/servers do not have the highy developed management systems available on mainframes.

If the application is mission critical and the business logic ill defined, the risk of a rewrite from a mainframe to client/server is also a major consideration. Often the documentation of the functional aspects of the mainframe is out-of-date or nonexisting. This makes the rewrite both expensive and dangerous. If there is a compelling reason to reengineer the function, then downsizing has to be considered seriously. The potential significant benefits of the reengineered applications have to be weighed against the risk of failure of the conversion.

At the other extreme of the batch world are users who do not currently have mainframes and have found available application packages that run on client/server; they are accomplishing their functional needs and have the capacity and scalability required. This is an easy decision for the user. There is no reason to consider a mainframe. There is still the need to select the right client/server hardware, operating system, and applications package. The choice of a particular applications package sometimes determines hardware and operating system choices. Examples of available securities industry applications packages that currently drive this type of decision are batch trading systems and portfolio analysis software. These examples tend to have on-line access associated with the batch process.

A user who has to build a custom application because no package exists should certainly lean toward client/server approaches unless some of the previously discussed significant factors are a requirement. With client/server technology now being mainstream and improvement being made at a rapid rate, it does not seem appropriate to ignore this economical, powerful architecture. Most new development is being done on client/server platforms.

Transaction Processing

Historically, transaction processing followed batch processing and was initially performed on the same type of mainframes as batch systems. The mainframe's hardware and operating systems had to be modified to accommodate this significant change in requirements. In particular, the operating systems had major suboperating systems written to control this very different environment. Many very successful systems were created in this way. Examples would be the NASDAQ trading system and many broker order-matching systems.

Subsequently a variant of the mainframe came into being from manufacturers such as Tandem and Stratus. Their hardware and operating systems were designed from the bottom up to be transaction processors. These systems will be called Transaction Processors in order to distinguish them from the function of transaction processing. (As part of what these manufacturers believed to be a requirement for transaction processing, the hardware and operating systems for these units were designed and built to have fault tolerance.) These Transaction Processors have proven to be very effective in providing highly reliable transaction processing. The latest client/server hardware and software are suitable for certain types of transaction processing and have high availability.

Three general categories of platforms are available for transaction processing, and the process of rightsizing means choosing among the three. There are significant differences in the cost, capacity, reliability, and openness of these alternatives.

As in the batch environment, large transaction systems built on mainframes many years ago at costs that go as high as tens of millions of dollars are still working reasonably well. The cost of rewriting these would be very great as would the risks involved in converting to a new system. Many of these transaction processing systems are mission critical to the users. Also some of these systems have very large input/output and database requirements that currently only can be handled by the capabilities of a large mainframe. Many of these users see rightsizing as merely an exercise in getting the right quantity of hardware from the mainframe manufacturer at the best price and optimizing the resulting configuration.

Even today, very high transaction rates might be best suited to mainframe processors. However, for some time many of newer systems have been built on the previously mentioned Transaction Processors. Sometimes mainframes are used in combination, with the Transaction Processor front-ending a mainframe and handling most of the communications and transaction load while the mainframe handles the business processing and files.

Sometimes a purchasable application that fulfills the user's need but is designed to operate only on a particular hardware and operating system environment in effect makes the choice for the user. Securities industry examples of these types of systems are real-time trading and order entry systems designed to operate on a particular Transaction Processor.

More recently, specialized transaction processing software has become available on client/server environments. Novell's Tuxedo is an example of this type of software. Tuxedo operates in both a Windows NT and a Unix environment. Database software manufacturers also supply transaction processing software capabilities for client/servers. Examples are Sybase, Oracle, Informix, and Microsoft.

Additionally, client/server hardware and operating systems have grown in capacity and stability though most would agree that they have not attained that of the larger systems. Some client/server manufacturers are building units with a high reliability and capacity that are well suited to transaction processing. They do not in general have the scalability of the transaction processors. Examples of these manufacturers are Tricord, Compaq, and Netframe. The two primary manufacturers of Transaction Processors (Tandem and Status) have added high availability client/servers with open operating systems to their product line. Again, packaged transaction processing applications programs have been built to work on a particular client/server and in effect dictate the platform to a user desiring the application.

As mentioned previously, there are significant differences in cost, capacity, reliability, and openness between these alternative platforms. Mainframes tend to be the most expensive to buy followed by Transaction Processors and then client/server. The cost platforms of both the mainframe and the Transaction Processor have de-creased considerably due to the competitive threat of the client/ servers; they are adopting new, more cost-effective technology. Client/server costs are also dropping. However, as mentioned previously, the support costs of the client/servers can be significantly greater.

Capacity considerations fall pretty much in the same order with one exception—the scalability of some of the Transaction Processors allows them to have a maximum capacity comparable to the mainframes for transaction processing. The continued rapid growth in client/server capacities bodes well for its future competitiveness.

The unique design features of the Transaction Processors make them the most reliable of the group but mainframe manufacturers have significantly improved their products' reliability over the years. In general, client/servers' reliability is not quite as high because of their lack of maturity and the fact that Unix (the operating system currently used by most) tends not to be as stable as the proprietary operating systems used on mainframes and Transaction Processors. Windows NT is somewhat new but reports on its stability are favorable.

Both mainframes and Transaction Processors have proprietary operating systems and are therefore closed systems. Client/server has Unix, Windows NT, or OS/2 for the most part. As previously discussed, Unix and Windows NT are open systems to varying degrees. IBM's OS/2 is not as open as the other client/server operating systems and functions only on one type of platform (the Intel processor) that is supplied by a number of companies.

Users have to consider all of the above in rightsizing a transaction processing system in addition to the other items previously mentioned if they have a major bearing on the application. Factors such as security or communications capability could have a significant effect on the selection process.

Database Services

Both client/server and mainframes do a very credible job in performing database services. The capabilities of the database software available for client/server are for the most part comparable to that for the mainframes. This may be in part due to the fact that many users have used client/server in database applications for some time and in turn pushed the manufacturers of the database software to produce capable database products.

This is where the previously noted differences in hardware capability between the mainframe and client/server come into play. The input/output transfer rate and scalability of disk storage associated with the client/server are not yet up to that of the mainframe. The general capabilities of both are increasing though that of client/server is increasing faster.

Another factor in the rightsizing of database systems is consistency of platform. All hardware and operating system selections have to consider the architectural plan of the organization. Only with very significant reasons should the rightsizing of a database system consider deviating from the plan. Most plans try to limit the number of different systems they have to reduce support costs. Assembling a wide variety of hardware, operating systems, and database systems is a self-defeating exercise.

A new approach to database systems now being considered or implemented by many firms is the data warehouse. The concept applies to a situation where a firm has multiple operational systems each part of which has pieces of the database and has been implemented in an inconsistent manner. To create the warehouse, data would be downloaded from the operational systems to a central system that would filter and rationalize the data and construct a proper corporate database.

This new integrated database can then serve as the source for management information. The processing load that this creates is separated from the systems providing operational processing to allow them to continue to perform their function properly. Data warehouses can be built on either client/server platforms or mainframes but a lot of consideration has to be given to scalability because corporate databases have a way of growing beyond original estimates. Since these are new systems, however, they should be developed on client/server if there is sufficient scalability.

In considering rightsizing of database systems, the user having very large databases with a requirement for excellent response times might have to also consider highly specialized computers built specifically for this purpose. An example of such a product is Teradata owned by NCR; this computer has not been highly popular.

Office Automation

The term *office automation* usually refers to the tasks involved in the day-to-day basic operation of an office, such as word processing, E-mail, desktop publishing, workgroup processing, file sharing, spread sheets, and scheduling. Prior to the advent of the PC and Mac, a limited amount of this type of processing was performed on terminals connected to mainframes. For example, IBM had an E-mail system using dumb terminals working into the mainframe and a word processing system that worked with the AS400. Wang had a fairly comprehensive office automation system that used dumb terminals working into a dedicated minicomputer.

When PCs (we include Macintosh computers in the term *PC*) became available, some of these office automation functions moved to them. When local area networks (LANs) started to become popular in the late 80s the possibility of them performing some of these functions became apparent. (A LAN is a communication capability within a location connecting PCs, servers, and in some cases mainframes together.) The advantage of the client/server platform is that processes can be shared and the LAN provides communication between the clients.

Today sharing office automation tasks between the client and the server is becoming commonplace. In this environment, rightsizing is balancing what programs go on the client and what go on the server. Those applications that require sharing or interclient communication most often go on the server; those that can stand alone can go either place and require some analysis. Considerations are the resource requirement of the application, the design of the application (some designs are uniquely client and others client/server), and in some cases the response time.

In summary, there are many considerations in rightsizing. Sometimes the answer is relatively easy as when the platform is dictated by the application either because it is readily available as a package or because of the enormous cost and/or risk involved in converting to a client/server platform. Sometimes the firm may require that new applications be on open systems. However, very frequently there is not this simple an answer and firms must perform an objective analysis to avoid a predisposition from determining the outcome.

Now we turn to the process of downsizing, the most common form of rightsizing. The topic is narrowed to downsizing from a mainframe to client/server.

DOWNSIZING FROM A MAINFRAME TO CLIENT/SERVER

Most rightsizing decisions today occur when organizations with significant investments in mainframes are contemplating major application changes (reengineering) and want to ensure that they are implemented on the right platform looking forward. Others occur when firms review their architectural plan and consider platform changes, or see opportunities for cost and/or operational improvements by moving some of their processing to a client/server environment. These are nonsimplistic decisions because there is still not a lot of concrete evidence to base such a decision on nor do a large number of people have comprehensive experience in performing such downsizing. There have been some successes and failures but the success rate seems to be improving.

There is also concern as to whether client/server is living up to some of the cost and capability claims. Reports indicate that the support cost for client/server offsets the cost advantage of the hardware and software. There are also presumed client/server advantages in ease of application program development and modification that is primarily attributable to the newer software developmental tools developed in the client/server environment. Object-oriented programming is an example of these tools. Object-oriented programming creates objects that are self-contained modules of data and its associated programs. These are reusable blocks of code that can reduce applications development time. There have been some favorable reports on containing developmental cost using these tools.

Almost everyone agrees that over the next three to five years there will be a significant movement away from the mainframe and toward client/server. No one wants to be too late in taking advantage of the growing effectiveness of that platform. The real question for most is not if, but when. With the rapid maturation of the client/server world, it would be reasonable for most concerns at least to put their toes in the water by converting some nonmission-critical areas to client/server platforms to gain the knowledge and experience of making an actual conversion. Data warehousing is an application that sometimes fits this situation.

A few securities firms have decided to make a significant effort to move the great majority of their applications to client/server. Most of the people directly involved claim success; many others are skeptical. There is no hard evidence either way; in fact, there is also no definition of what constitutes success. As client/server capabilities grow and the continued problems of multivendor interaction subside, success will become more commonplace.

Other firms have taken a more moderate stance. They are downsizing a limited number of more obvious applications and holding back a more far-reaching commitment until they have their sea legs and the advantages of client/server become more clearcut. This would seem a fair middle stance as long as the firm is not forced to substantially upgrade its legacy systems. If that should happen, the firm will have to make a rightsizing decision. There is good reason to go at a deliberate speed to both enhance your familiarity and wait until the products are more mature.

Finally, we explain how the Internet and Intranet relate to rightsizing. There has been some management level misunderstanding on this subject.

THE INTERNET AND INTRANETS

There is a misconception that the emergence of the Internet and the Intranet will significantly, affect the way the securities industry processes. The fact is that these new capabilities are primarily complementary to either mainframes or client/servers and will provide additional capabilities that were not previously available. Basically the Internet and Intranet represent an alternative network configuration with improved access and decreased costs. In the case of the Internet, the network connects to millions of people with whom a firm may or may not be interested in connecting. With the security concerns related to the Internet, it is not advisable at this time to have the firm's books and records or other critical systems connected to the Internet.

Generally Internet applications fall into three categories. The first is the accessing of pages of information. These pages could contain the information broadly available on the Web or specific information put out by an organization for its employees. The second application is the downloading of files. The third application is that of communications; E-mail is a prime example of this.

The Intranet connects a private group in a controlled communications environment. Both the Internet and the Intranet provide the user with a means to easily access information using very user-friendly browsers. Browsers provide a new and better way for users to access certain types of information. They are excellent at bringing up pages of information or moving from one server to another without any technical information. Their nature, however, is not suited to classical business applications. The primary use of these capabilities is to search for information, retrieve data, and communicate between users.

Thus when discussing the rightsizing of mainframes and client/servers, the Internet and Intranets enter the picture only in a peripheral way. This is not to minimize their value.

CONCLUSION

We have considered the subject of rightsizing from several management aspects. The differences between the constituent parts of mainframes and client/server-based systems were analyzed, and it was determined that these existed primarily in the areas of operating systems, network architecture, support costs, and in some hardware areas. The effect of these differences on rightsizing was described. Rightsizing was also considered from the point of view of a variety of typical applications. The importance of not moving from an acceptable working environment precipitously was emphasized. Also the value of being able to procure working applications sometimes outweighing the perfecting of the platform was described. The conditions that tend to make downsizing appropriate were developed with the understanding that this will be the general direction in the coming years. However, it was recognized that there will be an important place for mainframes for the foreseeable future. Finally, the complementary nature of the Internet and the Intranet were noted to clarify that they would not replace the primary types of processing currently being performed by mainframes and client/server-based systems.

⑥ EVALUATING AND
CONTRACTING
WITH VENDORS*

Mike Abbaei
Senior Vice President and Chief Information Officer
Legg Mason Wood Walker, Incorporated

Technology in the past 15 years has revolutionized the nature of many businesses. Specifically in the financial industry—and more visibly in brokerage and banking—technology has not only changed the business but also concurrently changed, created, or abolished relationships internal and external to all entities. For example, electronic funds transfer changed interbanking relationships; automated teller machines changed customer relationships; trading systems and broker workstations changed the relationships and interactions between the trading desks, sales force, and back-office; and various communication methods (electronic mail, fax, video conferencing, etc.) also changed many more relationships.

Probably the most critical impact of technology was on each firm's own technology department and its relationships. Thousands of persons saw their departments grow, be rightsized, outsource, grow again, and be reorganized as often as the chip producers came out with new products. Subsequently, these employees had to adjust their roles and relationships throughout different stages of each insourcing/outsourcing wave. It seems like every five years or so the insourcing/outsourcing trend shifts. Starting with the 1980–1985 period, the financial industry trend seemed to be in-house application development and information technology (IT) support.

---

*This chapter is dedicated to my friends Bob Donavan and Tim Scheve.

In the second half of the 80s, however, this trend was ostensibly reversed toward outsourcing. On the other hand, between 1990–1995 there seemed to be a more balanced approach to this issue.

The common denominator among all trends is business's dependency on IT vendors. With each trend the role of the vendors changed. As the technology evolved, new innovations were introduced and companies depended more on the vendors to deliver products and services. Hence, the relationship between the customers and the vendors also evolved throughout the past 15 years. Exhibit 3–1 depicts the customer/vendor relationship evolution.

Concurrent with this evolution, while businesses realized the importance of technology and their respect for the value of IT departments grew, the IT managers in turn realized the importance of their relationships with vendors and saw the value in an all-around partnership.

The goal in this chapter is to provide guidelines on how to decide on such partnerships, secure the terms of the partnership, begin the process, and grow each of these partnerships.

BUY VERSUS BUILD ANALYSIS

To build or not to build (buy)? This question goes through all IT managers' minds any time they are faced with a new project request. It is one of the most frustrating moments for systems managers who have to make such decisions. At times they wish the users would just tell them which way to go. Some firms have made it simple, they have set a hard and fast rule one way or another. Typically the size of the IT organization, especially the application development and support department, is a reflection of that rule. Ultimately, everyone is forced to exercise this judgment.

When we use the term *buy*, we mean the purchase of hardware and software, services, and outsourcing options.

As discussed before, the role of IT departments and information systems (IS) managers in the financial industry has changed in the past few years. They have found their role to be more of an integrator than developer. It used to be that the IT managers would brag about the number of people that they had to manage; now they talk about the number of vendor relationships they have to maintain. I personally like to think of the IT managers and chief information officers (CIOs) as conductors. They have to make sure

EXHIBIT 3-1

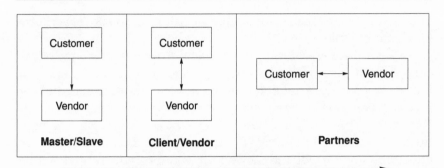

Vendor Relationship Evolution

that all the systems (instruments), developed and/or run (played) by various vendors (musicians), are integrated and work harmoniously (orchestra) so that the users (listeners) can benefit (enjoy) from the outcome (music) for which they have paid.

We must keep reminding ourselves that we are not in the software business. Our goal is to provide users with the best solutions to their needs; solutions that offer the most functionality at the best possible cost in a timely manner. Of course, there are times that the best solution is not through a vendor; then we must use our skills to either develop a solution from scratch or buy a solution and adapt it to our needs. To strengthen the argument on buying vendor solutions, let's review some of the criteria that should be considered while making the buy or build decision.

Resources

The definition of *resources* in the context of our discussion focuses on the IT staff that is required to develop and support various products, and to acquire the hardware and software necessary to support the infrastructure in which products must be developed and maintained.

In larger organizations with more established IT departments, the environmental issues are not much of a concern. They most likely have development tools and standards along with a proper operational environment to facilitate the ongoing maintenance. Staffing, although, is always a major issue.

In smaller organizations, the overall resources, staffing, and the environmental constraints are limited; therefore, when small organizations are faced with a build decision, the resources criteria play a bigger role.

Generally, regardless of the size of the organization, one of the benefits that vendors add to the equation is reduced reliance on internal resources. Therefore, by using vendors' products and/or services, we have utilized their resources without increasing our fixed costs. This solution also addresses the concern regarding high turnover and attrition in the IT departments. Keep in mind that we are increasing our dependency on the vendors, which can itself be an issue.

Costs

A major deciding factor in the buy versus build decision is costs. When we are analyzing the costs of a product or service, it is important to make sure that all costs are accounted for. In a build analysis, it is just as important to calculate the requirement gathering and user costs as it is to factor in the development cost. Furthermore, when we calculate the cost of building an application, occasionally we forget to add the cost of maintenance, both on the user side and IT side.

When we are purchasing a product, in addition to the cost of the product and maintenance, we must also consider whether any product customizations are required, and, if so, who will perform them and how much it will cost. Generally, the number of hidden or unknown costs are reduced when you are dealing with a vendor. It is in the vendor's best interest to disclose all the costs upfront, and they normally do; still you need to analyze your internal costs in supporting the vendor.

On most occasions, however, the costs of developing, or internalization costs as they are known, far exceed the vendor costs. There are two reasons for this: First, the costs to a vendor are normally shared among its customers, hence the costs per customer are reduced. Second, the vendors are in the technology business and they are in it to make money, so they will do whatever they can to reduce their own costs by utilizing tools to develop and deliver products and/or services.

Management

Even though the project management costs and resources are always considered when new projects are analyzed, what is sometimes missing from the picture is an intangible factor—the experience that a vendor can offer (normally at no cost) in managing the project. Vendors go through the process over and over again. They come in with a packaged set of procedures and a cookbook of definitions, processes, time lines, and steps. Even though every situation is different, the template always applies. For example, if a conversion is involved, they know the process and the routines; if training is needed, they should know when and how. In general, they can guide us through the steps.

In addition to the project management expertise, the vendor shares the risks with the client. It is to both parties' benefit for the project to be successful, so the vendor is committed as well. We discuss this aspect in more detail later on in the chapter.

Business Knowledge

One of the advantages that vendors have over any internal IT organization is the fact that they deal with more than one set of users. Therefore, their perspectives and knowledge base is widened. They sometimes can bring a breath of fresh air, points that were not considered or maybe even a different way of doing business. During a systems change, many firms take the opportunity to reengineer their processes. Vendors are willing to share information with the firms to accomplish that. By doing so, the vendors get to add to their repository and collection of business knowledge as well.

Of course, there are times that, due to the proprietary nature of a firm's business needs, the users are more knowledgeable and at times unwilling to share that knowledge with outsiders.

In summary, considering a combination of the resources, costs, management, and business knowledge in contrast to the entire project life cycle allows us to organize our thoughts and priorities while we make a decision on whether to buy or build.

Keep in mind that being a hero is not having a "We can do it better ourselves" attitude anymore; it is being a true business partner by making the right business decision for the firm.

RFP PROCESS

The first step prior to selecting a vendor is the request for proposal (RFP) process. The main purpose of the RFP is to solicit proposals from various vendors and utilize the RFP criteria for selecting the vendor of choice. In addition to the obvious purpose of the RFP, there are other benefits that the organization gains from conducting this process. In this section we review the RFP process step by step, then we briefly review RFP's benefits.

RFP Steps

The key to a comprehensive RFP is the requirements. Prior to preparation of the RFP, perform a thorough analysis and make sure to spend enough time on gathering all the information regarding the requirements.

Once the requirements are complete, prepare the RFP. Each RFP should include all the functional needs (including as much detail as possible), software and hardware platforms (if applicable), capacity and performance criteria (if applicable), logistical instructions such as: general ground rules, deadlines, response procedures (in writing and/or in person), plus any additional information that you deem important for the vendor to know or respond to.

Concurrent with RFP preparation, you must also conduct a vendor search so that you distribute the RFP only to those who have a high chance of being selected.

After the RFP is prepared, it must be reviewed by all parties involved: the users, the IT staff, senior management as well as any consultants involved in the process. The next step is to collect and incorporate the feedback from the reviews prior to distributing the RFP to the selected vendors.

The last step is to collect the responses in a timely manner. Make sure that the responses are all in writing. Sometimes it might be valuable to have the vendor present the response in person to allow time for questions and answers and to provide a better clarification of the key points. Although this by no means replaces the due diligence and selection process, it can facilitate the future steps.

Keep in mind that the process just described can be very time consuming and in some cases it might not be feasible to go through them all.

Potential Benefits of the RFP Process

Aside from providing a fair and accurate tool to select the best vendor for the job, the RFP also offers other benefits that might not always be obvious to everyone. The RFP process can be utilized to:

- **Evaluate the systems architecture**—You can take this opportunity to evaluate and maybe change or enhance the existing architecture.
- **Educate the staff and users**—The process can be an educational one for all parties to learn more about the business functions as well as the current and new technology.
- **Plan the implementation**—The RFP process will force you to think through and analyze the systems implementation plan.
- **Set expectations**—Since everyone will be involved with the RFP and the vendor evaluation process, they will know what to expect.
- **Build consensus**—By getting everyone to review and agree on the requirements and the expectations, you have built consensus among the users, IT staff, senior management, and potentially other vendors.
- **Get approvals**—You can use this process to receive the necessary approvals to continue with the project.

As mentioned before, although the RFP process might be a tedious and time consuming task, it has far more advantages that will pave the way for other tasks farther down the line.

VENDOR EVALUATION AND SELECTION

After the RFP is sent and the vendor responses have been collected, the next step is to evaluate the information and perform a comparison analysis. From the responses, you can quickly decide which vendors you need to evaluate in more detail. You may opt to review all of them, but keep in mind that this step also can be a long and tiring one. In any event, the RFP should be utilized to rank the vendors in the order that you would like to pursue.

One method of setting rankings is to adapt a weighting rating system. By assigning a weighting factor to each function and/or requirement in the RFP, and then rating the responses according to a preset scale, you can compare the overall ratings of the responses and then select the top two or three vendors for further evaluation. As your analysis expands, the ratings must be adjusted accordingly.

During this process, such different categories of data must be evaluated as the package or service, the technology, the vendor, and of course the costs. Let's review each one of these categories.

Evaluate the Package (Service)

Since the RFP is a reflection of the requirements needed, the package evaluation is somewhat simplified. By performing a gap analysis between the package and the requested functions, you can come up with a list of gaps, if any, that identify the shortcomings of the vendor's proposed system and/or services. Subsequently, for the existing functions, you can evaluate how well each function is supported by the package. As the gap analysis proceeds, you must prioritize the items on your list of gaps by their importance to you and the users, and then address them with the vendor. During this process, review the vendor's future plans as well as the history of the product. The history of a product is a reflection of the planning that goes into the product development. It also determines how organized the vendor is in releasing new features. You want to learn the product's release methodology as far as major enhancements and maintenance features are concerned.

Give additional considerations to the age of the product and whether the product is premature, mature, or old. Obviously most firms would like a mature product, but this is a judgment call that varies depending on the circumstances.

Review the Technology

From a business standpoint this criterion might not seem to be important, but the vendor's choice of technology can impact many aspects of implementation and support. If the technology is not reviewed properly, the results can be catastrophic. Points to focus on while reviewing the vendor's technology are as follows:

- **Do they follow industry standards?** If the vendor or
  the package deviates from the common standards, then
  support and maintenance can be an issue. Also it will be
  more difficult to integrate the package with other systems
  or environments. In addition, if they rely on third-party
  packages, then additional costs and support must also be
  considered.
- **Is their technology in line with your firm's standards?**
  This could be a major issue if you have to introduce a new
  technology or environment for just one system.
- **Is the package up-to-date?** You must make sure that the
  product is up to the current technology version or release.
  For example, even on the services side, if the outsourcing
  of services is being considered, the same rule applies. The
  services offered must support the current version of the
  technology needed.
- **What are their future technology plans?** Just as you
  considered and reviewed the future functional plans,
  review their technical plans and direction as well.
- **Is the technology leading edge, bleeding edge, or no
  edge?** Obviously there are risks and benefits to being in
  the forefront of technology. But there must be a balance
  among the benefits, risks, and costs of committing to
  unproven technology.
- **How technical is the organization?** The technical depth
  of the vendor indicates not only how well the product is
  designed but also determines the future support and
  product direction.

Evaluate the Vendor

As discussed before, the vendor/client relationship has evolved
into a partnership. Therefore, similar to selecting a partner, perform the same thorough due diligence on the vendor as you would
for new partners. The points to consider during this process are as
follows:

- **Study the vendor's financials (vendor viability)**—The last
  thing you want is a vendor that is here one day and gone

the next. Make sure the vendor has a viable business and can sustain reasonable downturns.

- **Monitor its business (is the vendor spread too thin?)**— Pay the vendor a visit and find out if it has adequate staffing and support. Find out about the organization, the marketing and sales efforts versus support and development. Request its current client base as well as the list of prospects in order to get a good indication of the vendor's commitments in comparison to its staffing.

- **Evaluate past performance**—One aspect of having a sound business is consistent growth and managing that growth. Too much or too little expansion can be attributed to lack of business direction or plan.

- **Check the references**—The best marketing tool is the vendor's clients. Normally, a vendor who has a good reputation and is customer oriented, encourages the prospects and the rest of the market to discuss their relationships, with current clients. Contact the references and if possible pay them a visit and ask as many detailed questions as possible.

- **Meet the vendor in person (build a relationship)**— Get to know the vendor and make sure there is a synergy between its organization and yours. The vendor will be part of your team. Strong relationships can overcome major obstacles down the road.

Evaluate the Costs

A major factor in deciding on the vendor is normally the costs. Be very cautious and make sure that in this process all costs are accounted for including your own internal costs. One way to simplify this effort is to require the vendor to include all the costs in its proposals. Hence, the RFP must include as many questions as possible to force the vendor to submit all costs.

In addition, during the vendor interviews ask as many questions as possible, even if you have to repeat the questions in different ways. This will assure you that the responses are the same no matter how they are presented. Also be sure that you are fully aware of the definition of the costs and that adequate clarification has been provided. You want to eliminate any surprises or any unknowns. Many vendors have creative cost structures and presentations; understanding every variation can be an art.

Once all the vendor costs are gathered, then you must evaluate your own internal costs. A lot of times a vendor's solution may require resources and time from you. Other vendors, specifically those that offer turn-key approaches, may not need any resources from the clients but normally their costs are higher. To be able to compare apples to apples you must include and understand all the costs.

Comparison Process

Once all the evaluations are complete, you must compare the results. But how do you do it? Is there a scientific approach to this? How can we objectively come up with the right answer? Who needs to be involved in the decision making?

The first step is to get the users involved. They must be part of the evaluation process as well as the selection process. Their buy-in can set the tone for the success of the project. Then utilize the RFP matrix of functions and requirements. Most probably this matrix has been enhanced and updated during the evaluation process. As mentioned before, create a weighting and scoring system based on the needs and priorities. The users should have a lot of input specifically in setting the weights for each function. As a result of the evaluations, the scores must be fine-tuned to reflect a more accurate standing of the vendors for each of the functions.

Additionally, consider the opinion of the industry experts. Various consulting services (such as Gartner Group, Meta Group, or Forrester) offer opinions and recommendations on many topics and/or vendors. You may want to add a score for this category as well, or you can use their opinion solely for validation and certification of the outcome.

Once all the scores are in, it is time to add them and come up with the final results. There are times that the scores are too close or there is a tie, that's when gut feeling and experience are critical; it goes back to synergy and the relationship.

CONTRACT NEGOTIATIONS

Contract negotiations can be the most dreadful and sometimes the most time-consuming part of the whole process. But it is one that has to be done and must be done in a methodical and calculated manner. If a point is missed or overlooked in this step, the results can be disastrous and at times fatal to a business. Therefore, it is imperative to remain patient during the negotiations and make sure that the proper legal reviews are undertaken. In this section, however, we will focus only on the business aspect of the negotiations with the understanding that the appropriate legal and administrative reviews must also take place. (See Chapter 6 for further discussion of legal considerations.)

Before you begin the process, do your homework. Proper preparation is key to formulating a better negotiating ground; you must gather information on competitive terms and costs. If possible, try to research negotiations that the same vendor has conducted with others. It might be very helpful to seek professional assistance from consulting firms, accounting firms, or individuals whose expertise is contract negotiation.

Furthermore, understand your alternatives and pick one that you are willing to exercise. There are times that you have to exercise your options, hence you must be prepared and clear on what they are. An opponent who believes that their firm is your only solution will have the upper hand and can take advantage of the situation. Another point that you must prepare for is setting your limits. You must know what you want and what your limits are prior to entering any negotiations. Just like purchasing a house or a car, it is important for you to set limits on every term and condition of the contract, including price, contract duration, service levels, maintenance, and support. Early in negotiations ensure that you raise the points that are important to you. Let it be known what points you are firm on and on which ones you are willing to compromise. This will give the vendor a chance to prepare different alternatives that can be workable for both parties. Always, try to see the vendor's point as well. Think of this as your first exercise in teamwork; one-sided negotiations do not produce the best results. People often ask when you should start the contract negotiations. I would start the negotiations concurrently with the evaluation process. Since this is a long iterative process, you should allow ample time to conduct it and not rush through it. However, this process should not finish prior to the completion of the evaluation and detailed analysis. We must include the resolution of the gaps as part of the contract and guarantee satisfactory coverage of all the limitations identified during the evaluation process.

Remember that you must treat the vendor as a partner. And as partners you must make sure that the deal is profitable for the vendor as well. You need and want a happy partner, one who constantly looks after your interests and pays attention to your needs. If the vendor, your partner, is not happy with the deal and is forced to accept terms that compromise its standards or business needs, its focus will not be on your business. You must make sure that the vendor feels and is indeed treated fairly. I call this a true partnership.

However, this does not mean that you should not be tough on your demands and stand firm. After all, you must be willing to walk away if your standards and limits are not met.

PREIMPLEMENTATION

Once you have picked your partner and the contract is in place, you must start preparing for the implementation of the project. Many points need to be addressed before you are ready to implement. For simplicity's sake, we skip over the normal project planning steps that have to deal with the actual planning and implementation of the project. These points are mentioned in other chapters. The focus here is on points that might not be obvious when a vendor is involved. During this process we must create a cooperative environment for all parties. The users as well as the management must be involved from the beginning. The team must include your resources as well as the vendor's, and you must treat their staff as a member of yours and vice versa.

Collectively, you must set realistic schedules and time lines. Working with the vendor to ensure that proper resources are in place to meet the expectations before committing to the dates and additional functions is important for both parties. Milestones are critical in measuring each other's progress; hence, set biweekly or semimonthly milestones. In addition, schedule timely status meetings with all parties and allow the vendor to present its own status. Try to reduce, as much as possible, the you-versus-us attitude. Each critical step and expectation must be documented in advance and agreed on with all parties. The responsibilities must be clear and documented as well so everyone has the same understanding. This method of project management reduces the confusion and eliminates any potential for mishap due to false assumptions.

IMPLEMENTATION

As in the previous section, this section explores only those key points in a project implementation step that might not be obvious or are different when you are dealing with a vendor. Consider the normal implementation step with a full understanding of the following observations.

During the implementation make sure that you keep the vendor's feet to the fire, but remember that you are accountable. In other words, although you may rely on the vendor to deliver, you must proactively manage the process. Keep your resources involved during the development and implementation even if they are not needed. This will assure continuity in case of emergencies.

There are only a few occasions when an implementation will be completed without any problem, on-time, and totally within the budget. Therefore it is highly likely that problems will occur, and you and the vendor must together manage the users' and the management's expectations. Continuously promote the teamwork even throughout stressful times. This is when synergy can play a key role.

Keep the communication lines open between the vendor and the users. Encourage direct dialogue between the two, while staying involved and abreast of the status. One of your responsibilities should be to clear the obstacles and to reduce any interference. You are the insider and the vendor has to depend on you to handle the political issues. The same is true with other members of your firm. They expect you to perform the vendor management and make sure that the vendor delivers. It is an artful task to be able to handle all these expectations especially during the stressful moments of any implementation that we all experience.

POSTIMPLEMENTATION

There isn't a better feeling than the gratification of the successful completion of a major project and observing the fruits of all the efforts that went into it. No matter what your involvement was and which side you were on, the intrinsic benefits achieved are invaluable. During this period, you must allow the vendor to also share the spotlight and be appreciated not only by you as the project manager, but also by the users and management.

At the same time, you need to start planning for the future. If there are day-two items or postimplementation and/or outstanding items that must be resolved, do not lose the momentum; stay on top of the vendor to ensure delivery of these items. Start planning for the internalization of the first-level support. Although the vendor might offer ongoing support as part of the agreement, it might be more beneficial to have some level of internal support.

Maintenance and enhancement releases must be scheduled and announced well in advance. The contents of each release must also be defined and agreed on by all parties. Furthermore, you should try to participate in setting the future direction of the product and the vendor, both from the technical and functional points of view. If there is a user group, your firm must get involved and be represented and active. This will assure that your interests and needs are considered as the vendor moves forward. And finally, help the vendor to be successful; remember that you are partners.

SUMMARY

This chapter outlined the steps involved with entering and continuing a vendor relationship. For the sake of time, we omitted the normal project-life-cycle concepts with the understanding that these concepts must be applied regardless of vendor participation. We emphasized that this relationship must be a partnership rather than a traditional client (requester)/vendor (provider) interaction. We also labeled the internal IT departments, in a nontechnical industry such as finance, as integrators first and developers second. The combination of the vendors and the internal integrators offers every business a superior set of resources at an attractive cost.

Furthermore, we analyzed the approaches that should be taken to make the ties stronger and provide protection on both sides. Again, we purposely limited our legal coverage of this topic since it deserves a full discussion of its own. Note that every relationship must be reviewed and consulted by appropriate legal advisors. We will continue to see the role of IT organizations change as their vendor relationships evolve. I predict that this evolution will result in more true partnerships where both parties will directly benefit from the risks and rewards of each other's business. Although they will remain separate entities, the dividing lines will become finer with closer organizational ties. We may even call them hybrid partners.

4

⑥ GLOBAL TECHNOLOGY MANAGEMENT

How to Staff, Manage, and Implement IT Projects

Russell D. Lewis
Chief Information Officer
Jefferies & Company

We are witnessing a trend within corporate America from a regionally independent organizational model to a globally interdependent model. Many departments and firms are restructuring their organizations to report and operate globally. The vast majority of organizations are wrestling with how to best position their firms for the future. An overwhelming variable in this equation is how to make the best use of a firm's technology investment. The cost to maintain a technology infrastructure will continue to increase at an alarming rate, and the challenge will be to find an effective way to manage these costs. The following pages lay out a strategy for tackling this problem—this strategy is global technology management (GTM). The examples given relate particularly to staffing, managing, and implementing technology projects within the securities industry, but the concepts should be universal to most businesses.

At the heart of GTM is the concept that the technology manager must learn to manage technology like a business. With the ever-increasing cost of technology and the pressure from outside vendors, it is even more important that technology is viewed in a significantly different way than in years past. Regardless of the legal structure of the firm or how the technology department is organized, the concepts of GTM should still be applicable. GTM embraces the concept of an internal customer, clearly defined products and services, full reallocation of all technology costs, and, most important, a mechanism to benchmark products to the outside. These concepts require multiple management and reporting tools to be in place to be truly effective. The biggest challenge in trying to implement this type of strategy will be trying to change how people view technology—changing people's mind-set will be the most difficult part of this process.

To begin, let's explore some of the business drivers responsible for this change in approach. Once we define what is motivating us to move in this direction, we can explore some of the tools necessary to implement these concepts.

BUSINESS DRIVERS

Globalization

The use of the term *globalization* is almost as overused as partnership is in the management lingo of the 1990s. Nonetheless, the trend toward expanding into the international marketplace is a significant challenge to how we view technology. Technology is the single largest obstacle to true globalization of our businesses, while at the same time, it is a key element to its success. This may seem a little harsh—if not confusing—but in my experience, most of the reasons why a business cannot conduct itself or view itself globally stem from limitations of its infrastructure (software, hardware, and/or networks). The business can fairly quickly reorganize itself and structure its compensation packages to encourage global thinking, but if technology cannot support this, then it is nothing more than window dressing.

A firm that truly wishes to grow its business globally must realize that doing so will significantly impact its technology budget. I am assuming that most firms have a large capital investment in their technology infrastructure. If a firm is a start-up or is already in the process of a major overhaul of its technology, there is a chance it can be done correctly from the beginning. The strategy to try to retrofit regionally developed and maintained systems or networks into a seamlessly functioning global system is immensely complex and expensive. When technology managers think about making their systems global, they tend to try to integrate already established systems together under the guise that this is their global strategy. If technology managers understand the business trends from the beginning, they should be able to anticipate or at least position their organization to support a global business. More often than not, technology managers tend to be reactive to these trends instead of understanding them and staying on top of them. Once a manager is reacting to a situation, it is probably already too late. Technology cannot react as quickly as the business units can. So, planning and anticipating business trends become an ever-increasingly important aspect of a technologist's job. Technology management historically is better at reacting to problems or opportunities than planning for them. The management of technology needs to become less of an art form and more of a science in order to stay in step with the business units. Over time, management's estimation and planning skills will improve to better position an organization to plan and anticipate change.

Technology as an Asset

As technology eats up more and more of a firm's budget dollars, it becomes increasingly important to manage it more as an investment and less like an expense. Technology can have a druglike effect on business—the more companies have, the more they want. To make the most effective use of the technology budget, firms must think of it as a strategic investment and not as just another expense of doing business. Technology is becoming an integral part of today's business products, so a clear plan should be put into effect and criteria should be established on how and where technology dollars are invested. If the corporation allows each business unit to drive technology independently of each other, the corporation as a whole will suffer. More times than not, economies of scale are not achieved because of a narrow view of the problem and a selfish approach to the solution.

GTM applies three criteria when looking at a business problem that requires a technology investment. Will this investment:

• **Increase revenue**—Can the investment use technology to bring in more dollars that impact the bottom line, regardless of the product sold? This should be measurable; a clear return on investment (ROI) calculation will determine if this is a wise investment of technology resources. The cost side of the equation should be provided by your technology organization, but the benefit component really needs to be owned and defended by the sponsoring business unit.

• **Manage risk**—Can the investment use technology either to control business exposure to outside regulators or to protect the shareholders' investment? With the explosion of technology and the trend toward decentralizing decisions to lower levels, it becomes even more important to manage firm risk. With the problems that major investment firms have experienced in the last couple of years and the increase in regulatory controls sweeping the business environment, it is imperative that technology becomes a means to control business exposure. The use of technology dollars to help manage risk should be viewed as the cost of doing business in this current environment.

• **Strategically position the firm**—Can the investment use technology assets to help a firm get into a new business, or position it to stay competitive in its current business? This is another effective use of technology dollars. In the securities industry, the push toward a shortened settlement cycle is a good example of how firms need to invest in technology to meet new regulatory requirements.

Noticeably absent from these criteria is the cost saving or efficiency argument for a technology investment. The concept of making technology investments based on streamlining work flow is flawed because rarely do these initiatives produce the desired cost saving. In most cases, the sunken cost of doing business (inefficiencies and all) are being funded by the current revenue stream. In some cases, improving the work flow will cut costs; but generally, considering the high cost of technology, the inefficiencies must be fairly extreme to warrant a significant technology investment. Also, efficiency of work flow becomes an outgrowth of applying technology based on the preceding three criteria. Efficiency of work flow will be a result of these efforts but should not be a driving factor. If all the outstanding technology opportunities are mapped to these three criteria (increase revenue, manage risk, position strategically), a technology manager will probably find a lot of projects that should be reevaluated. If after all the projects that map these criteria are completed, then, and only then, start expanding the firm's technology investment to improve the efficiency of the work flow.

Moving from Service Provider to Partner

As technology becomes an increasing percentage of the firm's over-all expenses, it becomes more important for the business units to view the technology department as a business partner. To be truly effective, the business units must take an active (dare we say pro-active) approach to technology. The smarter business unit managers (BUMs) will become more educated on the capabilities and limitations of technology on their business. The successful BUMs will require that technologists become more aware of the business issues and establish a partnership with technology.

GTM does not advocate a complete decentralization of the technology organization, but instead a model that keeps a central organization that has many dedicated groups that support each major business area. Each business unit should have a point person for all of its technology needs. This does not need to be purely a liaison role (as discussed later in the chapter), but should be some-one who fully understands the business problems and has a command of the capabilities of technology.

HOW TO BUILD A TECHNOLOGY TEAM

Staffing a Technology Team

The single, most important factor in deciding the success of a technology investment will be the people on the team. The group must be able to work as a team to successfully deliver the product. The process of team building must become the primary focus. Defining and then recruiting talent should be a manager's number one focus at the initial stages of the project. This is true almost regardless of the size of the project. No amount of budget dollars will make the sting of a poor technology decision fade.

A fairly recent trend has been to decentralize a large number of technology decisions. The rationale (which GTM fully supports) is that the people closest to the problem are the best judges of the appropriate solution. This requires qualified people throughout all aspects of an organization to be better prepared to make technology decisions.

College Recruiting

If at all possible, look to staff a technology team with internal talent. In cases where people need to be retooled, expect a long learning curve. The success rate for people to be retooled depends almost entirely on management's expectations. If management is willing to expect less than 100 percent efficiency for the first six to nine months while an individual learns a new skill set, then there is a greater chance that the retooling will be successful. Too often, management's expectations are not managed properly, and people are not given an appropriate opportunity to adjust to the new technology. As the rate of technology change increases, firms must be patient with individuals as they climb the learning curve. In most instances, people find it difficult to learn a new technology while at the same time trying to meet tight deadlines on a project.

When internal resources are not adequate, an excellent source of new talent can be found at the local colleges. A project manager should look to become active in partnering with the human resources department to develop a college recruiting program. Even though there are many excellent universities throughout the country, there are a number of advantages to looking at local schools. The local colleges in most metropolitan areas attempt to mirror the types of skills required in the surrounding marketplace. Their proximity allows for frequent recruiting trips, and candidates tend to be more familiar with the surrounding area.

When looking at statewide colleges, focus on schools that have a well-established recruiting center and that emphasize business as well as technical skills. One way to work with your local schools to improve their curricula is through participating on departmental advisory boards. Usually each department will have an advisory board made up of local businesspeople who consult with the faculty to help focus the curriculum on relevant topics. The time commitment is minimal and the results can be significant.

Larger organizations should look to college recruiting as an excellent method to bring new people and ideas into an organization. Management should establish certain recruiting guidelines to keep new talent flowing into the organization. Management should target a certain percentage of their new jobs to be filled through the college recruiting program. Another outgrowth of college recruiting is that it provides an excellent mechanism to start making inroads into establishing a diverse organization.

With very little effort, a well-thought out college recruiting program can provide a pipeline to diversify an organization. Colleges tend to have a diverse pool of candidates eager for a challenge.

Interview Process

The historical method of how people are hired is archaic and wrought with inefficiencies. Based on a self-assessment of an individual's skills (resumé), companies determine whether to interview the individual. Determination of whether a job offer will be extended is often based on having a person meet a representative of the corporation to talk for a half hour to an hour.

The current interview process is as accurate as trying to read tarot cards before asking an individual to make a career decision. Justice is being done to neither the individual nor the corporation by following this process. The current process does not encourage creative thought and tends to be biased against individuals who may express different views than the interviewer. It is human nature for the interviewer to be attracted to people that have the same likes and dislikes. People tend to like people who have the same views and thinking processes that they do. This unintended bias unknowingly filters out a lot of qualified candidates, and in the long run, will impact the diversity of the organization.

Regardless of how much sensitivity training interviewers receive, the draw of liking people who are like themselves is very strong. Likes attract likes, and this natural process will continue unless measures are taken to help counteract them.

Assessment Centers and Team Building

One of the most effective mechanisms for building a strong and diverse team is through the use of an assessment center. The assessment center concept is increasingly being used for the staffing of technology organizations. Typically, assessment centers span two or more days, and during this time, a true indication of a candidate's skills becomes apparent. On the flip side of that, a firm's true culture comes out as candidates meet more people in the firm.

Assessment centers challenge potential candidates on a number of fronts and allow management the luxury of viewing candidates in a number of different situations. One of the single, most important (and one of the most variable) aspects of being able to successfully develop a technology project is the ability for people to work well in a team environment. Very few aspects of technology are based on the accomplishments of a single individual. Because of this, assessment centers make the most sense for team-based projects/businesses. Assessment centers typically work better when multiple employment opportunities exist.

Assessment centers provide a mechanism for candidates to get a full understanding of an employer and give the employer better information about the candidate prior to making a job offer. Typically, assessments centers have four segments:

- Multiple interviews with different individuals within the firm.
- Testing of verbal, math, technical, and logic skills.
- Team exercises.
- Social situations where candidates interact with other candidates and firm members (e.g., lunch or dinner).

Each candidate is observed and graded based on previously agreed-on criteria for the position. The pool of candidates that successfully complete the assessment center experience will be a more diverse group and will lay an excellent foundation for a technology team. By far, the most important technology investment a firm can make is in the people. The assessment center process is more expensive and time consuming than the traditional interview process, but the results are well worth the extra effort. The retention rate for candidates hired from assessment centers is noticeably higher than through the traditional interview process.

PRODUCT MANAGEMENT

Project Management

GTM assumes a degree of competence in the area of project management. A number of excellent books have been written over the last five years on the subject of how to manage technology projects effectively. The typical tools of project management must be

- A project planning tool.
- A system-development life cycle.
- Budgeting tools.
- A communication tool to users and management.

These tools are not really optional when a firm is looking to invest seriously in technology. This aspect of technology management is really the foundation of any successful project. Without these tools, it is impractical to assume that a technology project will be completed on time and within budget. GTM really expects that most of these items are in place and functioning prior to investing in any significant way in technology.

Buy, Build, or Outsource Decision

Buy, build, or outsource is the age-old question that most technology managers face sooner or later. The approach to this problem should be very open and business-oriented. Technology managers should determine which core competencies are provided by their particular organizations and focus on strengthening these areas. They should make a conscientious effort to look at the other areas of technology and determine if the firm would be better off buying these services. A particular focus should be on areas of technology that can be considered commoditized. Avoid the franchise mentality that many technology departments have as it relates to outside companies providing technology products and services to internal customers.

A technology manager does not need to manage and staff all functions that relate to technology for the firm. Pick the areas that can provide value added by having them in-house. Most technology shops should take a hard look at which technology functions can be better served by an outside provider. Technology's focus must always stay in line with the overall business strategy, and by constantly reviewing the buy-versus-build option, focus the decision more on the business drivers than the technical issues. Technology managers who structure and manage their organizations properly should be able to react to changing market conditions. Like other businesspeople, technology managers must keep a keen eye on the overall business environment and not be bogged down in the complexities of running a technology organization or project.

Technology managers who are able to walk this fine line will earn the respect of senior management. In order for internal technology departments to survive into the next century, technologists must focus on effectiveness and not efficiencies. A good method to do this is to integrate the buy-versus-build equation into each technology decision.

Outsourcing Issues

The current trend of outsourcing should be a welcome consideration to most savvy technology managers. For years, internal technology organizations have been targeted as being huge, expensive, nonproductive organizations that are more concerned about self-indulging in technology than adding to the bottom line. Senior managers do not want to take the time to understand the complexities and/or risks of embarking on a technology project. Coupled with this is the uneducated sense that things should be able to be done more quickly and more cheaply; thus, we have the poor perception that a lot of technology organizations enjoy today. GTM helps technology organizations to manage these issues more directly. GTM forces technology managers to understand their financials more fully, requires business (not technology) sponsorship for projects, and, most important, makes business or product managers out of technologists. Most technology managers of today have some degree of technical background, and more than likely, worked themselves up through the ranks. Successful technology managers of the future must have more of a business focus on how their organizations operate.

Technology managers should view outsourcing as a way of controlling costs and providing value-added services. Outsourcing should not be considered if a firm cannot accurately determine and track its technology expense as explained in the "Financial Management" section. Managers must be able to understand current costs before being able to effectively weigh outsourcing options.

Some common pitfalls and issues of outsourcing must be understood before deciding to outsource part or all of a technology function:

- The targeted client base must be a fairly sophisticated user of technology. A client base that requires a lot of hand-holding or encouragement to use technology tends to be unsatisfied with outsourced support.

- Outsourcing tends to be a one-way street. Once a technology function is outsourced, experienced staff is lost and it becomes cost prohibitive to rebuild this skill set from scratch. The technology infrastructure and processes that were in place to support this function decay to the point of no return within one to two years. Outsourcing decisions must be considered a long-term commitment. Of course, outsourcing firms will tell senior management that they have release clauses, but in reality, there is no turning back.

- Service levels will be impacted because more processes will be overlaid onto the current structure. To be successful, outsourcing firms must be able to manage and measure their effectiveness. They tend to do this through very structured management methodologies that give users the perception of reduced service levels.

- An outsourcing contract must have incentive clauses for the outsourcing firm to be tied to the firm's overall success. It is imperative that your outsourcing partner be tied financially to you. Provide incentives for the outsourcing firm to help manage technology expenses and business needs.

- Cost savings in the first five years are not indicative of future long-term costs. Most pricing schedules provide an incentive for saving in the first five years, because outsourcing firms realize that few firms ever take back an outsourced function. There is nothing wrong with this approach; just be aware of this factor when determining the financial viability of outsourcing.

FINANCIAL MANAGEMENT

A very important component of GTM is the financial management aspect of how technology expenses are accounted and reported. The increase in the rate of change of technology and the increase in the size of technology budgets has made financial management a mandatory skill of today's technologist. If technology is to be run like a business, then a plan must be formulated to manage its financials like any other business unit. No longer is it acceptable to just plod through the annual budget cycle and then spend the rest of the year explaining variances. All aspects of the expenses and cost structure must be understood. As the outsourcing industry matures, technologists will come under increasing pressure to compete with outside entities. This should be welcomed because only through competition will the true value of a technology group be realized.

The proper financial management tools must be provided to manage technology competitively. Technology expenses must be uncoupled from other costs so that we can ascertain the true cost of doing business. Before a decision can be made about the effectiveness of outsourcing, the proper financial tools must be in place:

- Be assured of the accuracy and completeness of technology's expense data as part of the client's/firm's profit and loss statement (P&L).
- Provide for central management of technology expenses (CMEs) by the technology organization.
- Provide a technology bill that represents technology provider services to help clients to understand and manage their technology investment.
- Provide the ability to benchmark technology to the marketplace.
- Have the ability to perform cost/benefit analysis.
- Be positioned to perform trend analysis on expenses.
- Participate in business planning for technology.

More often than not, technology expense buckets and allocation methodologies were probably established long ago with rules that may no longer be valid. Managers must clarify each technology expense, therefore, and understand the origin of each expense. How these buckets are defined and what goes into them is the foundation to manage technology properly. GTM breaks these expense buckets into three subbusinesses:

Technology Business Management   The technology business management bucket captures all costs related to administrating the technology business, such as administrative head-count, organizational development, strategic planning, and financial analysis and planning. These costs should be considered the overhead costs of administrating the organization. Such costs are best distributed out as a firmwide expense of doing business. Keeping these costs in check is very important, since this line item usually becomes an easy target in cost-cutting times. Staff should be kept to a minimum and consultants are better used for specialized expertise that is not available in-house. This business should focus on leveraging the capabilities of the organization instead of building teams to facilitate its efforts.

Core Services   Core services create the infrastructure or uncontrollable costs of being in business. Certain inherent costs of being in any business are neither volume nor economically sensitive. These costs can include things like telephone usage, legacy systems, WAN/LAN, and so forth. This bucket should capture these core expenses, and they should be billed out based on an allocation methodology. Generally, these costs tend to be fixed but do have some ties to the level of activity generated in application development work or a significant expansion of any one particular business. This business is the heart of any technology shop. Without a well-thought-out plan to bill and fully recover core services, technology expenses in this business can easily escalate out of control.

Business-Sponsored Support Services   Projects directly sponsored and billed to the end client are business-sponsored support services. These costs tend to vary based on the end client's desire to sponsor technology projects—these projects usually tend to be software development. These variable expenses can expand and contract based on the business demand. Business sponsorship is critical in this business. As stated earlier, technology must not fund and sponsor projects in this business sector without approval. Even the best of intended projects will fail without proper financial and management support.

To be effective, a technology manager must understand how the technology expense buckets are represented to the user's P&L. What other costs are added in? Who determines what goes where? What pieces are controllable? All of this information must be made available to technology managers if they are expected to manage competitive businesses.

Part of a technology group's responsibility should be to have responsibility for CMEs (e.g., network, market data, phones). CMEs tend to be a significant percentage of the overall technology expenses, but since they are normally billed direct, they are not always included in the centrally managed technology budget. CMEs should be identified and clearly decoupled from other costs. Separate expense buckets should be established for each CME, and a technologist should be responsible for managing that expense. Vendor relationships, service level agreements, and optimization efforts are some of the advantages of having CMEs centrally managed. The real benefit to the firm, though, is a clear understanding of its true technology costs.

A monthly or quarterly technology bill representing all technology products and/or services should be reviewed with technology's customers. As a support division, GTM assumes technology expenses will be 100 percent recoverable. Technology expenses are defined costs incurred by the firm or any business unit for technology, plus the cost of the technology department. To properly manage technology like a business, the technology department must understand how to allocate expenses to the (1) client (technology sponsor), (2) product/service, or (3) function or CME.

A key component in producing a technology bill is knowing how the products are understood by the end client and in the marketplace. If products are defined either too narrowly or too technically, the bill becomes meaningless. Products and services should be defined in nontechnical terminology and must be actionable from the client's perspective. If products/services are defined too uniquely, then it will become impossible to benchmark to outside firms when evaluating outsourcing opportunities.

GTM positions technologists to make intelligent business decisions on where to invest technology dollars. The ability to price and, therefore, compare internally developed products/services with external vendors is an important part of a technologist's job. This approach to financial management positions a technology department to

1. Make buy versus build decisions.
2. Benchmark outsourcing opportunities.
3. Perform ROI or cost/benefit analysis.

Once the expense buckets are defined and priced (based on fully allocated costs and 100 percent recoverability), the question of which pieces make sense to outsource becomes more quantifiable. The argument that an internal technology service is more efficient or provides a strategic competitive advantage can be more easily determined with this methodology.

Once time-tracking mechanisms are in place to bucket and bill for technology time expended, technology managers can begin to proactively manage their businesses. Trend analysis can be done by product and by customer to best understand the ebb and flow of a particular business. In this way, managers can make projections on how to best manage the technology dollars. If the financial management tools are mature enough, incentive pricing can be used to encourage certain behavior. If managers want to discourage customers from using a particular product/service, it can be priced accordingly. Rates to establish a price must include all aspects of the expense and may be real or market based. Remember, the end game is 100 percent recoverability.

ORGANIZATIONAL DEVELOPMENT

GTM places a significant amount of emphasis on planning and organizational development. So much of the success of a technology project is determined by the people on the team. To not focus effort on the resources that will make a project successful is shortsighted and just plain bad business. A well-thought-out plan and approach to managing an organization should be part of any long-term technology strategy. A few suggestions for putting together a plan to promote a technology organization follow.

Encourage Technologists to Be Active in the Industry   The pace of technology is changing so fast that not to be networking within the industry to share and promote ideas is foolish. The cost of encouraging outside participation in the industry is minimal compared to the potential payback.

Try to Stay Away from Establishing Liaison Roles within a Technology Organization   These are roles that historically act as a buffer between user and client. These roles tend to be self-perpetuating and add little value to the end product. They tend to develop because of communication or personality issues between the technologist and the end client. The concept of partnering with the business units will be hampered by this unnecessary level of process overhead. The more distance between the technology team and the user community, the more difficult it will be to establish a meaningful partnership. Technology must be further embraced by the business units—not buffered from them—if technology is to move organizations to new productivity heights. If this type of role is requested, do some detailed root-cause analysis on why the responsible technologist cannot get this job done without a liaison role in place. If the issue is with the project manager, make that person aware of the issue and explain why the cost of a liaison role was necessary. This manager should rotate out of supporting this user at the first opportunity. If the issue is with the user, it tends to be because of a lack of savvy or understanding on what to do with technology. Sometimes, a little user education can go a long way in helping diffuse this type of problem.

Use of Staff Positions   A common practice among technology management is the use of staff positions. Staff positions are encouraged—but use them sparingly. A staff position should have a very specific scope, and the position should be eliminated once the charter has been completed. GTM encourages these types of positions on a rotational basis because it

- Provides rotational opportunities for management.
- Requires managers to rely on their skills instead of their employees for results.
- Tends to have the effect of breaking up little fiefdoms that may develop in organizations.
- Keeps managers motivated and on their toes.

In reality, staff positions tend to be a common dumping ground for problem employees. Instead of dealing with the problem directly and professionally, technology organizations tend to have more than their share of these positions without a specific charter or need. This misuse of staff positions reflects poorly on the entire organization and will create a negative perception from senior management if left unchecked.

In conclusion, what if the status quo is maintained? The consequences of not implementing a global model like GTM will cause a significant impact on the technology organization and overall business for years in the future. Some of the consequences are

- Costs will increase, and any previously eliminated costs will creep back in due to a lack of financial controls.
- The ability to react to the overall global trend will become harder because most technology firms are aligned regionally and functionally.
- The establishment and commitment to a business-driven technology strategy becomes more difficult because of a lack of formal partnership with the business model.
- An uncontrolled decentralization of technology functions will lead to increased overall technology costs.

It is of paramount importance that a technology organization embark on an effort to manage staff, and manage and implement technology in the future in order for firms to be competitive into the next century. No longer will it be acceptable to plod along on a tactical path as an order filler. Technologists must be proactive and open to new ways to manage technology in the future.

Of course, no change comes without its downside. Certain inherent risks are associated with implementing any major organizational change. The initial start-up costs and increased administration of new processes may be a difficult pill for business units to swallow in the face of increasing pressure for new technologies. The customers/users that are satisfied with the existing structure and processes may be unhappy with change. Resistance to change by the technology staff will result in lower morale and feelings of displacement and confusion. These are all necessary evils to achieve new technology heights. As Will Rogers once said, "Even if you're on the right track, you'll still get run over if you don't keep moving."

5

⑥ FINANCIAL EVALUATION OF TRANSITION TECHNOLOGIES

C. Warren Axelrod, Ph.D.
President
C.W. Axelrod Associates, Inc.

There was a time when it seemed relatively straightforward to develop proposals for mainframe-based batch systems. Costs were fairly well known in advance, with the usual allowance of 10–20 percent for contingency, and benefits were mostly in the form of readily defined cost savings. Evaluation became more complex with the emergence of technologies such as on-line and real-time systems, because greater implementation risk was incurred. The cost variance increased to the 30–60 percent range. At the same time, more of the benefits moved into the realm of the intangible, with value-added systems becoming the key phrase. These trends have accelerated as systems developers have adopted the client/server model. Now cost variances of 50–150 percent are common; a study by The Standish Group International found that 53 percent of client/server projects surveyed were over budget an average of 89 percent. It is often virtually impossible to define the real benefits of many of these systems since the systems are most often oriented toward customers, markets, and revenue production; statements of value in these cases are generally highly subjective.

There is an old saying: "If you don't know where you're going, any road will get you there." In this context, the saying might be: "If you cannot measure the costs and benefits of a new system, any method of evaluation will do, since none will yield an accurate answer." Even though we might believe that we are embarking on an impossible task, we should proceed anyway because if we can achieve some answers, however inadequate, they will be better than nothing at all.

We begin by defining various categories of costs and benefits in general terms, then we propose how they might be measured, and finally develop evaluation methods that will explicitly determine whether the firm should embark on a particular project. Often, in practice, this process is intuitive. Here we attempt to introduce more formal procedures.

Since we are all quite familiar with the traditional evaluation approaches, we shall not spend much time on them. Instead we shall concentrate on the particular aspects that have risen to prominence with newfangled technologies such as multitier architectures, object-oriented design and programming, and the Internet. It is eminently clear that the headlong rush into such technologies as these is often not the result of careful and precise analysis but results from the visceral feel of those in control of the purse strings. Not that this is necessarily the wrong approach in many cases— much innovation would wither on the vine were it to await the conclusions of detailed studies. However, there are particular costs and benefits that have assumed extraordinary importance at this time, and it would be a mistake to omit them. These comprise the category *transition* costs and benefits. This chapter concentrates on the definition, makeup, determination, and analysis of transition costs and transition benefits.

THE TRANSITION FACTORS

The 1995 Software Development Tools Market Report from Sentry Market/Research listed these obstacles to timely completion of client/server projects in priority order:

1. Underestimated time and staff required.
2. Change in corporate strategic direction.
3. Shift in technology management.
4. Unstable technology.
5. Overrated project benefits.
6. Too expensive to implement.[1]

---

1. _____, In "Fast-Tracking to Enterprise Client/Server Applications," A special advertising supplement from USoft. "Why Is Client/Server So Difficult?" *Client/Server Computing,*vol. 3, no. 1 (January 1996), pp.48–49.

Clearly, several of these factors are exogenous—such as changes in direction of corporate strategy and technology management. While these cannot be controlled, they can be allowed for. The remaining factors are, at least theoretically, under the control of management and should be specifically considered in any project evaluation.

Underestimated Time and Staff

To some extent (but not one-to-one), time and resources can be substituted for each other. The fewer resources, usually the longer a project takes. But not always. There is always a point at which too many cooks spoil the broth. However, to the extent that a particular project can be broken down into discrete and/or independent modules that can be developed in parallel, then adding appropriate staff can indeed reduce time to completion.

Considering that, in the majority of cases, time and effort are underestimated (only 16 percent of the surveyed projects were completed on time and within budget), it behooves the estimator to allow for more of both. It is suspected that significant cushions are already embedded in plans for projects which actually hit their targets.

One should not underestimate the importance of prior experience in a particular technology. If you, or someone on your staff, has worked with a particular technology before, the quality of project time and staffing estimates will be much more accurate than if the technology is entirely new. A general rule should be: If you are embarking on new technology and do not have closely related experience available, a 50 to 100 percent contingency on time and staff is not unreasonable.

Change in Corporate Strategic Direction

Companies today are frequently changing the businesses they are in, either through internal development or through acquisition or merger. The marketplace is demanding that firms move quickly with the times and respond rapidly to market influences. This calls for flexibility in both the business units and the computer systems that support them. Consequently there is a premium on systems which are highly flexible and readily adaptable.

A key benefit of many of the newer technologies is that they offer much greater flexibility than their predecessors. Such technologies include relational database management systems (RDBMS), fourth-generation languages (4GL), object-oriented programming (OOP), rapid application development (RAD) environments, multidimensional databases (MDD), and on-line analytic processing (OLAP).

Future Benefits   The responsiveness engendered by these technologies is a benefit that should be included in any evaluation. Often, the first implementation of a particular technology cannot be justified economically. It is only when subsequent implementations and changes are needed that the initial investment is leveraged. For example, setting up a data warehouse based on a relational database can be extremely costly and will undoubtedly take much more time and effort than anticipated. However, once the RDBMS is in place, systems and reports can be developed in a fraction of the time required for traditional methods.

It is important, therefore, to add a factor for savings to be derived from future applications of a technology. Care must be taken not to double count these benefits.

Shift in Technology Management

The managers of information technology have been a particularly mobile group—either voluntarily or forced. The high demand for specific skills has produced an active market for individuals with those popular abilities. On the other hand, the difficulty in implementing such technologies often leads to general management's dissatisfaction and consequent removal of those responsible.

Whatever the reason, it is very common for major projects to be started by one management team and to be taken over by another team or teams—the latter either continuing with the original approach or, more likely, dumping the inherited project and starting out on something new.

From the point of view of general management, rather than information technology (IT) management, projects should be broken down into shorter-term modules. In this way, were there to be a replacement of IT management or a change in the philosophy of existing IT management, there would be a good chance that something useful will have been delivered. On the other hand, IT management tends to favor an approach with long-term deliverables since it allows for greater flexibility within the department with regard to adjusting priorities and resources and also it puts off the final day of reckoning.

Clearly, from a corporate perspective, there are benefits to be derived from implementing systems that can be delivered as well-defined components and using methods that can be incorporated into a broad range of other technologies.

The financial evaluation should include benefits for modular design and short-term deliverables and for adaptability of the technology for other environments. For example, the vendors of the most popular relational databases—such as Oracle, Sybase, Informix—are continually developing new tools and establishing alliances with other software houses to keep their products fresh and to expand capabilities so that changes in direction will not make prior investments (in establishing databases and applications based on those databases) obsolete.

Unstable Technology

It is a fact of life that new technologies seldom work the way they were meant to originally. That is the main reasoning behind vendors' practically giving away beta versions of software and equipment that are put out selectively into the marketplace for a limited number of potential customers to test.

No matter how careful a software developer or equipment manufacturer may be and how intense their testing and quality assurance programs are, errors still slip through, especially as systems become increasingly complex. It is just not reasonable to expect a brand new system to operate flawlessly right out of the box.

What are the implications for project evaluation? Clearly some allowance must be made for the instability of pioneering systems since such unstable behavior results in costs to both the selling and buying entities. The costs might be due to the unavailability of certain key features or even the system in its entirety for a certain period of time. This might result in lost opportunities, such as not booking new business, beating the competition, or realizing anticipated savings from the new system. The vendor also might be incurring costs due to the delay and the need to rework the product. If the vendor is financially healthy and can sustain the costs and losses in revenue, then the vendor costs may not affect the customer. If, however, the delay were to put the vendor out of business, the impact on a customer dependent on the new system—one that never is completed—can be considerable.

The instability of the technology applies equally to in-house development. Whereas the underlying equipment and software might be proven, the use of software and equipment by in-house novices can result in unreliable and unpredictable systems, as can any unusual combinations of components.

And the most disturbing scenario of all—which is surprisingly common—is the combination of new, untried vendor products and inexperienced in-house and external staff. Regrettably, this situation is almost always doomed to outright failure or, at the very least, to a complete reworking of the system.

Overrated Project Benefits

There is a very strong tendency of those proposing the development and implementation of new systems to exaggerate the potential benefits. This occurs primarily because the proponents want to ensure approval of their proposal. After all, if they did not believe in the proposed system they would not support it. However, the proposal itself will not include the personal benefits to those who will implement the system—such as learning new technologies, receiving high exposure to decision makers, and working on something interesting. Career enhancement (or revenue generation for consultants) can be a strong motivator to put a prospective system in its best light.

From the perspective of the person presenting the proposal, the main advantage of overstating benefits—versus understating costs—is that the former is much easier to fudge because many benefits are highly subjective and cannot readily be disproved ahead of time, whereas costs are generally more tangible and can be more easily questioned.

Too Expensive to Implement

It is almost always cheaper to modify an existing system rather than starting fresh with a new technology. And, indeed, unless there is a compelling reason to do so, my advice is to utilize existing technology to the extent possible, assuming that it makes economic and practical sense.

Converting to new technologies can indeed be a very expensive endeavor fraught with cost overruns and implementation delays. If the benefits from future savings in application development and the ability of the technologies to adapt to changing business and IT management environments are neglected or understated, it is understandable that projects will be rejected on the basis of cost. There is a premium to be paid for any conversion to a new technology. That premium is often paid in anticipation of future benefits.

As a matter of course, projects should not be eliminated from consideration based purely on well-defined costs. Less measurable transition costs must be added—but so also must the benefits of moving into a more productive and flexible environment.

DETERMINATION OF COSTS AND BENEFITS

Let us look at the implications of the above factors on the evaluations themselves. The transition cost and benefit components are shown in bold type. The cost components are as follows:

Purchase and installation of equipment
Processors
Mainframes
Central
Departmental
Minicomputers
Central
Departmental
Microcomputers
Servers
Desktop
Laptop
Peripherals
Disk drives
Tape drives
Printers
Central
Personal

Communications
  Modems
  Switches
  Routers
Cables
  Local direct lines
  Local-area networks
Circuits
  Public
  Private

Third-party software
  Applications
  Tools
  Utilities
  Operating systems

Internal staff
  Business analysts
  Systems analysts
  Programmers
  Technical support
  Operations

External staff
  Vendor support
  Business consultants
  Technical consultants
  Programmers

Other
  Travel and accommodation
  Supplies
  Contingency

Costs of obsolescence
  **Diminishing pool of required skills leading to
    inflated costs**
  **High and increasing maintenance costs for older
    equipment**
  High and increasing support costs for older software
  Risk of discontinuation of vendor support

Lack of new features that are now taken for granted

Transition costs
Hiring of knowledgeable staff (high-salaried
   individuals)
Training of existing and new staff
On-the-job learning (reduced productivity)
Cost of complexity in design, development, technical
   support and operation
Cost of redoing or reworking initial efforts
Loss of credibility from missed deadlines and
   inadequate systems
Lack of adequate system management and data tools

The benefit components are as follows:

Direct cost savings
   Staff salaries and benefits
   Equipment and software maintenance
   Space rental
   Supplies
   Travel and accommodation
   Overhead

Time savings
   Project duration
   Task duration

Intangible benefits
   Increased revenues
   More competitive
   Reputation for leading-edge approaches

Benefits of Obsolescence
   Initially, abundant cheap equipment
   Stable, unchanging software

Transition benefits
   Implementation of infrastructure for future development
   Establishment of knowledgeable team
   More flexible, adaptable technologies
   Availability of advanced design and development tools
   Building of career-enhancing credentials

MEASUREMENT OF COSTS AND BENEFITS

The goal is to come up with accurate estimates in as many categories as possible, showing one-time and recurring costs and benefits with the time distribution of the costs and benefits laid out. Probability distributions of the costs and benefits and timings should also be specified, if possible, since some components are known accurately with narrow variances whereas others have very broad variances. Exhibit 5–1 compares the relative levels and variances of various costs and benefits for existing legacy systems and systems involving emerging technologies.

COST AND BENEFITS RELATIONSHIPS

Trends and Cycles

Whereas direct costs and benefits tend to follow general market trends (e.g., microprocessors halve price-performance every 18 to 24 months), transition costs and benefits and obsolescence costs

E X H I B I T 5–1

	Legacy Systems		Emerging Technologies	
	Relative Level	Variance	Relative Level	Variance
Costs				
Equipment	High on per-unit basis	Low	Low to moderate	High
Software	Moderate to high	Low	Moderate	High
Staff resources	Moderate	Moderate	High	Very high
Obsolescence	Moderate to high	High	Not applicable	Not applicable
Transition	Not applicable	Not applicable	High	Very high
Benefits				
Costs savings	Moderate	Low	Low	High
Time savings	Moderate	Low	Low	High
Intangible	Moderate	Moderate	Moderate	High
Transition	Not applicable	Not applicable	Very high	Very high

EXHIBIT 5–2

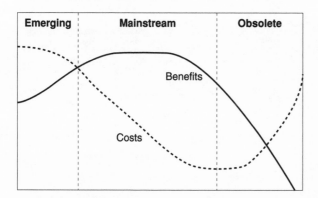

track the technology cycle. As new technologies emerge, the transition costs for the early adopters can be very high—with a relatively high percentage of outright failures—and the transition benefits are spotty at best. Gradually, as experience is gained, the transition costs fall, and the transition benefits can be more readily asserted. Coincidentally, obsolescence costs on former technologies begin to increase and vendors and staff abandon the older technology in favor of the potentially more lucrative emerging technologies. There is a brief period during which the cost of obsolete equipment falls precipitously and may be a real bargain for those wishing to extend the lives of legacy systems, especially for those systems that are not changing much and meet a stable need. Soon, however, the low cost of equipment is more than offset by the high cost of maintenance. And on the software side, the legacy software is less and less able to meet new requirements, especially those that have been precipitated by the capabilities of newer technologies. Also, as more and more customers adopt the new technologies, the costs of maintaining and supporting older technologies accelerate as the pools of expertise diminish and parts are no longer manufactured. These trends are illustrated in Exhibits 5–2 and 5–3.

In Exhibit 5–2 we see how costs and benefits vary over time as a technology goes through its emergent, mainstream, and obsolete phases. During the emergent phase, costs are high due to the dominance of transition costs. As a technology becomes mainstream, the transition costs diminish rapidly. Then, as newer technologies make the current mainstream technology obsolete, costs related to obsolescence have an increasing impact. With regard to benefits,

EXHIBIT   5–3

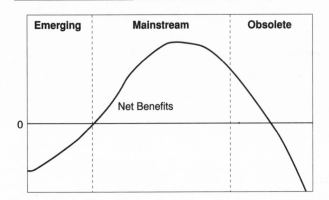

frequently transition benefits are fairly low as companies begin to see how they might gain from the new technologies. Occasionally, a small number of companies really exploit the technology and do extraordinarily well for themselves (examples include Wang Laboratories, Microsoft, Lotus, Netscape) during the emergent phase. The highest aggregate benefits are realized during the period when the technology is mainstream. As the technology becomes obsolete, the benefits fall off.

Exhibit 5–3 shows the net benefits. Here we see that often there may be a negative benefit (or loss) during the emergent phase. One might ask why anyone would adopt new technologies during this phase if the expectation is one of negative benefits. The answer is likely that gambling instincts may come into play, with early adopters believing that they might be one of the small minority that reaps huge benefits as mentioned above. During the mainstream phase, net benefits are positive and usually peak near the time an emerging replacement technology appears on the scene. Into the third stage, costs begin to outweigh the benefits. As the fall in net benefits accelerates, organizations are forced to consider the latest in emerging technologies. The hope is that by the time the costs of obsolescence become too much of a burden, the new technologies will have passed through their emergent phase so that the move to the newer technologies is less painful.

It is interesting to note that the early birds often lose money on their transition projects. How might this happen? The likely answer is that they grossly underestimate—or ignore completely—the transition costs and exaggerate the transition benefits in their evaluation. They may also be fooled by the brief period of growing obsolescence benefits when older technologies become really cheap only to turn expensive a little later.

Conversely, late adopters often keep modifying and enhancing systems that are becoming increasingly expensive to support when it would seem to make more sense to convert to a newer technology. This occurs because obsolescence costs are not fairly estimated. What will be the most significant obsolescence cost in history will result from the changes needed to handle the year 2000, and clearly these costs have not been factored into the maintenance of thousands of legacy systems. If they had, there would have already been a much greater push toward adopting emerging technologies and the replacement of older systems before there is the need to modify them for the millennium.

Compression of Work Plans

Reviewing Exhibit 5–2, we see that it may pay to compress the time schedules (by adding resources) so that the benefits can be realized before the technology begins to obsolesce. Clearly, at some point during the obsolescence phase even work-plan compression will not result in positive net value. However, once the initial learning phase with its casualties is passed, it may well pay to accelerate the development process for newer technologies so that systems can be operational during a period of high positive returns.

EVALUATION OF PROJECTS

The most informative analytic approach is to simulate thousands of different scenarios and to come up with probability distributions of costs and benefits, discounted to the present, for the range of timings that are considered feasible. However, many managers are not comfortable with probabilistic approaches and cannot visualize the impact of additional dimensions such as time compression. Consequently, an analysis using most likely values may be more practical and can provide significant insight. The next level of sophistication might be to provide upper and lower limits at, say, the 90th and 10th percentiles.

Nevertheless, the particular evaluation method used is overshadowed by the accuracy, completeness, and precision of the underlying costs and benefits. The omission of a major cost or cost category, for example, or a significant computational error can have more impact on a decision than the methodology selected.

CHAPTER

6

⑥ LEGAL CONSIDERATIONS[1]

Jeff Monassebian
Partner
Lieberman & Nowak, New York

System procurement agreements define the vendor's obligations with respect to functionality, delivery, maintenance, and support.[1] Similarly, confidentiality and payment obligations as well as your rights to use, modify, and otherwise implement the system will be expressly specified.

This chapter analyzes the various clauses that comprise the salient rights and obligations expressed in system procurement agreements in the context of (*a*) software license, (*b*) software development, (*c*) hardware, and (*d*) software maintenance agreements.[2] The deliberate focus on software reflects its pivotal role in the system procurement process.

DELIVERABLES

The deliverables clause identifies what the vendor has committed to furnish. This section of the agreement should clearly describe what is being procured in sufficient detail. Otherwise you may find yourself paying additional fees for material or services you thought were included in the price.

---

1. ©Jeff Monassebian 1996. All Rights Reserved
2. The clauses reviewed in this chapter assume that individual agreements are executed for each component of the system as opposed to a turnkey solution. However, the analysis is generally applicable to both types of agreements.

Prepackaged Software and Hardware

Computer hardware and prepackaged software deliverables are straightforward and simple to define. Prepackaged software can be defined by reference to the user manual for the software version being licensed, a copy of which should be attached as a schedule to the agreement. Likewise, computer hardware can be readily described by features and model numbers. In addition, when the vendor has submitted a proposal in response to your request for proposal (RFP), the deliverable should be further identified by reference to this document.[3] Although a user's guide or a functional specification may accurately describe the system, you still need to refer to your RFP and make sure that it takes precedence.

Custom Software Development

Custom software poses greater difficulty in defining the deliverable because the software does not yet exist. For this type of procurement, the requirements definition you develop is essential to the preparation of a system design and functional specification. In the same way that architectural plans define a house yet to be built, the functional specification and system design delineate the functions and capabilities of the software program. Consequently, the requirements definition should be referenced in and attached as a schedule to the agreement.

Customized Software Development

Defining the customized software deliverable presents many of the same issues related to custom software. In addition, customized software procurement requires consideration of sales tax consequences. It is advisable to execute a license agreement for the prepackaged software and a separate agreement for the required customization in order to limit the incidence of sales tax.[4]

---

3. This approach is applicable to and recommended for the procurement of customized and custom software as well.
4. Because some of the vendor's deliverable obligations cannot be validated for compliance until the customized software development work is completed, their acceptance should be deferred until the work defined in the agreement for customized software development services is completed.

Third-Party Software

In certain cases, proper operation of the vendor's application software (prepackaged, customized, or custom) may require software programs licensed by other entities. A relational database management system (RDBMS) is the third-party software most often required. Regardless of whether you are negotiating an individual license agreement for the vendor's software or a turnkey solution, the vendor should be made responsible for delivering the necessary third-party software, its relevant documentation, and license for its use.

SOFTWARE LICENSE

Common Licensing Provisions

As opposed to computer hardware where title to equipment is transferred to the customer, software is generally licensed. Software development is a lengthy and capital intensive endeavor. The low cost and ease of duplication presents vendors with both an opportunity for and a risk to recovering their investment. By maintaining title, vendors can control the use, duplication, modification, and distribution through appropriately circumscribed licensing provisions. Common restrictions found in licensing agreements include limitations on the (a) maximum number of concurrent users that can access the software; (b) use; (c) type and/or number of central processing units (CPUs) upon which the software can be executed; (d) number of copies that can be made; and (e) access to source code. Knowing the practical ramifications of these restrictions allows you to negotiate a licensing clause appropriate to your contemplated use. Each is discussed next.

Limited Users

When negotiating the licensing clause, it is obviously preferable for there to be no limitation on the maximum number of concurrent users. In particular, where the licensing clause limits execution of the software to a particular CPU, an argument can be made that a user limitation is superfluous. Each CPU has its respective maximum processing capacity as well as the maximum number of terminal devices it can support. If too many users are accessing the software, hardware capacity can be exceeded and software performance can be significantly degraded.

When the vendor nevertheless insists on such a limitation, consider the total number of users expected to use the software (concurrently and sequentially) increased by a percentage representing future growth of your business. This approach to establishing the maximum number of users will delay the imposition of additional license fees until the economic conditions of your business warrant them.

Normal Business Operation
License agreements often limit use to "normal business operation as presently conducted." When source code is licensed, a restriction of this nature may be appropriate. Access to source code allows you to modify the software to the point where it can support different requirements from those originally contemplated. The fact that software programs frequently use a RDBMS today makes modifications even easier to accomplish. For example, a time-scheduling software program could be modified to perform client billing as well. When the vendor markets time scheduling and client billing as two separate programs and receives a license fee for each, it suffers an economic loss from this type of modification.

Justification for the limitation is more difficult when only an object-code license is granted. Since you are not able to enhance or otherwise modify the software program, why should you be prevented from using it as creatively as possible? Besides, the vendor would seem to be adequately protected if the licensing provision is limited to a particular CPU (discussed in next section).

Regardless of whether a source- or object-code license is granted, a limitation on use can and usually does create problems of interpretation. What is meant by "normal business operation as presently conducted"? Courts generally interpret ambiguous limitations narrowly and usually against the vendor. Unfortunately, the presence of this language gives the vendor leverage unless you are willing to test its enforceability in court.

From the vendor's perspective, the use limitation does protect a legitimate concern, which is to prevent your use of the software to process another firm's data. However, this concern should be addressed specifically by the following sentence: *Customer shall have the right to use the SOFTWARE only to process its own data. In no event shall Customer process the data of any other entity.*

Designated CPU

Generally, the price of computer hardware has a direct relationship to its processing power. As processing power increases, so does price. Similarly, many software vendors, in particular RDBMS and operating system software vendors, impose a higher license fee based on the hardware's processing power.

A pricing strategy tied to processing power results in an equitable distribution of license fees and allows the vendor to reach a broader segment of the market. For example, assume the vendor charged a license fee of $50,000 regardless of the hardware platform. Customer A that processes 10,000 transactions per day would pay the same license fee as Customer B that processes 500 daily transactions. It is likely that Customer B would not be able to justify the license fee, resulting in lost revenue to the vendor. In addition, such a pricing strategy discriminates against customers with fewer transactions. A tiered pricing strategy pegged to hardware processing power allows the vendor to accomplish both goals of market penetration and fair pricing.

When the license agreement contains a CPU limitation, exercise care to ensure your continued use of the software is not interrupted if the designated CPU becomes inoperable or is replaced with equal or greater processing power.

Copies

Duplication of software is a fairly simple process and unless appropriately controlled can result in lost revenue to the vendor. Uncontrolled duplication will also prejudice the vendor's ability to claim the software as a trade secret.

Uninterrupted use of the software by the customer must be weighed against the vendor's desire to control duplication. Therefore, the license clause should allow you to make a limited number of copies so that the software can be restored if the main copy is damaged, destroyed, or is otherwise inaccessible. A clause that allows the customer to make up to two copies of the software usually strikes a fair compromise giving each party the necessary protection desired.

Reverse Engineering

Object code is unintelligible to humans and therefore software is generally licensed in object-code format to preserve the trade secret and confidential nature of its structure, sequence, architecture, and algorithms. Reverse engineering is the process by which the software's object code is dissected and converted to a form readily understandable to individuals in order for them to uncover the process by which it was developed. Because it can frustrate the vendor's legitimate efforts to maintain confidentiality, a restriction against reverse engineering is appropriate for the vendor's protection and commonly found in the licensing clause.

Site and Corporate Licenses

When business plans envision continued deployment of the system throughout your organization, consider investing in a corporate or site license. A corporate license allows you to execute the software on any CPU located anywhere in your organization. Site licenses are limited to CPUs located at a defined location. Because corporate or site licenses carry better margins for the vendor, usually you can more easily negotiate away restrictions limiting use.

Shrink-Wrap Licenses

Prepackaged software that can be mass marketed is usually sold through mail order and retail stores. Consequently it is not practical to negotiate the terms and conditions of each license and require each user to sign the agreement. Therefore, vendors seek to narrowly define the scope of use to which the software may be put and at the same time limit liability and warranty obligations by resorting to shrink-wrap or self-executing licenses.

A shrink-wrap license agreement is printed on paper placed on the outside of the software package and covered with clear plastic wrap, so that the agreement may be read by the user prior to opening the package. The agreement typically provides that opening the plastic wrap and/or using the software constitutes acceptance of the terms and conditions of the license agreement.

The enforceability of shrink-wrap licenses is questionable.[5] Courts that have ruled on the subject have reached similar results based on various legal theories. Some courts have decided that the "take it or leave it" nature of shrink-wrap licenses is a akin to a contract of adhesion and therefore against public policy. Other courts have denied enforcement of shrink-wrap licenses on the basis that there cannot be an acceptance of the agreement's terms by the mere opening of the software package.[6] We have not devoted much discussion to shrink-wrap licenses because such agreements by their nature are nonnegotiable.

DOCUMENTATION

After devoting a considerable amount of time, money, and resources, you now have the Rolls Royce of systems. However, when you do not know how to drive and an operator's manual is not provided, your new and expensive car is unlikely to fulfill your requirements. Likewise, comprehensive documentation will, to a large degree, determine the extent to which the system implementation is successful, adopted by your personnel, and used effectively and efficiently.

All too often documentation takes a backseat to software development. Because it is usually one of the last tasks scheduled in the development process, it is usually completed in a haphazard manner. Unfortunately, you do not realize the consequences of inadequate documentation until the time you need it most. To avoid this pitfall, standards for the type, structure, content, and quality of documentation to be produced by the vendor should be specified in the agreement.

Procurement agreements usually call for documentation to be "of the highest quality" or "state of the art." In some cases, an independent source for standards is referenced. However, either approach may not adequately define the documentation standard. *Highest quality* or *state of the art* are subjective terms and require their own definition. Although referencing independent standards

---

5. This may change if the proposed amendments to the Uniform Commercial Code are adopted. Specifically, the American Law Institute has suggested a provision, Section 2-2203 that would make standard form shrink-wrap licenses enforceable in certain cases.

6. In a recent case decided by the United States District Court for the Western District of Wisconsin, the court held that a contract was formed at the time the software was purchased and that the terms of a shrink-wrap license agreement subsequently discovered by the user could not be enforced against the user. *ProCD, Inc.* v. *Zeidenberg* (W.D. Wis. 1996).

is objective and therefore preferable, considerations leading to their formulation may have little or no relevance to the type of software being developed or how and by whom it will be used. It behooves you therefore to independently prepare documentation standards. Enlisting the assistance of a consultant for this purpose is recommended unless you have in-house expertise. If the vendor takes on this responsibility, you should have the right of review and approval.

Examples

Documentation can be used to refer to a variety of different materials useful to the design, development, operation, maintenance, and modification of the system. Documentation can include:

Functional Specification
Software design and development begin with a detailed description of the business functions expected to be performed. Therefore, this document must be carefully prepared to ensure all of your requirements are properly supported. Completion of the functional specification will be facilitated if a comprehensive requirements definition was prepared.

System Design Specifications
The logical operation of how data will be processed by the system is identified in a system design specification. This document should describe (*a*) each process affecting data entry, manipulation, comparison, storage and retrieval;[7] (*b*) record, file, report, and screen formats; (*c*) programming language and standards; (*d*) RDBMS requirements and integration; (*e*) computer hardware and operating system environment; (*f*) system performance including response-time requirements; (*g*) interfaces to all required third-party systems and information services, and (*h*) system diagnostic procedures including error detection.

User Manual
Clear and concise directions describing how the system is to be used is a basic and fundamental prerequisite to its adoption and use in an effective and efficient manner.

---

7. Flow charts depicting each process as well as a written description should be provided by the vendor.

Operations Manual

The operations document is intended for use by system adminis-tration personnel and should describe procedures for day-to-day system operation, including start-up and shut-down, routine main-tenance, and troubleshooting.

Training Manual

Vendors generally provide training in the system's use and opera-tion upon implementation. Inevitable personnel changes, however, require an ongoing training program. Although you can rely on the vendor to perform this task, consider its associated cost and the vendor's ongoing availability to provide the service. Alternatively, requiring the vendor to provide a comprehensive training manual obviates cost and availability considerations.

Source Listings

Recall that instructions which direct the software's execution are written in a human-readable computer language and referred to as source code. Source code is generally annotated so that program-mers, other than the person creating the program, can later main-tain, enhance, or otherwise modify the program. Source listings should include a full printout of the source code instructions together with all annotations.

The composition of the procured system will, to a large extent, determine which of the previously described materials should be included as part of the vendor's deliverables. Regardless of the type of documentation provided, you should request a copy in printed format as well as computer readable media such as disk or tape.

Prepackaged Software and Hardware

User, operations, and training documentation usually exists and can be readily identified as a deliverable when prepackaged soft-ware or hardware is procured. However, a functional specification should nevertheless be developed by the vendor with the cus-tomer's assistance. The functional specification is generally com-prised of the requirements definition, the request for proposal (RFP), and the existing user manual. The functional specification helps flesh out the system's required capabilities by forcing a function-by-function review by both parties.[8] In addition, the system design specification and source listings should be delivered to the escrow agent in accordance with the escrow agreement when only the object code has been licensed.

Custom Software Development

Prepackaged software and, to a lesser extent, customized software offers the advantage of regular program updates. The economics of custom software, however, render updates costly and less certain, posing a risk as your business grows and new requirements evolve.[9] Functional specifications and, more to the point, system design specifications will give you the flexibility to decide how and by whom updates are developed. Therefore, comprehensive documentation is particularly important when custom software is procured.

Customized Software Development

Documentation requirements for customized software are similar to those for custom software. For ease of reference, however, user, operations, and training manuals should be produced for the complete software program, as customized. Also, documentation standards may be easier to define by reference to existing documentation for the prepackaged software, as long as such documentation is satisfactory.

PRICING AND PAYMENT TERMS

After weeks of negotiating, the vendor has finally acceded to the price you offered. However, the agreement requires payment of a majority of the total procurement price three weeks before the

---

8. If you agree to simply reference existing documentation, make sure to review its content, sequence, and structure to ensure that it is complete and easily understandable.
9. Custom software is developed for your particular requirements and therefore may not be suitable for other companies. Besides, competitive advantages may counsel against allowing competitors to similarly benefit. Because the vendor cannot amortize the development cost across multiple customer-sites, it has to levy a higher fee for updates to recover its development cost and a reasonable profit margin.

system is to be delivered, let alone installed and tested. You've made the required payments but delivery of the system was late and never passed the acceptance tests. Unfortunately, the vendor filed for protection under the bankruptcy laws shortly thereafter. The foregoing may be an extreme example but it serves to illustrate that price should never be viewed in a vacuum. A pure bottom-line approach also may cause you to overlook the possibility that an otherwise budget-breaking software-license fee may be payable in installments as a royalty over a specified period of time.

Pricing and payment terms will vary depending on the items being procured, their respective states of completion, your negotiating abilities and creativity. A common principle that is applicable to all agreements, however, cautions that payments be tendered only against milestones that have been achieved. Payment milestones for prepackaged software, hardware, or custom and customized software differ only in the number and type of milestones. When custom or customized software is procured, the payment schedule should be weighted more toward the end of the implementation cycle with the final payment held back until the warranty period has expired.

PRICE PROTECTION

"You have negotiated price to the bone. No other customer will ever be given a lower price." Vendors may make the foregoing claim and many times it is genuine. Still, how can you be sure? An effective provision, commonly referred to as a "most favored customer clause," is useful in ensuring that you will benefit from a lower price at which the vendor may sell and / or license the system in the future. If the vendor's protestations are indeed real, it should have no objection to the following provision.

ABC warrants that the terms of this Agreement are comparable to or better than the terms offered by ABC to any of its present commercial customers of equal or lesser size for comparable deliverables and/or services. If ABC offers more favorable terms to its commercial customers during the period commencing on the date hereof and expiring one year thereafter, such terms shall also be made available to Customer together with any resulting refund within thirty (30) days from the execution of such agreement.

The one-year term during which the provision is effective should afford you sufficient protection without having the effect of penalizing the vendor. It is a fact of life that technological capability and price seem to have an inverse relationship; therefore it is reasonable to expect that the system you acquire today may cost less in the future.

OWNERSHIP

Earlier we discussed the general practice of licensing software whereas title to computer hardware vests in the customer upon purchase. Although it is unlikely and cost prohibitive to acquire title to prepackaged software, title is a reasonable issue for negotiation in connection with customized custom software. Clearly, ownership is the best way to ensure that you exclusively benefit from the time, resources, and money invested in software procurement.

Because software is an intangible, any ownership interest must be clearly defined to include copyright as well as the software program's underlying ideas and concepts. Copyright ownership confers the exclusive right to reproduce the software program and extends only to the manner in which the program *is expressed*. Copyright does not protect ideas, procedures, concepts, or techniques. Therefore, another program can perform all of the same functions and, as long as the manner in which it is *expressed or presented* is the result of independent development, there is no copyright infringement.

The apparent gap in copyright protection limits its effectiveness. Therefore, when custom software is developed, the vendor should also be precluded from using your ideas, procedures, and concepts to develop a similar software program.

CONFIDENTIALITY

The RFP includes information describing your business operation, requirements, and the objectives expected to be accomplished by the system. All of this information is confidential. Likewise, each response to your RFP will include confidential information describing the proposed system's functionality, technical design, pricing, and contract conditions. Therefore, prior to delivery of the RFP, the parties should execute a confidentiality agreement. Selected key provisions usually found in such agreements are discussed next.

Purpose

The use of confidential information by either party should be limited to the specific purpose defined in the agreement. For example, you would not want the vendor to use confidential information relating to the operation of your business to develop application software which could then be made available to your competitors.

Oral Disclosure

Confidential information should be disclosed in written form. However, during the course of marketing presentations or other meetings, confidential information may be disclosed orally. When this occurs, the information about to be disclosed should be identified as confidential and promptly documented in writing to the recipient afterward.

Exclusions

Information is not confidential merely because one party says it is. To be recognized as confidential, appropriate steps should be taken to preserve confidentiality. Even if the test for confidentiality is satisfied at the time of disclosure, information can subsequently lose such standing if it is indiscriminately disclosed.

Independent Development

Your evaluation of available application software programs may lead you to conclude that your requirements can only be satisfied by custom software. During the design and specification stage, you will most likely incorporate methodologies used in your day-to-day business operations, some of which may also be contained in software programs previously evaluated. To avoid a claim of misappropriation, the confidentiality agreement should acknowledge your prior knowledge of such information and recognize your right to use it in the development of new software programs.

Procedures

Confidentiality agreements usually require the receiving party to use "the highest degree of care" to safeguard the confidentiality of information received from the other party. The obligation imposed by such language, as well as the extent of compliance, is difficult to measure. Since it is in each party's best commercial interest to use effective means to protect its own confidential information, requiring the other party's information to be protected in a similar manner provides both a more effective and measurable standard.

SITE PREPARATION

Computer hardware installation and operation usually require a special environment that can consist of raised flooring, power supplies, electric-current conditioners, climate control, and extensive cabling. The extent to which the site must be prepared is mostly a function of the type of hardware, with personal and mainframe computers being at opposite ends of the spectrum.

Site preparation is generally the responsibility of the customer and if not performed properly can delay installation, cause system failures, and vitiate warranty coverage. Therefore, detailed site preparation requirements should be attached as a schedule to the hardware procurement agreement. In addition, the vendor should inspect the site with a view toward obtaining its written approval prior to shipment.

DELIVERY

Delivery time-frames for the various deliverables comprising the system must be effectively coordinated so that they occur at their prescribed times. Delay in the delivery of any item will disrupt the entire implementation schedule and cause working capital to be tied up and/or finance charges to be incurred for the other items delivered on schedule.

Unfortunately, it is common for delivery schedules to slip. Therefore, you should allow for possible delays in your planning process. Although the agreement should afford the vendor reasonable grace periods, additional resources or personnel should be devoted by the vendor to minimize delays and, beyond the applicable grace period, afford you the remedy of termination and/or liquidated damages.[10]

INSTALLATION

Installation can be performed by either the vendor or the customer. However, improper installation may result in the vendor disclaiming its warranty obligation. Therefore, for the more complex systems, it is recommended that installation be performed by the vendor.

In most agreements, installation can trigger a payment obligation and/or commencement of the warranty period. However, installation alone does not necessarily mean the system is error free and can be used productively. Although it may be appropriate for the vendor to require a partial payment upon installation, in no event should the warranty commence until the system has been accepted (which is the topic of the next section).

Computer Hardware

Installation of computer hardware usually is defined in standard vendor agreements as the date upon which the hardware has successfully operated the vendor's standard installation tests and programs. The vendor's test programs should be reviewed with an eye toward completeness and applicability to your contemplated use. Alternatively, as with acceptance tests, it is to your advantage to independently develop and attach to the agreement the test plans required to demonstrate that installation has occurred.

Software

As with hardware, installation tests should be agreed upon and attached as a schedule to the agreement. Software installation tests should demonstrate that each of the data screens within the software can be displayed although data do not necessarily have to be processed at this point.

---

10. Liquidated damages is discussed under "Remedies" in this chapter; termination is discussed under "Termination."

ACCEPTANCE

Acceptance is an important milestone in the implementation process, often causing a significant portion of the system price to become payable as well as fixing the warranty period's commencement date. Therefore, each major deliverable should be subjected to well-defined and comprehensive acceptance-test procedures.

Although additional work will be required on your part, it behooves you to prepare and perform the test plans by which the various deliverables will be measured. This is because (a) you know better than anyone else how the system will be used and therefore how test plans can replicate each process; and (b) particularly with respect to software, the vendor is too close to the program to objectively and vigorously test each function.[11] Assistance from a consultant can expedite preparation of the test plans.

An effective acceptance test strategy will include parallel processing for the duration of the acceptance test and for a limited period of time thereafter. During parallel processing, data are processed using both the then current processing methodology and the new system. Results from each are then compared for possible discrepancies and their causes.

Computer Hardware

Acceptance tests for computer hardware should be designed to demonstrate reliability and, when agreed to by the vendor, performance and compatibility with application software.

Reliability
Computer hardware should be capable of operating without interruption for reasonable periods of time. Particularly with respect to on-line processing hardware, availability is critical. Therefore, one aspect of the acceptance test should identify the percentage of time the hardware is not available due to malfunction or for required maintenance.[12]

---

11. This is not meant to in any way impugn the integrity of vendors but rather to make sure that the proper operation of any process is not assumed.
12. Vendors often refer to the hardware's MTBF which is the mean time between failures. MTBF identifies, for a defined period, the total amount of time the hardware is

Performance

Vendors publish performance and response-time statistics in connection with the various hardware configurations they sell. These statistics may have little value in determining how effectively the hardware executes the application software. Moreover, when the hardware vendor is not furnishing application software, it is unlikely to include performance and response-time criteria in the acceptance test because it has no familiarity with the software. A solution to this problem is possible when prepackaged software is procured and the hardware vendor can obtain a temporary license to execute performance and response-time tests.[13]

Compatibility

When the RFP has identified compatibility requirements, hardware acceptance tests should not be deemed complete until the application software is installed and shown to properly execute on the hardware.

Documentation

Ideally all system documentation should be developed and attached to the procurement agreement prior to execution. More often than not, however, functional and system design specifications for custom and customized software are prepared later. Therefore, such documentation also should be subjected to acceptance procedures.

Software

Since software is the result of a problem-solving process, it is unlikely to be completely error free. In some cases an error condition lies dormant until activated by the execution of a specific set of processes in a particular order. Acceptance test plans should therefore contemplate the manner in which each software function will

---

operational divided by the total number of failures. Similar measurements include the mean time between outages (MTBO), mean time to repair (MTTR), and mean time to service restoral (MTSR).

13. Under a turnkey-solution agreement, however, the vendor can be expected to warrant hardware performance and response time in connection with specific application software programs.

be used to confirm that it operates properly. In addition, acceptance tests should confirm that the software accurately performs data and system backup, data verification, and recovery functions.

For the same reasons given by hardware vendors, software vendors are reticent to provide performance and response time commitments. However, when you are buying custom and customized software the vendor necessarily becomes intimately knowledgeable with respect to the hardware platform upon which the program is developed. Therefore, it is not unreasonable to require performance and response-time criteria in the software-acceptance test.

TRAINING

As with documentation, a comprehensive and structured training program is essential to the efficient and effective use of the system. Training can take the form of one or both of the programs described next. Regardless of the training program selected, the agreement should require the vendor to provide a training manual allowing you to decide how ongoing training programs should be structured.

Training the Trainers

Under this program, the vendor trains a limited number of staff who will then be responsible for providing initial and ongoing training for all employees. Training the trainers is particularly useful in cases where the population of users is large and/or turnover of staff is frequent.

User Training

The most common form of training is direct-user training where the vendor trains all customer personnel in the use and operation of the system. Vendor agreements generally express the training obligation in terms of person days. For example, *ABC shall provide five (5) person days of training in the use and operation of the System.* Terminology of this type is ambiguous and invites disputes. Rather than person days, training should be expressed in terms of hours.

Business must continue during system implementation, therefore the maximum and minimum number of hours of training per day should be specified, as well as the number of instructors and their respective competencies.

WARRANTY AND MAINTENANCE

This section covers the issues applicable to both the warranty and maintenance obligations of the vendor. Vendors frequently make statements with respect to performance, functionality, and other system features during marketing and sales presentations. Representations can be either verbal or in writing, such as brochures, cover letters, and even advertising. To the extent relied upon in making your decision, these statements can be considered express warranties. However, as will be discussed in connection with the integration clause, such statements can be superseded unless specifically included in the warranty and maintenance services clause.[14]

At least two axioms are applicable to negotiation of warranty and maintenance service provisions. First, the vendor endeavors to define the scope of its warranty as narrowly as possible.[15] Second, the customer endeavors to obtain the broadest possible coverage. Somewhere in the middle, the two must meet since neither position is reasonably possible.

Warranty and maintenance provisions often specify that the deliverable will be produced in "good workmanlike manner." In addition, the warranty may be conditioned upon "use under normal operating conditions." The problem with phrases of this type is the lack of an objective standard. Here again, the use of an RFP as well as comprehensive functional and system design documentation is invaluable.

The vendor's response to your RFP caused your consideration of the proposed system. Therefore it is appropriate that the RFP be referenced and used to define the breadth of the vendor's warranty

---

14. Integration clauses are discussed under "General Provisions."
15. Vendor agreements typically disclaim the warranty of merchantability and fitness for a particular purpose as well as any other warranty not specifically contained in the agreement. These disclaimers are generally enforced by the courts to the extent they are conspicuously noted in the agreement.

and maintenance obligations. Vendors may resist incorporating the RFP for this purpose over concern that it lacks sufficient detail regarding the system's use and operation. This legitimate concern should not preclude the RFP's use. Rather, the warranty and maintenance services clause also should reference and incorporate the functional and system design specifications (for software procurement) or performance, throughput, compatibility, and/or continuous operation requirements (for hardware procurement). Strategically, this puts the onus on the vendor to ensure that the agreement identifies functions, capabilities, and/or features required by the RFP but, which the parties have agreed, will not be included in the system as implemented. In the event of an inconsistency between the RFP and the functional or system design specifications, the RFP should prevail.

The standard against which warranty and maintenance services are measured is only one of the important issues that should be negotiated and included in the procurement agreement. Others are discussed next.

Commencement

Commencement of the warranty period should begin only upon system acceptance in order to receive the full benefit of warranty services. Similarly, the maintenance-services term should begin upon the later of expiration of the warranty period or correction of all error conditions reported during the warranty period.

Warranty Term

Warranty length is strictly a function of negotiation with 90 days being the most common. However, where custom or customized software is procured, a longer warranty period is appropriate inasmuch as certain error conditions remain dormant until a particular sequence of processes is executed. The vendor may suggest that error conditions occurring after the warranty period will be corrected under the maintenance services agreement. Although this is true, services under the maintenance agreement are provided for a fee, whereas warranty services are included in the fee paid for system procurement.

Response Time

The time within which the vendor should diagnose and correct an error condition will vary with the type of system implemented and should be specified in the warranty and maintenance services clause. For example, every minute that an on-line system is down can result in lost revenue and increased costs. At the other end of the spectrum, a personal computer that is one of several within a network will most likely not impede normal business operations while under repair.

When warranty or maintenance service is contracted for in connection with software that has been licensed with its source code, you should have the right to employ a third party or your own qualified employees to correct error conditions that continue beyond specified response time parameters.[16] Furthermore, the vendor should reimburse you for your associated repair costs. Vendors may resist such a provision expressing concern that the error condition may not be properly corrected and/or possibly exacerbated. In cases where the vendor agrees to such a request, expect it to try to condition its consent upon the right to charge you for any additional work, material, or expenses it incurs as a result of services improperly performed by such a third party or your employees. This is a reasonable position for the vendor to take. However, if the vendor repeatedly fails to perform within the response-time parameters, it should be deemed to have assumed the risk and costs associated with work that is improperly performed.

Location

The location where warranty or maintenance services are performed will directly affect how quickly you can once again use the system. Generally, for more complex systems, work is performed at the customer site. However, when standard service requires work to be performed at the vendor's premises, on-site service usually can be contracted for at an additional fee—which may be a wise

---

16. When the vendor has failed to correct error conditions in software licensed in object-code format, you should have the right to demand access to the source code deposited in accordance with the escrow agreement.

use of money when you consider that your business data leave with the system when it is shipped to the vendor.

Certain software programs, such as on-line software applications, lend themselves to warranty and maintenance services through telecommunication services. Therefore, the vendor can logon to the software program remotely, diagnose the error condition, and directly transmit and install the necessary corrections. Although convenient, you should take care to make sure that you know about and consent to the vendor's access.

Updates

During the warranty and maintenance-services term, the vendor will likely develop updates to the software programs. Updates can take the form of (*a*) technical enhancements that correct program errors or improve how the software processes data; or (*b*) functional enhancements that add new capabilities or functions. At a minimum, technical enhancements should be licensed or otherwise made available to you during the warranty and maintenance periods at no additional charge. Functional enhancements on the other hand are generally made available for an additional license fee.

Year 2000

As the new millennium approaches, many computer users will find that their software programs were not designed and developed to accommodate the year 2000 as a valid date. Many software programs currently use two digits instead of four to represent the year, making the assumption that the year is in the 1900s. Therefore, commencing with the year 2000, many of the financial calculations or any other function that is based on a date may result in erroneous information. To avoid the problems associated with date calculations, the vendor should guarantee that the system can process date information that includes the year 2000 and beyond.

Virus Protection

Certain irresponsible people have created computer viruses that can cause your system to malfunction. A virus is a software program that can disable or destroy other software programs as well as data. Viruses can be transmitted to your system during the process of copying files from an external source such as diskettes, the Internet, or other service provider of data and/or programs. Unfortunately, unless you have installed a virus checking program, you may be completely unaware that your system has been infected until the damage is already done. Many viruses remain dormant until activated by some particular function, others are triggered by date or time. The infamous Michaelangelo virus, for example, is activated on his birthday. To guard against the possibility of an infection, insist that the vendor check and warrant that the system shall be free of all viruses prior to installation.

INTELLECTUAL PROPERTY RIGHTS INDEMNITY

The competitive nature of the computer industry compels vendors to vigorously investigate and prosecute any instances where their intellectual property rights (IPRs) may have been infringed.[17] Although infringement actions are mainly commenced against vendors, customers usually are named as codefendants. Therefore, the agreement should contain an indemnity clause addressing the following issues.

Defense

Retaining legal representation to defend against an infringement action is expensive and the facts required for a proper defense are in the vendor's possession. Therefore, the vendor should undertake defense efforts immediately after a claim has been asserted or an action commenced.

Indemnity

If the claim is successful or a settlement is reached, reasonable royalties for use of the system may become payable to the plaintiff. In addition, in the event the system is replaced, you will incur conversion, training, and other implementation costs. The vendor should take full responsibility for payment and/or reimbursement of all such amounts.

---

17. IPRs can and usually are in the form of a trade secret, copyright, patent, or trademark.

Continued Use

Infringement claims usually include a request for injunctive relief which, if granted by the court, would deny your continued use of the system until a decision is rendered on the merits of the case. Such a ruling could have a devastating effect on your business. Therefore, the vendor, at its own cost, should be required to secure an interim license from the plaintiff allowing your continued use. Since you are the innocent user of the system, the plaintiff will most likely agree to such a request. Besides, depending on the outcome of the action, you may be the plaintiff's future customer.

Replacement

When continued use of the system, either while the action is pending or after its resolution, cannot be arranged, the infringing elements should be replaced, at the vendor's cost, with noninfringing substitutes providing the same capabilities. However, the majority of IPR indemnity clauses drafted by vendors provide that when continued use or replacement cannot be provided at reasonable cost, the vendor has the right to terminate the agreement and refund the fees paid on a predefined depreciated basis. For example, if the system is deemed to have a five-year useful life and an action is commenced two years after acceptance which ultimately causes the vendor to terminate the agreement, the vendor would only be obligated to refund three-fifths of the fees paid for the system. The economic justification usually given for such a clause is that the customer had use of the system for two years and should therefore pay for such use. However, this fails to take into account the opportunity cost associated with the implementation of a new system and should be avoided.

Assistance

In the course of defending the infringement action, the vendor may seek your assistance in certain aspects of the case. While it behooves you to do so, the vendor should compensate you for time lost in managing your business.

Counsel

If the vendor fails to retain counsel or engages an attorney who is not reasonably qualified to represent your interest, you should have the right to select and appoint alternative counsel. The vendor should pay all reasonable costs and expenses for legal counsel.

REMEDIES

As with warranties, vendors attempt to narrow the remedies available to a customer in the event of a failed system-procurement. And, as with warranties, the customer's interest is just the opposite. A dose of practical commercial reality is particularly necessary when negotiating the remedy clause. Let's say the vendor agrees to assume unlimited liability if it fails to perform. Chances are, unless the vendor has very deep pockets, you have negotiated an empty remedy clause. In addition, the long-term business viability of any vendor that would agree to such a clause should raise a red flag. Procurement failures occur and such a clause could easily bankrupt a vendor the first time it is invoked. Each party should recognize the inherent risk associated with any commercial transaction and fairly balance these risks through a remedy clause designed to provide compensation for foreseeable losses.

Standard procurement agreements generally contain a remedy clause limiting the vendor's responsibility for system failures to either repair or replacement of the defective element. In addition, the vendor's overall liability for all causes is limited to a fixed dollar amount, usually equal to the purchase price or license fee. Liability for incidental and consequential damages is specifically excluded.[18] Remedy provisions of this type do not adequately protect the customer. Although the vendor's standard remedy clause

---

18. Damages the could be awarded against a vendor resulting from a failed system implementation include (*a*) direct damages that represent the additional sum of money the customer would have to pay to procure an alternative system of equivalent capability and functionality; (*b*) incidental damages that represent expenses incurred by the customer for evaluation, inspection, transportation, care, and custody of the system; and (*c*) consequential damages that represent losses suffered by the customer which, at the time the agreement was executed, the vendor had reason to know or reasonably foresee.

can be used as the starting point for discussion purposes, the final clause negotiated should be qualified by the following caveats.

Termination

Limiting remedies to repair and replacement of defective system elements does not address the possibility that it may not be possible to repair or replace the defect either within a reasonable time or at all. Therefore, you should have the right to terminate the agreement and seek damages if the defect continues beyond a defined period of time.

Confidentiality

Limiting remedies to repair and replacement also fails to afford a viable remedy when information is disclosed in contravention of the agreement's confidentiality and nondisclosure obligations. In such a case, the only effective remedy is a court order enjoining further disclosures.

IPR Indemnity

Liability and defense costs for intellectual property rights (IPR) infringement can be substantial, easily using up the entire amount specified as the limit of the vendor's liability. Therefore, amounts payable by the vendor in discharging its obligations under the IPR indemnity clause should not be included in the calculation of, or subject to, liability limits expressed in the agreement.

Injury

Liability limits should only apply to the vendor's failure to perform under the agreement. Recovery for damages and/or injuries to individuals, real or personal property resulting from the commission of willful and/or negligent acts should likewise not be included in the calculation of, or subject to, liability limits expressed in the agreement.

Liquidated Damages

When damages are difficult to calculate, the parties can agree to a reasonable amount that they believe is a fair approximation of the financial injury to be suffered by a party upon the other party's failure to perform under the agreement.[19] Particularly since negotiated procurement agreements generally excuse the vendor from consequential and incidental damages, a liquidated-damages clause can be very effective in recovering lost profits or time and money expended when an alternative system must be procured. Liability limits should therefore be defined with the possibility of liquidated damages in mind.

Vendors are generally reluctant to accept liquidated-damage provisions. However, if profits will be negatively affected by a tardy or failed system implementation, profits will likely be enhanced by an early implementation. Allocating a portion of such profit for payment under a bonus clause rewarding the vendor for early implementation may make the liquidated-damages clause palatable to the vendor. When negotiations lead to inclusion of a bonus clause in favor of the vendor, the bonus should only be paid after the applicable warranty period has expired to ensure that the system is free of defects and fully functional.

CHANGE IN SCOPE

As customized or custom software is developed, it is not unusual for the functional and/or system design specifications to be revised periodically. Revisions may be the result of more efficient processing methodologies, a change in business requirements, or changes in the hardware or its operating systems. The agreement should therefore contemplate the possibility of revisions and provide a mechanism by which they can be incorporated.

TERMINATION

Termination of a system-procurement agreement is an extreme remedy which should only be invoked when it is clear that a party to the agreement will be unable to satisfy its material obligations after a reasonable cure period has been afforded. Termination however, should not necessarily end your right to use the system. Moreover, the agreement should specifically address each of the following considerations.

---

19. If the amount specified appears distorted to the high side, a court may rule that the amount is intended as a penalty and therefore unenforceable.

Wind-Down Period

The time and cost associated with conversion to a new system has been referred to earlier. The entire system-selection process must be repeated and your data will have to be converted to a new format compatible with the new system. During the transition period, operation of your business must continue uninterrupted. Therefore, the agreement should allow for a wind-down period during which time a vendor can be selected and conversion to the new system proceed in an orderly fashion.

Cause of Default

System-procurement agreements impose a variety of material obligations on the vendor, the failure of any one of which can have damaging consequences to your business. Conversely, there is really only one material obligation on your part, payment of fees. Because your business depends on the system's continued availability, a balancing of the equities favors termination by the vendor only in the event that you have failed to pay the fees due within the prescribed time frame and applicable cure period.

Vendor Default

Termination of the agreement when the vendor has defaulted may not always be a viable remedy if termination results in no longer having access to the system. Obviously if termination occurs due to system defects and/or failures, this will not be an issue. However, where the system is operational but the vendor has failed to perform other material obligations (for example, confidentiality or dedicated project-personnel), your continued use of the system should be permitted notwithstanding termination.

Ownership

Termination of customized or custom software-procurement agreements when the vendor has defaulted should not affect ownership rights to the software, documentation, or the related intellectual property. Ownership should vest in the customer immediately upon creation regardless of whether the agreement is successfully concluded.

GENERAL PROVISIONS

Procurement agreements generally have a catch-all section comprised of a number of independent clauses describing administrative aspects of the agreement. Nine of these clauses are reviewed in the pages that follow.

Amendments

It is common for agreements to be amended from time to time to reflect changed business terms and conditions. However, each change should be reflected in a written amendment signed by all parties. Otherwise, conduct contrary to express written provisions of the agreement could be interpreted by a court as an amendment to the agreement. Unfortunately, the court's interpretation of the parties' conduct may not necessarily reflect their actual intentions.

Assignment

Standard vendor-agreements usually prevent the customer from assigning the agreement to a third party. Although the vendor has a legitimate interest in prohibiting assignment in certain cases (for example, the creditworthiness of the proposed assignee), a blanket restriction is not appropriate and, in fact, the vendor's right to assign should likewise be circumscribed.

From the customer's point of view, assignment should be allowed where a subsidiary, parent, or other affiliated company now in existence or to be formed at some later date may be a user of the system. In addition, where the system is procured in a lease transaction, the leasing company must have the right to assign the warranty, indemnity, purchase option, and other rights under the system-procurement agreement (between the vendor and the leasing company).

Assignment by the vendor should likewise be addressed. In particular, with custom or customized software, the customer relies on the vendor's unique skill, knowledge, and experience to develop and maintain the software. Assignment by the vendor should therefore be prohibited in order for the customer to realize the benefits of such reliance.

Escrow

Although a separate source-code escrow agreement is usually executed, the software-procurement agreement should likewise make
reference to the vendor's deposit obligations to preserve your rights
to seek damages and/or terminate the procurement agreement in
the event the vendor fails to comply with the escrow agreement.

Project Personnel

During the course of system evaluation, preparation of functional
and system design specifications, and through your investment of
time with the vendor, vendor personnel learn your business, its
operation, and requirements. This valuable asset can facilitate the
system's efficient implementation. To make the most use of this
asset, the vendor should agree that it will not reassign its key personnel until their scheduled tasks have been completed.

Notice

Standard vendor-agreements generally allow written notice to be
given by regular mail or facsimile transmission with notice deemed
given within a few days after notice has been sent. Such a clause
can expose you to the possibility of being deemed to have received
notice without actual receipt. Therefore, the agreement should
require that all notices be sent in a form that requires a receipt
acknowledgment (for example, certified mail, overnight express
mail, or delivery by courier) and that notice is deemed given only
upon actual receipt.

Injunctive Relief

When an agreement is breached, the nondefaulting party's damages usually can be calculated and satisfied by the payment of
money. In system-procurement agreements however, a breach of
the confidentiality and nondisclosure provisions may not be com-
pensable through money damages alone. The nondefaulting party
may have to seek a court order preventing further violations. Standard vendor-agreements usually allow only the vendor to seek
injunctive relief and further attempt to secure the customer's prior
consent to its imposition. Clearly, the customer has an interest in

preserving its confidential information as well. Therefore, both parties should be entitled to seek injunctive relief. However, its availability should not be predetermined. The party requesting injunctive relief should first have to prove monetary damages alone are not a sufficient remedy.

Nonwaiver

In an ideal world, all system-procurement agreements would be successfully completed without any problems. Problems and issues do arise however and many are resolved between the parties while implementation continues. In situations where a resolution is not reached, the mere fact that the parties continued with the implementation effort and did not immediately resort to their contractual remedies should not be used by one party to claim a waiver by the other. Such a result would discourage negotiation. Therefore, agreements generally contain a nonwaiver clause that preserves a party's remedies even though those remedies were previously available but not invoked.

Force Majeure

A commercial risk which all parties to an agreement must take is that some event over which a party has no control can disrupt, delay, or prevent successful system implementation. When such an event occurs and continues, the agreement should not penalize the affected party but instead should allow a suspension of that portion of the work that cannot continue until the problem is abated.

A party claiming force majeure should nevertheless give the other parties notice of the effect anticipated by such delay and the steps being taken to alleviate the consequent problems. Ultimately, there must be a way for the parties to terminate the agreement if the event of force majeure continues beyond a prescribed period of time.

Integration Clause

Standard vendor-agreements generally contain a clause stating that the entire agreement of the parties, including all of the vendor's representations and warranties, are contained in the agreement as executed. The intention is to prevent reliance on any statements made or material provided by the vendor during marketing efforts. Although such a clause is appropriate and serves a useful purpose, take care that all material you relied on in selecting the system is attached or clearly referred to in the executed agreement or its schedules.

In conclusion, negotiation of a system-procurement agreement, like any other agreement, should take into account each party's reasonable business objectives and constraints. A negotiating posture that seeks to exact the maximum number of concessions from the other party certainly does not foster a spirit of mutual cooperation.

In this chapter, factors you should consider in negotiating the system procurement were reviewed together with an insight into the vendor's motivation, where applicable. Understanding these competing interests will help you negotiate a fair and balanced agreement for all parties.

INVESTMENT TECHNOLOGY APPLICATIONS

7

⑥ ELECTRONIC MARKET MECHANISMS

James T. Leman
Vice President
Salomon Brothers, Inc

Over the last 25 years, the securities industry and especially the institutional customer business has witnessed and provoked substantial changes. Technology's ability to meet the appetite for well-organized, timely, and effectively delivered information and services has enabled the institutional components of the securities markets to meet the challenges presented.

Technology has had a large role in those solutions, and dependence on technology-assisted solutions is evident in every facet of the business. Some significant products and services provided by vendors, exchanges, and brokers/customer groups have become reality. The future shape of these markets will of necessity be touched by these bodies and, of course, the regulators; but technology and its accelerating advances promise to make the next 25 years even more dynamic and revolutionary than the last 25 years.

The essential elements of electronic market mechanisms obviously began with manual processes that eventually gave way to faster and more effective ways to communicate. Additionally, the appetite for more efficient ways to manage the process was an objective of institutional customers as the marketplace catered more to the needs of this growing asset pool.

This chapter focuses on those technologies that helped shape the electronic market we enjoy currently. It addresses the development of five major categories: research, liquidity indicators, electronic order delivery, integration of trade management, and post-trade processes. Also, the assessment of market impact on the transactions affected caused transaction cost analysis to be an important component to be reviewed.

RESEARCH

Obviously, we need to discuss the component elements that make up research as a product delivered by institutional brokers for consumption by the money management community. The obvious initial method of delivery is verbal and that continues today as in the past. For speed and communication clarity you can't beat the phone. However, today's world is more complex. Full-text research indexed by ticker, industry groups, and related participation in various markets is still largely created for presentation on paper at various time intervals with certain attendant time delays due to creation, printing text, graphics and quantitative statistics, compliance review, delivery, and prioritization by the reader. Morning meeting notes, which are usually summaries of fast-breaking information, are more succinct text documents and are issued along with earnings estimates.

One of the first electronic tools provided to assist the institutional buyer in sorting through research materials was the First Call system created by Thomson Financial in the 1980s. This software application, linked to a database, gave institutional customers access to a variety of brokers' research indexed in a way that eased the burden of identifying needed information in an organized way. First Call became more and more dominant as customers began to expect their brokers to supply research to it. It included morning meeting notes and has matured over the years to be deployed to international customers and offers information on a wide variety of domestic and international markets. Bloomberg, a large market information vendor, and Bridge also offer brokers the ability to deliver research information to their terminal users. With these events, the selection options open to customers for viewing multiple brokers' research arose and the element of how customers paid for research became more complicated.

Over the last several years electronic improvements in the delivery of research have become substantial. Thomson Financial, the owner of First Call, created a new service called Research Direct.

This service utilized Adobe and Acrobat software modules. These permit full-image presentation of research on a PC screen. These images, in complete color, represent the same document that was traditionally printed with graphics charts and tabular data. In addition, this product allows notations to be included by a sender and further highlighting by the receiving party. Another key element is the indexing of every word in the document. This allows the user to create random word searches to retrieve documents addressing particular topics. This system and that of another vendor, Multex, using similar Adobe and Acrobat technology, hold the promise of eliminating the need to retain hard or paper copies of all research and greatly accelerate the assembling of relevant information. These services are increasing their user bases both by deploying hardware and software solutions that incorporate local area networking to empower all designated personnel at a particular institution, and by gathering more contributing brokers. Brokers are being prodded by potential savings in printing costs and the opportunity to get reports on who is reading the various research publications, since both Thomson and Multex promote a feedback mechanism to brokers. The next steps in broadly distributing the research are occurring, for example, with Multex research, which is available across Bloomberg terminals. Research Direct can be expected to follow suit through other dominant market data vendors or through the newest emerging medium—the Internet.

Almost any entity managing data and information on a customer's desk can be a display device for research. This will broaden brokers' avenues of distribution and enable customers to have a wider array of discrete solutions that will best complement their own needs.

LIQUIDITY INDICATORS

As with research, the initial method of delivering information about liquidity information was verbal. Messages were carried back from the New York Stock Exchange's (NYSE) specialist post by brokers to be relayed to traders, then to salespersons, and on to institutional customers. As institutional traders evidenced their dominance due to the size of their trades and their sensitivity to efficient executions, they provoked upstairs brokers to attempt to match one large customer's need to transact with the needs of other large institutional traders who sought offsetting liquidity. Initially this was accomplished by a trader working a large order to buy for Customer A by getting his institutional sales force on the phones to learn of sell interest from those who had previously traded the stock in question with his firm, but also through the dialogues his salespeople had with customers. This process was in-tense since timely action was essential, given that market information would leak out and the security could begin to reflect price changes.

Out of this necessity for more information, Autex was created. Autex, the original product, was a system allowing brokers to type their interest to buy or sell securities into a terminal. That entry would then appear on Autex terminals located on the desks of institutional buy-side customers. This advance enabled customers to view multiple-broker indications, organized by security, in one place, thereby giving a consolidated view of liquidity opportunities. Three types of messages became standard: a super message—individual messages initiated by traders based on active orders in hand; advertisements—reports of consummated trades placed on the tape evidencing real activity with the intimation of more to do; and interest messages—those messages which are traders' shopping lists that advertise their potential interest. Those listings of interest by each trader are retransmitted several times a day with the intent of demonstrating active interest, and in order to appear regularly in the windows displaying this activity in the Autex terminal display.

Providing rapid, diverse distribution of liquidity information, Autex complemented telephone calls and became a key electronic tool for institutional investors to efficiently assess liquidity. Bridge Information System also offers a liquidity advertising service as part of its market-data-delivery platform and analytic service. Both Autex and Bridge are prominent fixtures on brokers' desks where indications, advertisements, and interest lists are input by operators and some traders. Either or both devices occupy essentially all institutional buy-side trading desks unless an organization is predominantly quantitatively driven or follows a pure index-tracking strategy. Both Autex and Bridge continue to modify their products to present information more effectively or in a more integrated way. Once liquidity is identified, however, the traditional phone call to a broker ensues and a trade occurs if the merchandise is still available.

One other limitation of these systems is that they are only as good as the information they contain. Over time many institutional customers complained to Autex and Bridge about brokers making up activity to conduct fishing expeditions (looking for a trade on the institutional side of the business). There are no definitive statistics on what proportion of messages generate actual trades but the message activity is heavy and the terminal population on both the institutional and brokerage sides continues to grow. As of December 1995, the brokerage terminal total was more than several thousand.

The most recent development in the indication-of-interest arena is the creation of the Financial Information Exchange (FIX) protocol by a group of institutional firms and brokers. This protocol enables brokers to send indication messages in a defined format to customers whose internal or vendor-provided systems can read these messages and deliver them in an integrated way into their internal order system. Customers are more actively seeking to integrate their order data with indications so that they only deal with matches that interest them.

The protocol will allow customers to customize how they use the data, far beyond methods currently in use, by employing logic that takes the data, compares it to orders in progress, and then provides a conversation with the sending broker. Uninteresting and fishing-expedition messages will not receive attention. This advance will greatly accelerate the discovery of liquidity and should change broker habits.

ELECTRONIC ORDER DELIVERY

Because institutional orders were by their nature large, they demanded high levels of service. While that business was growing, the New York Stock Exchange (NYSE) was experiencing increasing levels of volume and persistent congestion in the booths that ringed the NYSE floor. To address these levels of volume, large wirehouses—whose names arose from the use of the telephone and telegraph to relay orders from branches to a centralized order room, and from there to booths on the floor of the exchange—used teletype machines to receive and report on orders being executed

The exchange saw value in the concept but took it to another level and created the designated order turnaround (DOT) system in the 1970s. The DOT system was originally conceived to handle small orders, those below 500 shares. The orders would be sent in a standard format called common message switch (CMS). The exchange would accept the message, route it to the specialist post where the stock was traded, and print out a turnaround document to be completed by the specialist. The cards used to record these orders and served as turnaround documents placed in a mark-sensitive card reader; the execution details were routed back through the CMS computer on to the network of the broker. This process saved time, took the load off the booths where institutional order flow was growing, reduced errors, assisted greatly in handling higher levels of volume, and increased customer service. Functionality was added to the DOT system to handle higher levels of volume. Share levels were increased in the early 1980s to accommodate the AT&T breakup. The system was enhanced to handle up to 10,099 shares per order, and new classes of orders were included such as market-on-close (MOC) and market-on-open (OPG) orders. These levels were eventually increased to 30,099 shares for market orders and 99,999 for limit orders.

DOT was an extremely significant electronic step forward because it liberated the brokers from treating each order exactly the same. Efficiencies were gained as well when institutional customers began to embrace the concept of index tracking. The S&P 500 index required up to 500 orders to be entered concurrently and executed within a relatively short time. This occurred since brokers who were completing orders from customers usually utilized S&P 500 futures contracts to equitize customer cash balances and would then eliminate the futures and replace them with the underlying equity securities. Speed was essential to minimize the disparity between the cash market and the futures contract trading levels. DOT throughput speed was increased along the way and the devices provided by the exchange to deploy and manage orders were enhanced substantially. Brokers and customers increasingly used DOT's fast order-delivery capability to facilitate program trading to take advantage of disparities between the cash and derivative markets which included listed options, index options, futures, and options on futures.

By the end of 1995 DOT trades accounted for close to 80 percent of the exchange's order flow and approximately 45 percent of its share volume. Regional exchanges also created electronic order delivery facilities; while each employs a CMS formatted protocol, they each are distinct in how orders are managed and executed by regional specialists. Because of DOT's attractive features, it began to be demanded by institutions as a direct entry tool on their desks by late 1989. Initially, large wirehouse brokers with institutional customer bases provided DOT access to their customers. Soon, in a matter of several years, at least six large brokers were providing their own DOT access devices to their institutional customers. DOT systems in the hands of customers addressed several issues. Brokers wanted to expand their market share without significant staff increases; brokers were under pressure to transact trades more cost effectively, and DOT provided that opportunity. It was fast, relatively error free, and required minimal upstairs support and no floor personnel aside from occasional exception trades.

Customers wanted more control of the order process and wanted cheaper commissions, especially on index types of managed funds, where advisory fees were lean. Customers were becoming more experienced as traders, and were gaining a feel for the markets. Unfortunately, many customers wished to deal with several, and usually at least a dozen, brokers. To do this they needed several brokers' DOT switches and each had a different series of sometimes cumbersome commands needed to load orders, send orders, extract executions, and manage other details. A need was present for a more comprehensive way to address this process. It wasn't until 1992 that an opportunity to address this next level of electronic order handling came about in the form of the FIX protocol. Through the late 1980s, the quest for alternative sources of liquidity in listed and OTC securities were being sought by the institutional community. These efforts were propelled by the desire for less market-impact on orders being worked by brokers, and for lower commissions. The large money managers were insistent on better pricing, and two distinct products emerged: the Posit crossing system and the Instinet system.

Posit was created by and is still owned by the Jefferies Group. It was a daily cross effected to permit buy-side customers to cross stock with other institutions anonymously. Through this mechanism, customers could insert buy lists, sell lists, or be linked into the system; when the time was set for the cross, the software operated by Posit initiated the calculations needed to execute as many shares as possible at a mutually agreeable price. Posit became very effective for electronically oriented, low-commission-cost and low-impact-cost-sensitive customers. Only a modest fraction of the shares submitted to a cross are effectively crossed each day; however, it is still actively worked by institutions seeking liquidity opportunities with no broker involvement. In reaction to market interest and to potential competition from other crossing systems created in 1994 and 1995, Posit moved to four distinct crosses at 10:30 AM, 11:30 AM, 1:30 PM, and traditional 3:00 PM.

In addition, Posit decided to permit brokers to participate in its intraday crosses to access another liquidity pool. This action was started in late 1994 and initially was resisted by institutional customers. After the inclusion of an initial pilot group of brokers demonstrated that no severe problems resulted, more brokers were added; today more than 100 brokers regularly participate in the crosses. However, customers can still elect to have their cross opportunities hidden from brokers and many still do. Posit system administrators continue to improve their product in terms of efficiency. They have upgraded software to enable cancellation of selected issues previously submitted for potential crossing up until shortly before the cross is completed.

This helps since previously the customer's only option was to amend a list over the phone, which was time consuming, error prone, and manually intensive for the Posit staff. Additionally Posit staff have adopted the FIX-protocol message format for the delivery of orders. This will further assist institutional money managers in controlling their orders on their own order-management software, and in routing orders and receiving execution reports seamlessly. Posit also has aspirations to expand its service to international markets where liquidity concerns will exist as money flows into these markets, and where spreads are considered too wide or commissions are considered too expensive.

Instinet is the other system created to enable institutions to anonymously access liquidity during the course of the trading day. Instinet was created to permit institutions to trade stock with one another anonymously, but with a negotiation mechanism via the Instinet display. That display permitted two partners to offer alternate bids or offers to one another with certain rules set as to when others could then trade in the same security. This system has grown significantly over the last nine years and has had its most significant impact on securities traded in the OTC/NASDAQ marketplace. Over-the-counter (OTC) securities are not listed on an exchange, but instead trade on the system administered by the National Association of Securities Dealers (NASD) and their automated quotation (NASDAQ) service. This market is a dealer market where many or few companies can become registered market makers in OTC issues. The number of market makers are generally indicative of the trading activity, customer interest (both retail and institutional), and the volatility of the issue involved. Instinet has captured a significant share of the NASD's trading volume, since institutional customers with large orders prize liquidity as well as anonymity and want to trade at prices better than advertised spreads. In recognition of this source of liquidity, the same brokers that serve as market makers on the NASD market utilize Instinet to access liquidity in anonymity. For this privilege they pay a commission to Instinet. Instinet, now owned by Reuters, also conducts an after-hours crossing session based on the New York Stock Exchange's closing price. That service began in 1988–1989 and its popularity grew as the liquidity it offered grew larger. Again, in the beginning it was accessible only to institutions and then later included brokers to foster greater liquidity. Again a fee was charged to process the trades and all those entries sent in where no match occurred were discarded with no disclosure to anyone.

INTEGRATION OF TRADE MANAGEMENT

As institutions experienced growth in their asset bases, they encountered day-to-day problems with managing the elements of data they needed to carry out their duties effectively. While certain tools were created to assist portfolio managers in selecting securities and tracking them in the portfolio, the process of handling transactions effectively and efficiently needed a lot of support. This, compounded by the availability of market data and information about liquidity, drove many buy-side institutions to seek more all-encompassing solutions utilizing technology.

Whether home grown or acquired from vendors, institutions sought technology to give them paperless order-management systems that would allow better control over order origination and tracking through execution. These systems usually enabled their portfolio managers to send orders to a buy-side trading desk for execution. The systems also contained basic compliance features such as limits on amounts of any one security to be purchased, selling only what was already owned, blocks to prevent inadvertent acquisition of off-limit or "sin" stocks for customers, and cash management tools.

These systems also attached to the portfolio management system already in use, as well as the back-end accounting and settlement process. Institutions integrated the ability to select a security and initiate an increase in holdings by selecting a percent-of-ownership target, and the system would advise how much needed to be acquired by each account to meet the threshold established. Many of these systems also simplified the process of allocation to specific subaccounts at the end of the day between the institution and their brokers. Later, the paperless order management systems began to create interfaces to systems such as Thomson's OASYS to further streamline the delivery of the allocation to the brokers electronically. In the early 1990s, the order-management-systems users sought greater integration by beginning to incorporate DOT execution capability directly from their system to selected brokers who offered interfaces, or to those who were working with certain vendors.

This was the initiation of the multiple-broker-access concept. Since many of the large institutions that needed paperless blotters to maintain better control also needed better small-order management and execution, it was a logical next step. Why have three different broker devices when a single device integrated with your system would be more effective? Brokers, of course, resisted this in many instances.

Brokers were understandably concerned because extending their terminal networks onto customer desks could create substantial technical challenges and would require effort to open those systems to modification. They also perceived that their position on the institutional customer's desk would be compromised if any changes took place to blend their functions with those of other brokers.

As the concept of multiple broker access grew, the creation of the Financial Information Exchange (FIX) committee set the stages for the next level of developmental change. The FIX protocol was created by a group of buy-side and sell-side firms to standardize the exchange of key elements of information between institutions and brokers. FIX was designed to be concerned with reliable exchange of data that previously was presented on individual broker or vendor screen displays, but was not previously presented so it could be integrated into an order management system or blotter. As a result of FIX's development beginning in 1992 and its practical production introduction in January 1995, a number of vendors marketing their own order-management solutions and a variety of their customers have committed to implement FIX as a standard. This event permits institutions either through their own staffs or through vendors to merge and present data previously spread across several terminals or systems.

That previous lack of integration held back efficiency and limited the degree to which applications could be enhanced to meet customer needs. Now a customer will be able to originate and control orders in a paperless fashion while also absorbing indications of interest directly into the order management system. The customer will be able to react to these indications selectively based on software logic and to send electronic orders in response to the indicating broker. The customer will also receive execution details back electronically, thereby eliminating rekeying of data. The customer will be able to send DOT orders to participating brokers from the same blotter and receive the execution details on these orders electronically. The customer will be able to record all of these messages along with their time stamps in a local database and will later be able to create management reports on the performance of its own traders and brokers. It will also make it easier to control the variety of processes such as step-out trades, prime-broker trades, and plan-sponsor-directed activities that customers need to track in the complex world of money management. Additionally, since Posit and Instinet have committed to follow the FIX formats, customers can integrate order delivery to these systems into their order management systems.

This integration is unprecedented and a strong evolutionary step toward the ultimate trading desk of the future. Being able to interact with portfolio managers, to receive indications of interest selectively and efficiently, to respond with electronic orders, to execute DOT orders, and to send orders to Instinet and Posit will reduce lost time from a buy-side trader's day. Coupling these advances with live pricing feeds and news services that offer shredding capabilities will present the most integrated solution package to the institutional customers.

These systems will develop to this state over the next few years and then will expand in international equity and fixed-income markets. For this to occur, the FIX protocol and other standards must evolve. This evolution will occur since buy-side institutions will continue to gather larger and larger bases of assets and will demand greater integration of data in order to streamline the investment process. Similarly all existing vendors, whether they are primarily market-data deliverers, research deliverers, or order management providers, will continue to evolve to offer institutional customers more integrated solutions to their needs. Customers will need to assess the adequacy and flexibility of their existing systems and how important these changes are to how they conduct their business. In some instances, minor notifications or attachment of an external vendor solution may be sufficient. In other situations, major changes may be required with a customized overhaul through the support of external consultants. Either way change will be needed to take advantage of the new opportunities and to maintain a competitive edge with an institutional customer or a broker's competition.

POST-TRADE PROCESSES

After the completion of a trade, an absolutely critical, yet all too often overlooked, set of steps must be carried out to ensure an error-free and timely completion of trade processing. This series of steps in the past was carried out exclusively over the telephone and later through an exchange of fax transmissions. Today, with shortened settlement cycles in place and monumental levels of trades occurring, customers and brokers have sought more expeditious ways to accurately and efficiently exchange data at the end of a busy trading day.

Traditionally in the institutional marketplace, an order given to a broker by an institutional money manager represents several orders in the same security for pools of money the portfolio manager is responsible for trading. At the completion of the trade, the broker provides the money manager or its trader with the detailed executions on the trade and the average price at which the entire trade was accomplished. The money manager uses the average price to uniformly provide each pool of funds involved in the order with an equitable execution. This also simplifies the settlement process in that only one settlement per security per account is required.

Verbal communication of this level of detail is cumbersome especially when it is concentrated at day's end. In addition, after receiving this information, the customer must determine on their own records how many shares each of their pools of money or sub-accounts should receive from each trade. After determining this, they must communicate back to their brokers in a timely fashion. The exact share quantity may not be determinable at the order's initiation since the customer may want to execute up to only a certain price or time and the market may move beyond that point before the completion of the order.

After receiving the allocation of the order with subaccounts identified, the broker must book the trades after identifying how that customer's accounts are named or numbered on the broker's records. Institutions vary widely in how many subaccounts are involved in any single order; as few as one and as many as 20 are common, with instances of 100 or 200 handled on a routine basis by brokers.

As trading volume began to grow in the mid- to late-1980s, services emerged that sought to assist this process through electronic mechanisms. In hindsight, these services were essential to the institutional business in tackling more volume with essentially no significant growth in support personnel. They also became essential as the transition to a T + 3 settlement date from a T + 5 settlement date occurred in June of 1995.

The first service created was Alert (Thomson Financial), which focused on streamlining the development of a database for institutional-customer-account details such as delivery instructions for different instruments, customer confirmation addresses, customer statement addressing, and other key data such as institutional delivery (ID) coding for the Depository Trust Company. Prior to Alert, brokers were notified of account details by mail, over the phone, and later via faxes. In many instances, trades being done on a given trading day would be allocated to, at least in part, accounts being opened on that day. This placed a greater burden on the broker to ensure that these new accounts with trades pending against them were promptly created and authorized by the salesperson and a registered principal. After Alert became more accepted as a standard way to deliver initial account setup information and subsequent updates to brokers, the stage was set for the next level of electronic system streamlining. Imagine 500 trades failing to settle because an agent bank clearing number was transcribed incorrectly. It happened quite a bit and created substantial extra work. Alert helped to address this. Incidentally, in late 1995, an estimated 80 percent of all U.S. money managers used the Alert system to deliver instructions to brokers. Virtually all brokers serving the institutional customer base had at least one terminal over which it received instructions on account details. Many brokers also moved to a computer interface to ease the transfer of data to its internal account databases.

A number of large money managers chose not to use Alert primarily because they had only a handful of accounts to oversee; while those accounts were very large, the number of accounts did not warrant the use of Alert.

In 1989 a group formed to address the problem of exchanging information at day's end on large block trades where a large number of subaccounts needed to be communicated to a broker. This information was either called over the phone to sales personnel or sales assistants, or sent via faxes. Whether a phone or fax was used to transmit the information, the potential for transcription errors was present; as volume grew, the magnitude of errors expanded causing the need for corrections to trades to cascade into the following day with revised confirmations being issued.

The solution posed by the group of institutional customers and brokers assembled by Thomson Financial was the creation of a service that enabled the customer to succinctly direct a message to a broker and detail the ticker, executed quantity, execution average price, subaccount affected, and the shares related to each subaccount along with the commission and other elements. The broker would be able to view the trade and accept or reject it based upon its accuracy. The service was called OASYS and was created over an eight-month period of meetings and design sessions. The product worked in conjunction with the Alert database, and would permit the broker to see the customer account detail identifications as the broker knew them to exist on the broker's records if the broker cross-referenced his account identifier to that of the customer. As originally conceived, the customer interface was a personal computer networked through Thomson's central computer to a freestanding single-user PC on the participating broker's desk. As participation grew, institutional customers created direct interfaces to Thomson's system using the OASYS import/export specification. Brokers similarly created interfaces to OASYS using the same import/export specification so that their ticketing and order management systems could interface seamlessly. This series of steps and the growth of this system from 1990 through 1995 enabled the growing level of institutional trading volume to be handled more efficiently, and to hold relatively stable the support staffs of both the buy-side and the sell-side.

A more internationally oriented version called Global OASYS was created three years ago and differed in several respects. After the broker initiates the electronic dialogue by sending block-level indicated messages on block executions, the customer acknowledges this as valid. Concurrently, the customer transmits the subaccount allocations to the broker, again optimally cross-referenced in Alert. The broker accepts or rejects the allocation and then responds with essentially an electronic confirmation for each subaccount including delivery instructions. The customer receives these detailed confirmations back and accepts or rejects them. If all items are accurate, including principal money, currency, commissions, appropriate taxes and fees, the transactions are essentially destined for a clean settlement. This system is not as widely used in Europe as OASYS is in the United States but it is growing along with several competing systems. It is also being used more in Japan and in the other Pacific Rim countries to streamline the communication of execution details on orders and the buyside's response with subaccount allocations. The broker's response with confirmation details then completes the essential communication of details and assists in smoother settlement processing.

In conclusion, creating synergy among the individuals involved in the investment process within an organization is a major benefit we have begun to experience through well-thought-out development of technology. Extending that synergy to include external parties such as brokers, markets, and liquidity concentrators will be the next strong integration trend we experience both domestically and internationally.

Many of the problems solved over the last 25 years seemed simple in concept but difficult in execution. Greater power within technology tools (i.e., FIX, ISITIC, and other standards) and more cooperative efforts among the players—customers, brokers, and vendors—will enable a much wider array of problems to be solved. The overall investment process will change as we know it, most likely for the better. One way to help guide that change is to become involved and stay involved for your company's sake, for the industry's sake, and for your own individual development.

ⓖ # INTEGRATED ORDER
MANAGEMENT SYSTEMS

Vincent A. Walsh
Vice President, Pershing Division
Donaldson, Lufkin & Jenrette Securities Corporation

> We need to clean up the clerical morass that our traders have to go through to execute a trade, link them to our portfolio managers, and give them both decision support tools to improve their efficiency.
>
> —Pension fund executive

For major investment firms to take full advantage of the rapidly evolving market mechanisms described in the previous chapter, they must have a platform that systematically integrates investment decisions, trading, and settlement processes. The need for integrated order management systems is critical in light of the growing size and complexity of portfolios and the resulting demands for liquidity for transactions both large and small in greater and greater transaction volumes. At the same time, regulatory scrutiny and well-publicized control problems at major firms have highlighted the need for pretrade on-line compliance screening of transactions.

While many institutions have some form of order management system for their traders, in the beginning of 1996, very few firms had large volumes of orders managed within fully integrated systems including all of the following elements:

- Paperless transmission of orders from portfolio managers to their trader's trade blotter.

- On-line compliance checking of orders prior to execution.
- A trader blotter to maintain open order status with relevant market data.
- Electronic links to key brokers for indications, orders, and execution reporting.
- Paperless post-trade links to allocate trades to appropriate subaccounts and update the accounting system.

There is broad recognition that integrating these elements offers investment firms significant competitive advantages. But integrated order management systems are significant technology developments with implications for the buy-side firm's internal processes and external communications. At the same time, order management needs and priorities vary widely among different investment firms based on size, trading style, regulatory requirements, and many other factors. As a result, it is not uncommon for initial implementation of order management systems to integrate only the components of most critical importance to the particular firm. Therefore, we look at each of these elements to help the many institutions that are currently striving to integrate their investment and trading decision making.

The objective of this chapter is to provide a broad outline of integrated order management systems, their functionality, and key benefits targeted to meet the needs of investment firm executives. It also will summarize practical insights based on the experience of professionals who have implemented either in-house or vendor systems. The system descriptions here are generic but are largely derived from documentation provided by Merrin Financial and MacGregor Group.

Besides building on the prior chapter concerning "Electronic Market Mechanisms," other chapters of particular importance to readers involved in building or implementing integrated order management systems may include "Evaluating and Contracting with Vendors" by Michael Abbaei, and "Global Technology Management" by Russ Lewis.

OVERVIEW OF INTEGRATED ORDER MANAGEMENT

For investment firms, integrated order management systems can provide a paperless linking process between portfolio managers and traders who have historically communicated their orders by phone or paper order lists. Instead, orders and trades are accessed by both portfolio managers and traders through shared access to common databases. More important, this integration provides both with the platform and electronic plumbing needed to deliver enhanced investment and trading tools to improve their control and decision making. As a result, it paves the way for meaningful interpretation of relevant market information, better access to natural liquidity in the marketplace, and more control over order flow and the execution process.

Nearly all stand-alone order management systems operate primarily as trade date intraday systems and links built around a common order management database. Exhibit 8–1 highlights some of the mechanisms integrated to this database. With the exception of linked historical databases, order databases typically start with a download from the firm's portfolio accounting system of the positions and cash balances by account based on the prior day's batch

E X H I B I T   8–1

Integrated Order Management System Block Diagram

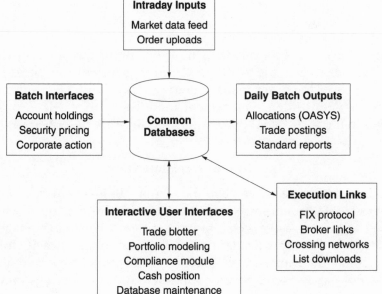

EXHIBIT 8–2
Integrated Order Management Investment Functions

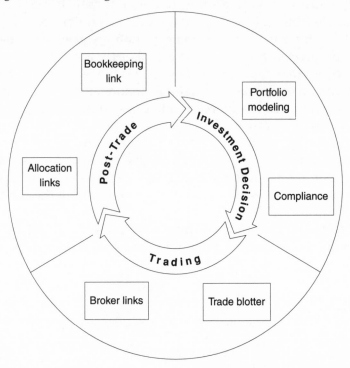

accounting cycle. Typically then at the end of the day, an upload of trade allocations to the portfolio accounting system completes the daily cycle of the order management process. Exhibit 8–2 summarizes common order management modules as they relate to the stages in the investment process. These stages are described next.

Investment Decision Stage

The investment decision stage focuses on decision support tools that generate orders implementing the portfolio managers' view based on their research, creativity, and insights. Portfolio managers and traders can apply portfolio modeling and compliance modules to translate their investment strategies into executable orders that must not violate regulatory or fund-defined rules or constraints. This allows for quicker decision making by systematically bringing investment decisions into conformity with established guidelines or exposure limitations.

Portfolio Modeling

Once the portfolio managers have expressed their view or defined theoretical portfolios, they can perform what-if analysis to assess the impact on the existing portfolios of specific trades. Through multiple iterations, the optimal realistic portfolio can be defined which reflects their investment view while meeting cash and other fund constraints. Then the appropriate orders are created to rebalance the portfolio.

Compliance

At the same time, a compliance module can carry out regulatory and other checks against orders to ensure that the orders are appropriate to the objectives and structure of the respective funds. This can highlight orders that might need to be blocked due to many reasons including fund restrictions or operational considerations such as restrictions against positions which have been loaned from the portfolio. At the same time, tracking of potential conflicts of interest in personal trading by traders or portfolio managers is increasingly important. Increasingly investment firms want a module to monitor personal trading by key employees such as fund managers and traders as well. On-line vendor systems provide on-line review for pretrade compliance. Other batch compliance software may review orders on a post-trade basis.

Trading Stage

The orders generated by the portfolio manager's decisions are transmitted to the trader for execution in a paperless way, generally through access to a common database. Common to this stage are the trade blotters and broker link modules.

Trade Blotter

Central to all automated order management systems is a trade blotter or list of open orders in which the trader can maintain real-time status of open orders and routed orders being executed. It is a screen, often in a spreadsheet format, that permits the trader to monitor which orders have been routed to particular brokers and that helps monitor the status of a number of orders at the same time. The average price of all routed orders for a given customer order is calculated and ultimately the allocation of the original order quantity is prorated to the respective executed quantity.

Broker Links
Completely paperless trading necessitates linking to key brokers electronically. Broker links have tended to be diverse and broker-specific; currently several evolving multibroker link products and the FIX protocol described in the prior chapter are dramatically changing this. Some links focus on automated execution of small orders permitting better focus on execution of working orders. At the same time, order management systems linked to broker block desks increasingly can receive execution reports and indications of interest electronically on working orders even while the trader continues to communicate by phone as well.

Post-Trade Stage

Completing the trade process depends on notifying brokers of allocations and related account details. After the trade, the order management system provides a vehicle for efficiently allocating executed quantities based on the funds represented by the portfolio manager to the full breadth of subaccounts they represent. Links to vendor allocation systems (i.e., Thomson OASYS and DTC's Institutional Instruction) as well as to custodians may be fed electronically to avoid multiple reinput stages. Allocations generally must be linked from intraday trading systems rather than accounting systems that process on an overnight batch basis. Further, the firm's agent bank must be notified of pending settlements, typically done from the accounting system rather than directly from the order management system or module.

BENEFITS OF INTEGRATED ORDER MANAGEMENT

Most firms still process orders and executions through the time-consuming and error-prone manual processing of ticket writing and input. Writing paper tickets, relaying executions, and doing calculations by hand will inevitably lead to errors. At the same time, you are at a very real information disadvantage in the absence of real-time positions. This can lead to costly mistakes such as overselling or violating compliance limits. Rekeying data into different computer systems for various post-trade clearing, custodial, and accounting purposes is redundant. Finally, time spent at the end-of-day reconciling for unaccounted trades or mistakes is a waste of a trader's time. The driving forces for increased interest in integrated order management among investment firms include the following:

- **Growing regulatory and risk awareness**—Pretrade compliance checking is increasingly critical due to growing regulatory visibility.
- **Shorter settlement cycles**—T + 3 settlement in 1995 dramatically changed behavior and highlighted the need for intraday allocation, confirmation, and affirmation efforts between brokers and institutions. Many industry leaders anticipate the further shortening of settlement cycles in the coming years. This drives the growing need for intraday integration between investment decisions and trading decisions to more efficiently initiate post-trade processing.
- **Rapid asset growth**—Investment assets continue to grow dramatically based on the increased savings among baby boomers and on rising markets over the past few years. These include the increasing need for compliance checking of trades before execution; increasing need for efficiencies, especially in rapidly growing firms where there is very limited support staff to compensate for inefficiencies. With a paperless order management system, firms can eliminate these problems and their costs while immediately increasing productivity and access to information.

The benefits of integrated order management accrue to both traders and portfolio managers:

- **Trading efficiency**—There is greater control over the order execution process with more time to spend on the larger, less liquid orders. At the same time, trading and portfolio management processes are improved through access to real-time position and profit-loss information with real-time risk management tools.

- **Operations efficiency**—Productivity is improved by eliminating multiple inputs of trade data, which helps to minimize errors, and to lead to less reconciliation based on single-point-of-input processing flows. In turn, less paper flow reduces back-office processing problems.

- **Flexibility**—More reliable and timely information on portfolios and commissions directed to specific brokers improve responsiveness to business requirements.

- **Capacity**—Integrated order management permits the firm to increase trading and processing capacity with existing staff.

PORTFOLIO MODELING

As noted before, portfolio modeling is a decision support process that translates the portfolio manager's investment decisions into the optimal list of orders through multiple iterations of approaches for executing the strategy. Because a large portfolio might represent changes in a number of positions which may represent a complex of numerous specific accounts, some order management systems provide this functionality. Technology frees the manager to be able to experiment with options before making a decision. Exhibit 8-3a provides an example of the portfolio modeling screens of the Merrin Financial Trading Platform. Portfolio modeling involves a what-if process followed by the rebalancing process.

What-If Modeling

Modeling takes place when portfolio managers enter potential trades based on percent or dollar increments to see the effect such trades will have on the composition of their portfolios. The potential trades might seek to align the portfolio to a theoretical or model portfolio that has been constructed to reflect corporate investment policy, optimal asset allocation, and so forth. The modeling process frequently involves adjusting models to see the effect of a wide

E X H I B I T 8–3A

Integrated Order Management

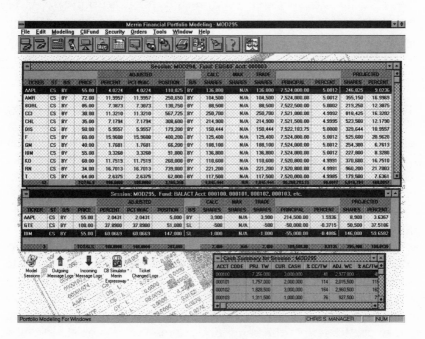

range of potential investment scenarios prior to execution. Doing it systematically has broadened the scope and added great flexibility to the process compared to manual processing. In the past, what-if analysis could not be done as freely by multiple iterations of calculations and subsequent analysis.

Rebalancing

Rebalancing portfolios is the term given to the process of aligning the actual portfolio to the model. The actual portfolio is reconstructed to reflect the underlying composition of the model even though the actual portfolio might contain different issues, dollar amounts, and clients from those in the model. Using a computer, in a matter of seconds or minutes, you can create several iterations of model portfolios using different investment criteria such as security types, issuers, or global exposure, and then rebalance a target portfolio to reflect the same weightings of components as those contained in the model. The resulting trades generated then can be passed to the trade blotter electronically for execution subject to compliance checking, which is increasingly integrated into the portfolio modeling process.

Compliance

The compliance module requires a message or process for alerting the trader or portfolio manager of possible violations of defined rules. To accomplish this, each of the orders must be compared on input against a set of decision rules in the form of defined restrictions for the specific securities. This process obviously needs a flexible application to define and update restrictions. Depending on the size and regulatory requirements of the investment firm, these may apply to specific securities or there may be dynamic rules subject to securities holdings, lists of recommended issues, or a trader's personal trades. Typically to facilitate regulatory reporting, this module should have a detailed audit trail and report writing capability and possibly a calendar of regulatory reporting key dates. Portfolios may be checked against all investment restrictions before trade orders are sent to the trader. At the same time, some systems or stand-alone compliance products function only on a post-trade basis. Merrin Financial's CompAlert product is the most widely installed vendor solution for on-line compliance checking although other vendor products such as MacGregor's Predator and Longview's LandMark have well developed compliance modules. They tend to include some or all of the following functions:

• **Trading system alerts**—Check that fund trades do not violate their prospectus limitations or SEC rules. It checks the trade before the fact. When employees wish to buy or sell specific securities, they enter the orders into a computer that checks each potential trade against the activities of the advisors' managed accounts. In contrast, manual checking of compliance rules is inefficient and labor-intensive. The automated system provides the needed advance notice before the trade goes through.

• **Restriction definition**—Customer-specific compliance tests are custom programmed using data items in the system's order and symbol databases.

• **Personal transaction screening**—The compliance module interfaces with the trading system. This is intended to defend against conflicts of interest among investment managers and the potential for adverse publicity. At many mutual funds, employees may be required to get approval for personal trades and to execute trades within a certain period and report back. The software could indicate when trades were not approved in advance. Further, it could highlight if employees bought anything that they also bought for a client within a short period of time. These programs are not specifically designed to catch portfolio managers in the act of front running. The software may hold the firm's code of ethics in its database and track every trade a manager makes. When a manager wants to trade, the program looks up the code, cross-references it against the trade, and checks to see if the manager has followed proper procedure, otherwise, flagging a potential problem. If not, there may be a problem.

• **Calendar reminders**—Calendar reminders facilitate timely reporting based on complex regulatory requirements from various sources.

• **Detailed audit trail and report writer**—A detailed audit trail provides flexible ad hoc reporting of transactions based on requests or internal requirements.

TRADE BLOTTER

A trade blotter provides a real-time tool for managing status of orders between portfolio managers and traders. By using a trade blotter, the trader can maintain the positions and status of orders being worked while the respective managers can monitor related reports. The trade blotter lists all the orders to be worked by a trader along with their respective status. It often is also linked to real-time market data. Exhibit 8–3b is an example of the trade blotters for a trader and portfolio manager.

The trade blotter provides a display or work area for the pending orders. It includes original order quantity and limits or instructions as provided by the portfolio manager as well as details of working order status information including broker and/or exchange routing, executions reported, and related "leaves quantity" (remaining shares not yet executed in an order). Also included

E X H I B I T   8–3B

Integrated Order Management *(concluded)*

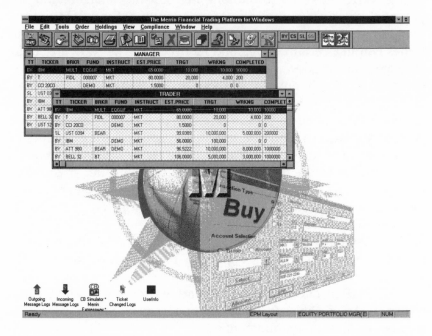

is the automatic calculation of the average price. Generally on a separate screen, planned allocation subaccounts, commissions, and related quantities will be displayed subject to final confirmation. Order input may take the form of simplified input by the trader or by way of direct linkages to portfolio managers.

Depending on the links to the particular system, execution reports may be entered by the trader based on phone calls or faxes from the executing broker or may be fed as part of specific broker links. Broker links preclude the need for the trader to enter orders off tickets, manage these orders manually on bits of paper, as well as reentry ticket writing and input at the end of the day.

Most order management systems integrate some market data on issues traded, although it may be limited to closing prices from the portfolio management system. In this case, at least it provides a standard for reasonableness of prices. Depending on the strategy of the investment manager, this may be sufficient to its needs.

Increasingly, buy-side systems are linking to real-time data feeds, or to broker or other third-party analytical tools such as Bloomberg to provide greater trading decision support. By linking to some sophisticated systems generally provided by brokers, the trade blotter can now be linked to real-time market data including volume weighted average price (VWAP) for the issue and historical trading volumes to identify

- Quality of execution.
- Alerts of orders subject to movements in the primary market.
- Size comparisons of orders to recent trading volume to identify orders for special handling.

BROKER LINKS

Based on the coverage of links to alternative sources of liquidity in the prior chapter, broker links are described only in passing here. An automated order management system is needed for investment firms to take advantage of execution and decision support services offered electronically by specific brokers. These linkages started with the need to execute numerous smaller orders, but increasingly the need for linkages for working orders and for receiving indications of interest from multiple brokers is the driving force on the buy side for integrated order management. This is clearest among a few leading mutual fund companies that have installed order management and that have demanded that their brokers link electronically.

Merrin Financial developed its Intermarket Trading Network (ITN) as an electronic link between the buy side and sell side; it is used for order delivery to brokers and receipt of trade execution reports by the money manager. This and other multibroker systems such as Bloomberg, Bridge, and Thomson TradeRoute are having an increasing impact on the marketplace.

The FIX protocol described in the last chapter appears to be increasingly the protocol of choice for order and indication messages for those firms with in-house integrated order management systems. While security issues need to be addressed, over time the comfort level will increase with the use of this Internet technology unless aggressive premature use of the technology leads to a well-publicized breakdown prior to the implementation of sufficient controls, which would tarnish the image of the Internet and delay use in financial services.

The process of order routing for automated execution in DOT, a broker's system, or a crossing network generally follows the pattern of buy-side orders being sent and sell-side acknowledgments and execution reports. For large blocks, there is greater variability. Some systems such as Merrin's ITN follow a similar process of electronic order routing and execution reporting for larger blocks. In contrast, major fund managers doing block orders have preferred a message flow calling for the buy-side trader to phone orders and to utilize electronic links for indication and execution reports primarily so that most messaging is generated by the sell-side trader. This avoids any additional input by the buy-side trader while recognizing the reality that most traders for the foreseeable future will be likely to still have the rapport with their sell-side counterpart on large blocks but would like the broker's input to match to the order in their system to ensure that there has been no misunderstanding in the booking based on the telephone discussion.

POST-TRADE LINKAGES

Most investment firms are batch or multibatch in the post-trade environment. The bulk of the firm's data resides in accounting systems often constrained to the availability of reporting and critical information intraday. These tend to be well-tested "basic plumbing" transaction processing systems with relatively inflexible functionality. Under this circumstance, a client/server order management system is all the more critical to bridge the gap of information for intraday decision support as well as for ad hoc analysis.

Allocation Process/ Vendor Links (OASYS/DTC-II)

Another variable in methodology involves whether allocations utilize the same network (as is the case in ITN and Instinet) or separate allocation systems such as Thomson's OASYS and DTC's Institutional Instruction. Most broker/institution links handle orders, executions, and indications of interest, but not allocations. As noted earlier, allocations tend to be fed from portfolio management systems rather than trading systems.

Bookkeeping Link/Portfolio Management Systems

Trader order-management systems typically have a download from portfolio management systems of prior-day close positions and an upload to bookkeeping or portfolio management systems after the end of the trading day. In choosing or building an order management application, it is best to take advantage of systems that have established links to the systems in use, if possible.

REFLECTIONS ON THE IMPLEMENTATION PROCESS

In this section, we try to distill insights from investment firms that have successfully implemented order management systems.

Get Management Buy-in

A firm's order management process is the life blood of an investment firm. Changing it requires management commitment as well as the willingness of portfolio managers and traders to dramatically change some of the tried and true methods for doing business and substituting it with a very different mode of business. Further, this process has a relatively long planning-horizon for system implementation regardless of whether it is an internal development or a vendor solution. This effort may be costly, time consuming, and may absorb the precious time of key management, so commitment is critical to success. The decision to proceed can sometimes be driven by a wide range of circumstances. In some firms it is the decision of a sponsoring executive while in others it may be driven by the demands of one or more customers. At the same time, it could be driven by management consensus reached as a result of a defining or bellwether industry event; for example, after the World Trade Center bombing. It is important to be realistic in setting objectives for the effort.

Prepare a Business Case and Needs Analysis

What benefits are anticipated? Can they be quantified? This analysis will be central to the main components of the request-for-proposal document if a vendor solution is to be considered, or otherwise to staff and initiate the specification of the necessary in-house systems development effort. Assessing needs in advance includes key elements such as:

- Constraints of existing infrastructure, trading desk real-estate and other systems.
- Mix of instruments traded (equity, fixed income, derivatives).
- Number, location, and roles of portfolio managers and traders.
- Typical trade flows including size of typical and complex trading strategies.
- Decision support tools to be integrated.
- Anticipated regulatory and compliance requirements.
- Availability of internal project and development resources.

Identify a Focal Point Liaison Group or Individual

To pursue paperless trading, focus is needed by a group or individual in order to solicit the necessary input from traders and portfolio managers and to translate it into a coherent set of requirements. However, a trader's skills of rapid decision making are often anathema to the methodical, detailed orientation needed to implement a new system. Therefore, key to the process is to have a focal point liaison to integrate user input into a technological solution. Some firms lack these resources and either hire consultants or depend on vendors to satisfy these needs. Particularly if an in-house development is planned, the skills embodied by this group or individual typically include

- Business experience to earn credibility among traders and portfolio managers.
- Ability to communicate effectively orally and in writing.
- Willingness to listen to input from key potential system users.
- Ability to deal with technology and existing alternatives.
- Project management skills.

Decide on a Build or Buy Approach

There are various possible combinations of in-house and out-sourced solutions to software development. Sometimes, the best approach is to combine an in-house development effort with an interim lease of a vendor solution. This may provide quicker start-up functionality as a good short-term stepping-stone to an in-house solution that helps identify needs and priorities while buying time for a tailored solution. Even those that may eventually develop in-house systems may choose a vendor system initially to gain knowledge and insight on the process. Large, complex firms should take a serious look at in-house implementation unless most of their needs are effectively addressed by a particular vendor solution. If a firm has the time, the people resources, and the management commitment to design and implement an in-house system solution, it is almost certainly the best long-term way to go, since each firm has its own unique investment flow that any vendor solution can only approximate. At the same time, some investment firms may be able to accomplish these developments using longer-term consulting engagements of a technology and software consulting firm. Further, with the evolution of client/server systems with graphical user interface development tools such as Visual Basic and X-Windows, that development can be done more efficiently today than in the past.

Identify and Screen the Potential Alternative Vendor Solutions

A number of vendor solutions are available for paperless trading systems as shown in the selected vendor list in Exhibit 8–4. Unless prior success for satisfaction with a particular vendor is definitive, the screening process may involve multiple steps, narrowing the field based on comparative functionality to the needs analysis or request for proposal (RFP). While a great deal of time is spent on an RFP and it is helpful to define needs, it is often difficult to identify a particular vendor who is head and shoulders above the rest. In general vendors interpret questionnaires most positively in terms of their own functionality, so positive answers to most questions can be anticipated. Further, it is extremely difficult to identify, in the context of the rapidly changing desktop technology, whether a

EXHIBIT 8-4

Select Buy-Side Order-Management-System Vendors (as of May 1996)

Vendor	Advent	Bloomberg LP	Data Exchange	Longview	MacGregor	Merrin Financial	Thomson Financial
Product	Moxy	Bloomberg Trade System	WinDX Trader	LandMark	Predator	Merrin Financial Trading Platform	TradeView
Telephone	415-543-7696	212-318-2000	212-809-6868	617-439-4545	617-423-6560	212-708-2700	617-345-2000
Ownership Structure	Advent Software Inc.	Private	Advent Software Inc.	Private	Private	ADP	Thomson Financial, subsidiary of Thomson Corporation
Operating Systems	M/S Windows	Proprietary	M/S Windows	M/S Windows NT, Unix	Unix, M/S Windows NT	M/S DOS and Windows	Unix server, M/S Windows
Networking OS	IPX/SPX Windows NT	Proprietary	IPX/SPX, TCP-IP	IPX/SPX, TCP-IP	TCP-IP	IPX/SPX, OS2	TCP-IP
Broker Links	Plan FIX Link	Direct broker links, Davidge, and FIX	Davidge	Plan FIX Link	ITG/Quantex, broker DOT systems; and Plan FIX Link	InterMarket Trading Network; Plan FIX Link	TradeRoute including BRASS; Plan FIX and Davidge Links

vendor has superior features, much less whether any advantage will exist in the future. New vendors are entering the market all the time and competitors rapidly leapfrog their competition based on the implementation of new features which quickly are copied by others. The comfort level of the investment firm, in depending on a particular vendor for such an important system, is sometimes a key concern particularly since some vendors to this market have historically been very small systems-development groups. At the same time, today's vendor start-up could possibly be tomorrow's technology leader given success in development, marketing, and implementation.

Arrange a Test of Leading Vendors

A useful process to differentiate between the viability of alternative vendors is to narrow the field to the most likely vendors and then for the survivors to arrange for input of test trades or scripts of typical transactions into each system. By using realistic test scripts processed through different vendor solutions, you can determine the limits of a system's functionality. The output from this process will identify differences in interpretation between how a vendor describes functionality versus how these functions would impact your business. Critical and potentially deal-killing issues can be identified by both you and the vendor early enough so that expectations will be realistic on both sides.

Choose Your First Implementation Strategically

Implement one area at a time, starting with select traders who have either a comfort level with technology or a pressing business need. Focus on the needs of the key decision area for the success of the product. This may vary from one firm to another and certainly varies from one function to another. Senior management may view the primary outcome as paperless trading or compliance monitoring. On the other hand, index-focused portfolio managers would be most concerned with a solution for portfolio modeling. For example, traders are less interested in paperless trading than they are in being able to link to multiple sources of liquidity so that small orders can be rapidly sent electronically, allowing them to focus on adding value to the largest orders.

BUILD VERSUS BUY?—THE IN-HOUSE VERSUS VENDOR DECISION

The vendor buy-versus-in-house-build decision can be a difficult choice in pursuing order management technology. This decision is generally not just a trade-off in incurring upfront cost versus ongoing lease or maintenance expenditures. From a timing perspective, if the investment firm's needs closely fit the function of the vendor's offering, the quicker and generally the cheaper strategy is to lease the software. While larger firms need to assess existing vendor solutions, smaller firms lacking support staff to consider an in-house development can take advantage of the accumulated wisdom and speed of implementation of an existing vendor system. The trade-off arises from the potential control and flexibility offered by an in-house firm-specific solution. At the same time, in choosing vendors, it is extremely diffuclt in the context of dynamic technology to predict which vendors will have the superior features and technology in the future.

Some of the largest mutual fund firms in the country have built their own trade order management systems. But that simply is not an option for most smaller firms with less capital and fewer technical personnel, unless these firms can hire an outside consulting firm to develop a client-specific solution. Since the nature of technical overhead among buy-side investment managers is typically limited, few buy-side firms have the critical mass, technical expertise, or desire to pursue an internal development of an order management system. Even those that may eventually develop such systems may consider using a vendor initially to develop knowledge of the inherent functionality. On the other hand, every investment firm uses its own order-management and decision-making process. The more unusual the firm and the more geographically spread out it is, the more necessary it is to pursue an in-house solution.

To assist in evaluating vendor solutions, Exhibit 8–4 provides an outline of selected vendors. This is of course only a cursory summary but it provides some points for comparison with regard to the experience and infrastructure of some of the firms. Most vendors of integrated order management systems are offering stand-alone software. However, a service bureau approach is currently available for fixed income from Bloomberg and it is likely that major market-data vendors will be expanding their offerings in this area.

LOOKING TO THE FUTURE

Within the next three years, paperless, integrated order management systems will become the standard among investment firms. While only a few firms have established fully integrated systems as of this writing, it has become a fact of life that high trading-volumes, complex and conflicting regulations, and risk management demand that the smooth handling of orders be done within linked systems. Buy-side traders were able to ignore paperless trading in the past but they are increasingly at a trading disadvantage to their better linked peers at firms with trading systems interconnected to multiple sources of liquidity. This will be the driving force to bring integration to the majority of investment firms.

However, even in a world of increasing client/servers and declining hardware and software costs, designing and implementing these systems, and getting them to be fully utilized is a very difficult process. If you do not have the resources and management commitment within your firm, a vendor solution can provide a cost-effective alternative.

CHAPTER

9

⑥ PORTFOLIO MANAGEMENT AND ACCOUNTING

Elizabeth C. Church
Vice President
Advent Software

Evaluating the options for portfolio accounting and performance measurement is a complex and time-consuming task. It is not a task most businesses care to take on more than once every 5 or 10 years; therefore most firms lack extensive experience in accomplishing the task. A good decision yields cost-effective flexibility, enabling long-term growth and profitability for the firm. A bad decision will be at best painful and expensive. Many will choose to endure system inefficiencies simply to avoid taking up the project again. "If it ain't broke don't fix it," is often code for "If it's not killing us let's ignore the problem because I know I can't live through another conversion." Our objective in this chapter is to articulate the alternatives, questions, and issues one might consider to make the best business decision possible.

The complexity of the evaluation is defined by:

1. The dynamics of the investment industry.
2. The rapid evolution of technology.
3. An investment business's need for flexibility to respond to changing regulatory requirements, market conditions, and increasing competition.
4. The myriad products and services offered for fulfilling the task.
5. Political dynamics within the firm itself.

181

Each issue will vary in importance from firm to firm, so we address them one by one, leaving the reader to assign appropriate weightings.

DYNAMICS OF THE INVESTMENT INDUSTRY

Employee Retirement Income Security Act (ERISA) legislation, Association of Investment Management and Research (AIMR) performance, Securities and Exchange Commission (SEC) regulations, the commoditization of investment and economic data, globalization—the list of industry influences out of our direct control is significant and growing. Increasing complexity has created enormous opportunities and challenges in the investment industry. The opportunity is manifest in the unprecedented growth in the number of registered investment advisors (RIAs) during the past 10 years; RIAs in-creased from 4,000 in 1983 to more than 20,000 in 1994. (See Exhibit 9–1.) The challenge has been and continues to be to establish a core infrastructure that enables the industry to maintain and measure quality in accounting that is sufficiently flexible to facilitate growth in new markets and new products. Not many legacy systems have been able to keep up. The management and accounting foundation laid 10, 15, or even 20 years ago invariably underestimated the rate of change in the investment industry. The industry composition has fragmented from the traditional bank trust department to RIAs, financial planners, brokers, mutual funds, asset allocators, hedge funds, limited partnerships, and family offices; all are approaching the same huge pool of assets from a slightly different angle. (See Exhibit 9–2.) Each new angle will require variations in accounting, management, client reporting, and service. And who knows what will happen in the next 5 years, much less 20? Some experts predict still greater competition, increased specialization, and more exotic products. (See Exhibit 9–3.) Other experts look at the same industry statistics and predict not only a massive consolidation in the number of investment advisors, but also an industry in which a few large firms will offer a variety of products under the same roof. From a portfolio management accounting standpoint, either prediction yields the same result: Change is a given, and the ability to adapt to the change efficiently is the key to prosperity.

E X H I B I T   9–1

Registered Investment Advisors

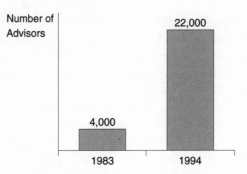

E X H I B I T   9–2

Assets Managed by U.S. Institutional Investors

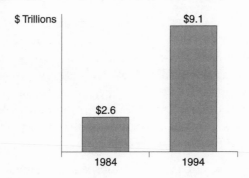

E X H I B I T   9–3

U.S. Institutional Investment in International Securities `

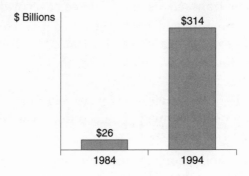

Assume, for example, that the industry continues to fragment, and product offerings become more and more exotic. The challenge of the supporting portfolio management systems will be twofold: First, to accurately account for new investment vehicles [e.g., derivatives, swaptions, interest-only securities (IOs), principal-only securities (POs)] and second, to present the information in such a way that it can be used easily to manage the assets and educate the client or prospect. An industry consolidation puts equal pressure on systems support, although in a slightly different way. While the accounting requirements probably would be more mainstream, the lack of product differentiation would put pressure on client service and would require more sophisticated presentation materials. Graphics, desktop publishing, and flexible report content and formats will become a market necessity.

CHANGE IN TECHNOLOGY

Mainframe, minicomputer, PC, client/server, DOS, Windows, Unix —most investment businesses believe that choosing between these is little more than rolling the dice. The best strategy is to focus on the business application and pick the technology that you can afford and support. After all is said and done, the technology is the means to an end and not the end in itself. The implementation of one platform or another is relevant only in its contribution to the growth of the business. (See Exhibit 9–4.) Each firm needs to consider:

- What are the current and anticipated business application requirements?
- How are those needs changing over time in terms of processing requirements? How many accounts, what volume of transactions, which types of securities?
- What staffing is available to support a given technology? Do you have a database administrator? An MIS staff?
- What is the internal climate for technology? Who uses computers and why?
- What other data services or software systems do you currently use? How will you need to transfer information from one system to another?

There are application, technology, and financial pros and cons to each configuration. The easiest way to get tripped up is to

EXHIBIT   9–4

Adoption of Enabling Technology

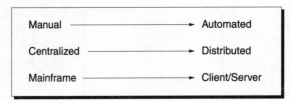

become enamored with technology that cannot be maintained by the existing staff. You want to anticipate the growth of the business in your evaluation without exceeding the users' capability to benefit today. The practicality of running the business should remain at the forefront: Either too much or too little power can frustrate the users' requirements, both because the system will not have the capacity to deliver, and because the user will not know how to harness the system's capacity. There is no definitive answer to the technology question. Any configuration you choose will eventually be out of date. Your best bet is to concentrate on business needs, to view technology simply as a means to achieving those needs, and to incorporate the cost of the technology (hardware, software, and personnel) into the cost/benefit analysis that you would make for any capital investment. More specialized instruments have a higher risk of obsolescence; vendors need either broad markets or high prices to sustain their own businesses. More mainstream investments have a greater likelihood of longevity, but you may need to tinker with the system a bit to tighten the fit to the special needs of your firm.

THE NEEDS OF THE BUSINESS

Determining the needs of your firm is the part that should be easy. And it is easy, to a point. (See Exhibit 9–5.) The first task is to define the investment process as it exists today. For example, is your firm's strategy set by an investment policy committee? Once it is set, who implements the strategy? What is the flexibility of the portfolio managers to calibrate the firm's, strategy to meet the investment objectives and restrictions set by specific clients? (See

EXHIBIT 9–5

Increasingly Complex Industry Requirements

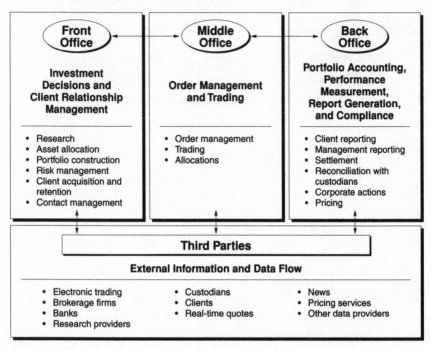

Exhibit 9–6.) What is the portfolio load of each manager, and how do those portfolios overlap in terms of investment requirements? Does each manager specialize in specific types of securities, such as fixed income or equities? How quickly do you need to rebalance and execute changes to portfolios based on changing economic and/or market conditions? (See Exhibit 9–7.) How do you communicate with your clients? What level of sophistication do they require in terms of reporting? Do you want to comply with AIMR performance standards? IMCA standards? ICI (Investment Company Institute) standards?

OPERATIONS

The operations group will have another set of issues: How many clients do you service? What is the frequency with which you send reports? What is your capacity to generate reports in-house? What

EXHIBIT 9–6

Challenge: Investment Decisions

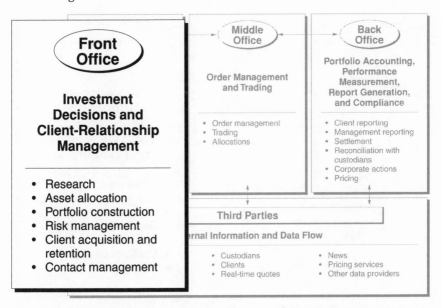

EXHIBIT 9–7

Challenge: Investment Execution

EXHIBIT 9–8

Challenge: Portfolio Record-keeping

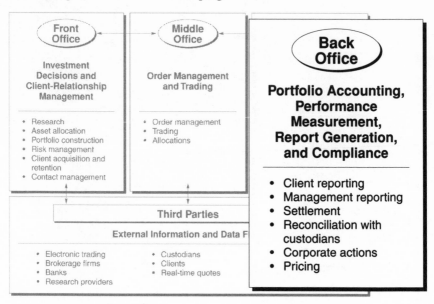

EXHIBIT 9–9

Challenge: Information Integration

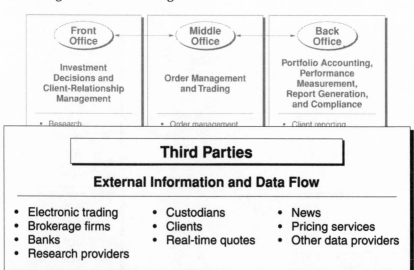

custodians do you work with? What is your process for reconcilia-tion? What external databases do you use? How do you plan to integrate your various sources of information? (See Exhibits 9–8 and 9–9.) Do you have an internal trading desk? How do your traders manage their order flow? How do your portfolio managers communicate with your traders? What is your turnover in adminis-trative staff? What training is required to maintain the process as is?

MARKETING

Who is the primary contact for the client? Is it the portfolio manager or do you have a marketing staff that takes responsibility for most client communication? What is your means of keeping track of com-munication with the client? What level of support do you offer your marketing and client-service staff? Do all clients get the same infor-mation with the same periodicity? Can your staff see reports on-line when clients call in with questions about reports which they have received? Can they create composites for presenting performance in a manner that conforms with what consultants need? What kind of graphics capabilities are available, and what gyrations are required to present data in a pie chart or bar chart or whatever format looks best? While not a comprehensive list, these are the types of ques-tions you will want to answer in the context of evaluating your existing systems and potential alternatives. The existing business process is your first focus, but the future of the business is an equally important consideration.

FUTURE BUSINESS NEEDS

We can only assume that the rate of change in the investment industry will continue at least at the pace we have experienced to date. The real debate is what that change will entail. Since the 1970s, when the industry was dominated by bank trust depart-ments, the increase in the number of registered investment advi-sors has been staggering. Fortunately, the assets managed by U.S. institutional investors have also grown from $2.6 trillion in 1984 to $9.1 trillion in 1994. Money managers have tried different strategies to differentiate their products and capture market share. Many have specialized in specific segments of the market, developing an expertise and reputation for performance in fixed income, equity, global management, or hedge funds. The business has become increasingly fragmented as more and more money managers pursue the same pool of assets. Most have found that while performance may be a key characteristic, it is by no means an assurance of winning new business. Money managers must provide satisfactory performance relative to the mix of assets and strategies their clients want. The manager can compete by offering a more mainstream strategy to a larger target market, or a more esoteric strategy to a smaller audience of interested investors. The systems requirements are stringent for each. For example, managers who opt for a more mainstream strategy of, say, balanced investments, will compete in a much larger target market against a larger number of competitors. They can differentiate their products by providing superior performance, superior client service, and superior reporting, and chances are, they'd better provide all three. In the event they opt for a more esoteric investment strategy, they will compete against fewer managers, but they will find a much smaller audience. They will still have to generate superior performance, but they will also have to be able to generate reports that educate their clients, and make them comfortable with the strategy employed. Superior client service is part and parcel of the product offering.

The money management industry could continue to expand, or it could contract. In either case fees are likely to come down. If the market continues to expand, then fees will be pressured by increasing competition for actively managed accounts. Institutions will be tempted to meet their return requirements by placing more assets in passive funds, which typically have lower management fees. If the market begins to consolidate, then larger money management firms will begin to offer a broader range of specialized products, limiting the need for plan sponsors to maintain relationships with multiple firms. Generally the industry trend has been to offer lower management fees for greater assets under management. It also seems likely that globalization of the industry will continue, meaning that competitors from overseas will increasingly compete for assets that historically have been managed domestically. Multicurrency accounting will be the standard, and some of the larger overseas firms will probably buy market share through acquisition. From a systems perspective, what this means is that while the demand will increase for more flexible reporting, multicurrency accounting, client reporting, performance reporting, and graphics, the fee revenues will be pressured by market conditions and increased competition. It's a business for the agile, not the faint of heart.

Your Firm's Future

Are you planning to start a mutual fund? Are you broadening your product offering? Are you building a professional marketing staff or allying with another firm's distribution network to minimize the client-service component of your portfolio managers' day? When you decided to evaluate your portfolio management systems did you think you would be reengineering your entire business strategy? Cost-effective flexibility is your best bet.

Your Firm's Options

Some would say that the availability of enabling technology has fueled the growth in the number of investment advisors. It is true that not long ago the need to invest in mainframe technology was a serious barrier to entry in the investment advisory business. Now there not only is no need to use a mainframe but there is also almost no barrier to entry. The number of vendors servicing this market has grown with the market itself. The task of vendor selection will be time consuming because of the number of options. But you should invest the time wisely because the long-term ramifications will be dramatic.

Once you have your business model detailed, you can consider the functionality that you need now and expect to need in the future. You can also give consideration to choosing the platform that will best serve those business needs in terms of processing capability, flexibility, staffing and training requirements, and implementation cost. This process will narrow the field to a short list of finalists, at which point you can begin to consider the vendors' references and corporate infrastructure.

References

Dig deep. Ask specific questions. Ask the references for names of other clients they may know that the vendor has not given you. Most clients will try to put the best face on their own situation, particularly if they have been selected by the vendor to tell you their experience. Most clients do not want to say bad things about their current vendors, so if you suspect they are generalizing to avoid saying something less than complimentary, you either need to probe more specifically or ask for more names. Keep in mind that almost any vendor can come up with three good references. Ask for 10. And ask for references who are running their businesses the way you plan to run yours.

Look for an Evolving Product

You expect your business to change over time. You need a vendor who can keep up with the change. The best way to evaluate that is to get specific information about how their own product lines have changed over time, and what new products they have added in anticipation of client needs, or as a response to client requests. What process do they follow to match the needs of the market to their product enhancements? What sources do they tap for industry information? Look for a methodology to the process that can be reflected in the design of the products. If you have used in-house legacy systems, you know how unwieldy they can become over time, usually because the development is reactive and undocumented. A software development company cannot sustain long-term growth on that basis. They must have the internal flexibility to accommodate client requests within the context of a long-term product plan that encompasses both a functional strategy and a technology strategy. Their clients will be able to tell you how their strategy is working because they will be the beneficiaries of it. Ask them about the sophistication of the enhancements and the quality of the code along with the number of enhancements that come out. The level of detail that they can provide will also give you a feel for the quality of the documentation, training, and service that accompanies the new features. A new enhancement that nobody knows about or that is difficult to use is of questionable value.

Ask to see user manuals and training materials. What internal training process is used to educate customer service reps? What is the turnover rate in the service department? A high level of turnover can mean one of two things: Either the software has bugs or there is no career path thought out for the service reps, so they can only advance by leaving. In the first instance, inadequately tested software will infuriate clients. Infuriated clients vent on their service reps. Service reps put in a position of continually calming angry clients soon leave. In the second instance, everybody suffers because your most experienced service reps are a great resource to the vendor as well as to the client. They know the product and the industry, and they can help specify needed product enhancements, train junior reps, as well as anticipate the needs of the client base. A forward-thinking firm focuses on ways to keep the position of a client service representative from being a dead-end job.

Corporate Infrastructure

Evaluate the vendor's corporation as if you were thinking of buying the stock. The best plans in the world do you no good if there is no capital—human or financial—to implement them. Meet the management. Study the financials. Is this a business on which you are willing to bet your business? You really are betting your business, because a vendor with inadequate books and records can quickly cause you to fail.

Some companies' managers believe that if they have access to source code they are safe. But any programmer will tell you that taking someone else's code and even following what they have done and why is a major task. Depending on the size of your IT staff and the integrity of the code, you could easily find it's not worth the effort. It's better to work with a vendor who has a better than average chance of thriving in business.

There are two basic business models from which to choose: service bureau and in-house. The service bureau model was introduced into the industry when the alternative was to buy a mainframe and hire a programming team. Over the years, this model has become generally less attrative particularly with the evolution of the PC. Typically, the service bureau will charge a monthly fee based on the number of accounts, transactions, and tax lots. An in-house system will require an initial license fee with an ongoing maintenance charge that is a percentage of the license. For the start-up that is not certain to make a go of it, the service bureau can be attractive because the initial cost typically is lower. If things do not work out for the business, the investment in systems has been minimized. Once the firm hits critical mass, the in-house system is almost always more cost effective, and local control of the data is desirable. If the specifications of the firm permit, it is to your advantage to use software developed by a third party. The additional overhead of an in-house development effort generally far outweighs the perceived advantage of internal control. In most cases, you want to be sure you have control over the data, not the software development. And at this point, there do not seem to be too many unique requirements of money management firms that cannot be customized to an existing core portfolio management product. Writing software is not magic. But if you don't need to do it, why bother?

Corporate Politics

Most firms do not have significant issues to deal with here. But for the ones who do, the issue can be debilitating. The primary question to consider is not just: What do you need? but Why do you need what you are asking for? Communication between the business unit and the technology staff is imperative, and prioritization of the needs of each will make life easier for all concerned.

A complex technology may be required to fulfill the requirements of the business unit. It also will mean that more staff, or more expensive staff, is required to implement and administer the solution. Every implementation will have its trade-offs. The important thing is to understand fully what the trade-offs are so you can make the appropriate decision.

In summary, this is one of the most important decisions you can make for your firm. Overlooking any detail in your analysis can have significant repercussions. The upside is that everyone in the industry is facing the same decision. Use all the sources of information you have, talk to colleagues who run similar businesses, and above all, use your common sense.

10

⑥ MEASURING TRADING/INVESTMENT PERFORMANCE & RISK*

Esther Eckerling Goodman
Chief Operating Officer, and Senior Executive Vice President
Kenmar Asset Allocation Inc.

Caroline Poplawski
Senior Research Analyst
Kenmar Asset Allocation Inc.

Joseph Rosen
Managing Director
Enterprise Technology Corporation

The terms and concepts of *risk, risk measurement,* and *risk management* in the financial trading arena have numerous and varied meanings and applications, depending on the context of the need as well as on the observer. Perhaps the importance of effective risk management—whatever that means—need not be pointed out again in times such as these, when a venerable institution like Barings can disappear almost in a flash due to poor or nonexistent risk management and controls.

Source: Reprinted from *Derivatives Risk and Responsibility,* eds. Robert A. Klein and Jess Lederman (Chicago: Irwin Professional Publishing, 1996), 85–118.
*Acknowledgments: Measurements of risk can most clearly be expressed in graphic formats. A special word of thanks is owed to Vicki Rabinowitz and Jean-Marc Merine of Kenmar, who provided assistance in the production of all visual aids. Their meticulous work and attention to detail supplied us with the nineteen illustrative graphs and charts the reader will find in this chapter. Thanks also to Jacquelyn Coffee, of Enterprise Technology Corporation, who carefully edited the manuscript.

RISK MANAGEMENT

One useful way of sorting through the various definitions of risk management is to look at it from the perspective of answers to four related, but still conceptually distinct, questions that in our estimation encompass nearly all of the generally accepted purposes of risk management. These questions include:

- What is?—How exposed and risky are our current positions?
- What if?—What could happen to our current exposures if various market parameters (e.g., interest rates, volatilities) change?
- What was?—How well did we perform, and what sorts of risks did we incur in the process?
- What do we want?—Which guidelines do we want to follow in our portfolio asset-allocation decisions—in particular, how much money do we give to which traders?

In this chapter we focus, though not exclusively, on the retrospective view, or post mortem, of the risks that were assumed by a particular trader or portfolio, and to a lesser extent, on how these risks should be incorporated into the portfolio construction/asset allocation process. One of the benefits of this type of risk measurement is that it more easily lends itself to cross-market analysis and comparison, which is not always the case with the other questions, where you often have the problem of comparing apples to oranges because of the different instruments.

Themes

A number of complementary themes and messages are threaded throughout this chapter. Most importantly, no single measure or ratio, concept, or formula can by itself adequately express, let alone manage, financial risk in a portfolio of assets. In other words, there are no magic bullets available to slay the risk dragon.

One must not lose sight of the reality that all of these algorithms and systems are only tools, and can never substitute for human thought, judgment, and common sense. We confess that much of our discussion is basic common sense. Unfortunately, events of the last couple of years suggest that all too often common sense rules are ignored. For example, even those organizations with the most sophisticated analytical systems are doomed to fail if they lack the other equally critical elements. Effective risk management requires and entails a holistic philosophy and a truly integrated set of components that must also include the requisite level of senior management involvement, organizational structure, and a culture that fosters cooperation. It also requires a compensation system that does not skew the risk-reward scale for traders so as to give them a "free option," which could encourage some to take untoward risks with the firm's capital.

Managed Futures as a Case Study

The various analyses and examples we present use real numbers from real traders from real Kenmar portfolios—though for obvious reasons trader anonymity is maintained. It is the authors' strongly held view—based on our combined track record of nearly half a century of successfully creating and utilizing risk-management systems to build and manage portfolios of external traders—that a great deal of risk-management technique can best be learned from practices within the managed futures industry.

The proof is in the pudding. As Exhibit 10–1 illustrates, this industry has experienced tremendous exponential growth over the last decade, increasing in assets by $22 billion, with approximately one thousand commodity trading advisors (CTAs)—the analogue to the registered investment advisors (RIAs) of the traditional money management world—trading mostly futures and options on global exchanges. Kenmar is in the class of industry firm called a CTA and trading manager—although affiliates are registered as an RIA and commodity pool operator (CPO)—whose primary business is the construction and management of multiadvisor, multisector portfolios of external traders for global institutions and large private investors.

Organization of the Chapter

This chapter comprises four additional sections. Following this introduction, we review a number of methods traditionally used to measure risk by both the RIA and CTA worlds, briefly describing

EXHIBIT 10–1

Growth of the Managed Futures Industry

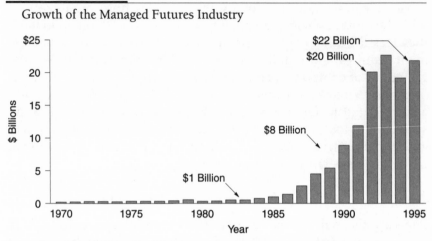

Source: Managed Account Reports, New York, NY.

for each the underlying concept and algorithm, plus key advantages and drawbacks. Next, we broaden the readers' horizons with more creative and innovative approaches to risk-adjusted performance measurement, and pay special attention to the use of graphical views for illustration of the concepts presented. This section also touches on a microlevel review of trade-by-trade risk and real-time exposure analysis, as well as the more qualitative—but still equally important—elements of monitoring and managing traders' risks and performance. The next section puts it all together and examines the portfolio approach to risk management in action. We conclude with a summary of our major points, and a reference list for those interested in additional research and readings.

LIES, DAMN LIES, AND STATISTICS

Many measures used for years to rate money managers are nothing short of woefully inadequate and irrelevant, even when applied with some thought. They are especially misleading when utilized blindly. The analysis of Trader A's annualized standard deviation presented in Exhibit 10–2 (we will have a lot more to say about standard deviation as a measure of risk further on) is a case in point. This trader is clearly penalized by extremely positive returns; note that if the five months with highest returns are excluded from

EXHIBIT 10–2

Various Views of Standard Deviation—Trader A

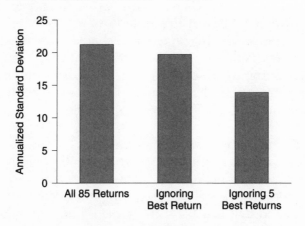

Annualized Standard Deviation	
All 85 monthly returns	21.42
Ignoring best monthly return	19.86
Ignoring five best monthly returns	14.38

Source: Kenmar Asset Allocation Inc.

the calculation, the trader's standard deviation actually *declines* by about *one-third*.

One-Dimensional Views and the Herd Mentality

Seven discrete statistics that purport to measure either risk, return, or both are described below. Some have clearly become industry standards for measuring trader/manager risk—especially by pension fund consultants. In fairness, we must admit that with all their defects noted below, these measures are still a step up from what is unfortunately the rule at many a major bank and trading house, where the only measure of risk and return is that of pure profit and loss in straight dollar terms.

Average Monthly Return

This sums all of a trader's monthly returns and divides by the total number of months traded to produce the mean or arithmetic average monthly return. This measure's major advantage is its intuitive appeal as well as its wide acceptance, often on an annualized basis, which is computed by simply multiplying by 12. It is also easy to obtain this information. In the managed futures industry, the Commodity Futures Trading Commission (CFTC) mandates that this data be provided directly by the trader, and in a format dictated by CFTC regulations. The big drawback, shared with other "return only" measures, is that there is little sense of the type and magnitude of risk borne to achieve the return. Furthermore, this figure may be very deceptive when it comes to total return because it does not take into account the effects of compounding.

Standard Deviation (of Monthly Return)
Standard deviation is simply the square root of the variance. This in turn is computed by taking the difference between each monthly return and the mean (see above), squaring this difference, summing the squares, and dividing the sum by the number of months. This measure represents how on average any month's return will vary from the mean (or expected return in statistical parlance), and shows the dispersion, or volatility, of monthly returns around the average. Standard deviation describes the riskiness of a trader's or portfolio's returns in the sense of consistency, or how likely you are to actually achieve the average monthly return in any given month. This measure is often annualized by multiplying by the square root of 12. As with the average monthly return described above, this measure can also be computed for differing periods, for example, daily returns and the standard deviation of daily returns (which in turn would be annualized by multiplying by 260 the approximate number of trading days in a year and the square root of 260, respectively).

Criticism of this measure is prevalent; we will limit ours to its most annoying features. First of all, in common with other risk only performance measures, standard deviation provides no clue to the returns associated with the risk. In addition, this measure does not distinguish between intermittent and consecutive losses, and it therefore does not accurately portray the actual risk of drawdowns, or losses in equity. But most frustrating to those who are still amazed by its pervasive use is the plain fact that it does not focus at all on the risk of loss, but rather includes both upside and downside volatility. In other words, returns that are too high (i.e., considerably above the mean) are by definition as risky as those that are significantly below the mean (see Exhibit 10–2).

Having said this, however, it is easy to believe that if a trader's mean monthly return is 3 percent and he or she is up 30 percent in a month, even if the worst drawdown has never been as great as –5 percent, more risk *must* exist. Intuitively, you can't make 30 percent in a month without taking risks. In other words, although upside volatility is not as bad as the downside variety, it still is risky, albeit in a different sense. This is just another way of looking at the basic relationship between risk and reward as taught in Finance 101.

Now that we have spoken a bit in defense of standard deviation, let's go back to pointing out its shortcomings. Another example will even more clearly illustrate the ludicrousness of this measure. Let's say that Trader 1 has 12 monthly returns, each of which is exactly equal to –2 percent (i.e., ignoring compounding, the trader has lost about 24 percent of your equity). Trader 2, by contrast, has incurred no losing months during the year, with monthly returns ranging between 2 and 5 percent. Well, guess what? In standard deviation terms, Trader 1 is preferred, because he or she has no risk (the standard deviation in this case is zero). To call this counterintuitive is an understatement; perverse seems more descriptive.

Sharpe Ratio

The Sharpe Ratio—named after economics Nobel Prize winner William Sharpe—is computed by simply dividing the average monthly return by its standard deviation, with purists first subtracting the monthly risk-free rate from the numerator (the monthly return). While an improvement on return-only or risk-only measures, it is still tainted by the deficiencies inherent in its denominator—monthly standard deviation.

Sterling Ratio

The Sterling Ratio is calculated by computing the average annual return over the last three years, and then dividing by the sum of 10 percent and the average of each of the last three years' drawdowns (we dwell at greater length on the subject of drawdown analyses in the next section). On the one hand this measure has the same benefit as the Sharpe Ratio: that of synthesizing both risk and return. However, this measure has its criticisms as well. First of all, it may be unrepresentative of the true downside risk because it only measures the depth, but not the frequency or duration, of drawdowns. Likewise, regarding both return and drawdown, it somewhat arbitrarily restricts the analysis to three years of a trader's track record. Another problem with the Sterling Ratio is its arbitrary use of the 10 percent figure in the denominator. Finally, this measure may also omit larger drawdowns that span *calendar years* (more on this issue below).

MAR Ratio

One computes the MAR Ratio by dividing the average annual return by the maximum peak-to-valley decline (drawdown). While the return component is more representative than that of the Sterling Ratio, specifically for traders with more than three years of history, the reverse is the case with the risk component, because only one figure is used.

Compounded Annual Return and Unit Value

Unit (asset) value is how much an initial $1,000 investment in a trader or portfolio is worth today (this is sometimes called Value Added Monthly Index [VAMI]). As a simple example, assume that after three years of trading the initial value of $1,000 has grown to $1,953. In this case, the compounded annual return is exactly 25 percent: $(1 + 0.25)^3 = 1.953$. The total return for the three-year period is then 95.3 percent (rounded to the nearest tenth).

While compounded return is usually viewed as the truest of average return measures, it is still lacking an explicit measure of risk; likewise with the unit value figure. However, as we shall see in our discussion of drawdown analyses below, a time-series presentation of unit values by period—especially as a line graph —is information rich indeed, and clearly illustrates downside risk via the peaks and valleys associated with each drawdown and recovery.

Percentage/Number of Months Profitable

Finally, while useful as an indicator of trader consistency, this measure lacks magnitude of risk as well as return.

This short list of statistical measures is just a sampling. There are, of course, many more measures that can be employed to analyze trading performance.

GRAPHICAL AND OTHER VIEWS OF
RISK/RETURN IN TANDEM

In this section, we discuss a number of different but complementary approaches to analyzing risk, which, together with some graphics, facilitate cross-trader comparisons.

Windows Analysis

As we all well know, numbers, especially those describing investment performance, can quite often mislead more than they inform. Let's consider again the standard measure: average annual return. Exhibit 10–3 depicts seven years of trading history for Trader A, with the average annual return equal to approximately 30 percent.

Clearly, this number does not tell the whole story about expected return, nor about what is going on during the year. For example, what would happen if an investor either exited or entered the trader's program in the middle of a calendar year? A basic problem is that the measure is based on a calendar year—a constraint that is not usually imposed on investors.

A truer and more realistic picture of expected return, as well as risk, can be presented by using a windows, or rolling returns,

E X H I B I T   10–3

Annual Returns (1988–1994)—Trader A

Source: Kenmar Asset Allocation Inc.

analysis. This analysis focuses on a particular length of time—typically 12 months—and then computes the total return for each consecutive 12-month period in a trader's history. It then calculates a series of statistics based on the entire set of rolling, or window, periods.

Some of these derived statistics include (1) average 12-month rolling return, (2) last 12-month rolling return, (3) best and worst of all rolling returns, and (4) the percentage and number of all 12-month periods profitable. These analyses clearly tend to dampen the exaggerated influence of outlier periods of unusually high or low returns. In addition, they are tailor-made for graphical displays. One drawback, or more precisely a complicating factor, is the need for relatively more data to make it meaningful, since you have only N-11 rolling 12-month periods, where N is the number of months of history for the trader in question. For example, a trader with a track record of 15 months will only have 4 rolling 12-month periods available to analyze.

Many experts consider this to be one of the best syntheses of risk and reward, as it combines in one set of measures the consistency, magnitude, and riskiness of a trader's performance over time. It also overcomes the calendar year problem, and therefore enables one to specify precisely what the maximum annual gain or loss would have been for any 12-month period. Exhibit 10–4 illustrates this concept for the same Trader A, over the same period in question. Note that the average 12-month rolling return is substantially greater than the average annual return.

A Picture Is Worth a Thousand Words

The above adage is especially true when it comes to measuring, analyzing, and managing financial trading risk. As we never hesitate to point out, numbers alone are usually necessary, but certainly not sufficient, for proper risk management. Exhibits 10–5 to 10–8 illustrate the explanatory power of raw rates of return numbers when combined with graphical displays.

The time-series graphs in Exhibits 10–5 and 10–6 depict the actual daily percentage changes in account equity, overlaid with a unit asset value growth line, for two traders over the same time period. While the performance numbers themselves are clearly

E X H I B I T   10–4

12-Month Rolling Returns (1988–1994)—Trader A

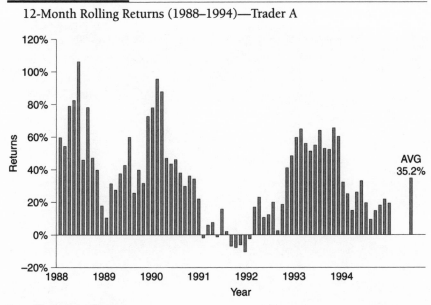

Source: Kenmar Asset Allocation Inc.

material—obviously given your druthers you'd prefer to see stable performance that results in a smooth capital growth curve over time, as opposed to extremely volatile moves, especially on the downside—it is the pattern, however, that is most instructive. What may be perfectly acceptable and normal for one trader and style may not be for a trader with a different style. Here, again, we touch on the qualitative aspect, which we will discuss at length below. Some of this is not easily quantifiable, but with enough experience and knowledge of both the markets traded and the individual traders involved, it is possible to sense and feel that something is wrong, and to actually see it when the pattern of returns changes dramatically without justifiable reason.

Looking back at Exhibits 10–5 and 10–6, we see that Trader A is more volatile than Trader B—on both the upside and the downside. This is not inherently an undesirable characteristic. In fact, Trader A outperforms Trader B over this time period. The relevant aspect of these two figures lies in understanding the why of the volatility of each of these traders and in particular, any outliers. It is

E X H I B I T   10–5

Daily Rates of Return—Trader A

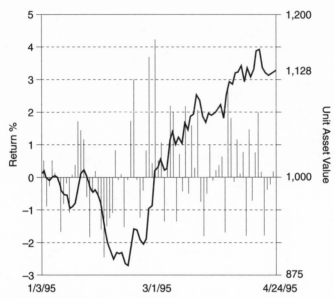

Source: Kenmar Asset Allocation Inc.

just as important to understand these answers for the less volatile trader as it is for the more volatile trader. In general, recouping a large outlying loss is more challenging for a less aggressive trader than for a very aggressive trader.

Notice how we have used words and concepts like *experience, due diligence, judgment,* and *knowing your traders,* for which numbers are just no substitute. It is one thing to read statistics about daily trading activity, but quite another to actually have it presented before your eyes and see how far off the outliers really are. While this is obviously not rocket science, it is every bit as dependent on advanced information technology as is crunching numbers for the latest algorithms and models.

In fact, a reasonably good argument can be made that not only is it easier in some sense to look at the data pictorially, but that in this age of information overload, visual scanning will allow the seasoned observer to quickly discern anomalies that might otherwise be missed. In other words, it can help to both see and feel what

E X H I B I T   10–6

Daily Rates of Return—Trader B

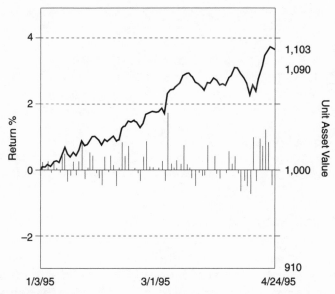

Source: Kenmar Asset Allocation Inc.

is normal and abnormal for a given trader and a given market/
environment.

Once again, we feel obliged to point out to readers how so
much of this is basic common sense. With this in mind, it is nothing
short of amazing how few firms actually use these relatively simple
yet extremely powerful tools to help manage their traders' perfor-
mances and associated risks.

Assuming adequate computer horsepower—which we believe
to be a given in our industry, when a recent survey estimates that
U.S. banks will have spent some $17 billion on technology in 1995
—it is just a matter of creativity to decide how best to convert the
data into graphical views and what time periods to use.[1]

For example, the simple histogram shown in Exhibit 10–7
speaks volumes on what are reasonable expectations for this trader's
monthly returns, and what outliers should signal red flags that

---

1. "Waste Not, Want Not," *USBanker,* March 1995.

EXHIBIT 10–7

Distribution of Monthly Returns (1993–1994)—Trader A

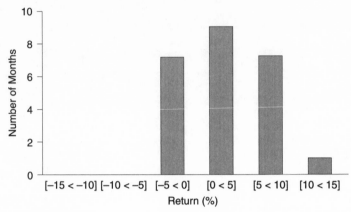

Source: Kenmar Asset Allocation Inc.

demand more-detailed investigations of the trader's positions and overall trading strategy. Perhaps the trader has totally changed his or her methodology and style without bothering to fill you in.

Flexibility is another key factor in successfully monitoring and managing trading risks. Do not be dogmatic or unidimensional in your approach and analysis. For example, even though your specific time frame is an important element in how you do your analysis, you should not arbitrarily restrict yourself to only one particular period and interval of time. Exhibit 10–8 depicts the same trader's distribution of returns, but this time on a daily basis. Clearly, both views are important to prevent the forest and trees problem.

Let us also return for a moment to one of our major messages; that there is no one right number or measure or tool appropriate by itself and in all instances. You must have both macro and micro views on various levels and across different time periods and intervals. This could include anything from the percentage of trades in gold futures that were profitable and their average gain, to the trader's best and worst ever 12-month rolling (window) return. You must be able to go back and forth, and especially drill down when necessary. The trick is knowing which technique is most suitable when, and likewise, what are or are not acceptable numbers in a

EXHIBIT 10–8

Distribution of Daily Returns (1993–1994)—Trader A

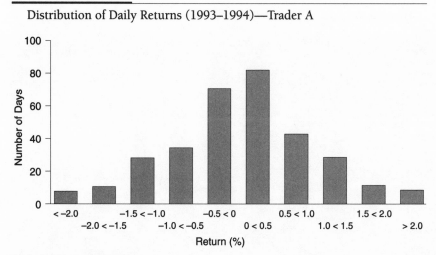

Source: Kenmar Asset Allocation Inc.

given environment. And once again, for better or worse, this to some extent comes only with experience.

We should also reiterate that basically all of the analytical techniques in our toolkit can and should be used to select traders for inclusion in a portfolio as well as to monitor their continued suitability on an ongoing basis.

Drawdown Analysis

Another deceptively simple, but nevertheless powerful, concept is that of drawdown, or decline in equity. The unit asset-value graph in Exhibit 10–9 illustrates this approach to measuring risk. Note the various highs/lows and peaks/valleys in this trader's performance, and—equally important—the respective time intervals in getting from one to the other.

This type of analysis is viewed by many as the truest and most comprehensive measure of downside risk in the classical sense, the risk of losing significant amounts of equity. A drawdown is typically defined as a peak-to-trough percentage drop in equity (as measured

E X H I B I T   10–9

Unit Asset-Value (1988–1994)—Trader A

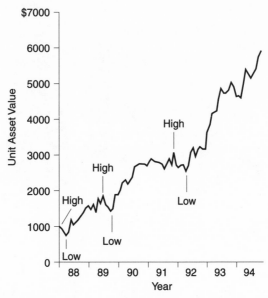

Source: Kenmar Asset Allocation Inc.

by unit value). The time period involved may be one or more months before the previous high (peak) is achieved or surpassed.

Conceptually, drawdown analysis presents, among other perspectives, that of the worst case. In other words, if you were unfortunate enough to have invested with a particular trader at the start of his or her worst-ever period of performance, then how bad would it have been? And how long would it have lasted?

While the graphical display of unit value—particularly when it is labeled with drawdown start-and-end periods—is very useful, when it is combined with a number of derived measures it is unsurpassed in utility. In addition to magnitude, measures of drawdown frequency and duration are also of prime interest. These measures would usually include:

• Worst percentage drawdown ever.
• Recovery period from worst drawdown (to previous peak or more).

EXHIBIT 10–10

Drawdown & Recovery Analysis—Trader A

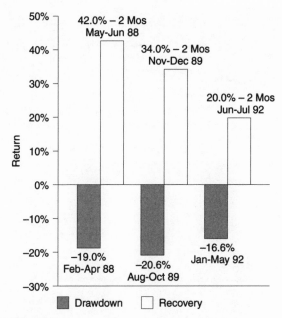

Source: Kenmar Asset Allocation Inc.

- Longest recovery period from any drawdown.
- Average drawdown in magnitude, duration, and recovery period.
- Total number of drawdowns.

Exhibits 10–10 and 10–11 display graphically and list in a table format, respectively, some of these derived statistics.

Replacing Standard Deviation

It appears that slowly but surely the tide is turning away from standard deviation as *the* measure of investment risk, notwithstanding its relatively long tenure. In fact, a growing literature —both of the scholarly variety (i.e., a lot of equations in academic journals) and in the more mainstream business and financial press—has sprouted to suggest a number of very attractive

E X H I B I T   10–11

Additional Drawdown/Recovery Analysis
February 1988 through March 1995

	Percent Decline	Months to Decline	Months to Recovery*	Percent Return During Recovery*
Peak-Valley Drawdowns				
Largest	−20.6%	3	2	34%
Second	−19.0	3	2	42
Third	−16.6	5	2	20
Consecutive Losses				
Largest	−20.6	3	2	34
Second	−19.0	3	2	42
Third	−13.5	2	5	16
Single Losses				
Largest	−11.8	1	4	20
Second	−11.0	1	6	13
Third	−10.7	1	2	42

Source: Kenmar Asset Allocation Inc.
*Recovery is defined as the period from a valley to a new peak equity (or unit asset-value) level.

alternative methodologies that capture the useful aspects of standard deviation without its flaws.

These measures go by various names, from *semivariance* and *semideviation* to *downside risk* and *downside probability* or *shortfall risk*. What they all have in common is that they do not penalize a trader or portfolio for volatility on the upside, usually defined as returns that are above the mean, or at least positive. In other words they distinguish between good and bad volatility. The more sophisticated ones allow the user to specify a target return to use in the analysis, which could be the risk-free rate, or perhaps an actuarially significant rate of return for a pension fund. These measures are also very important when optimizing the allocation of a portfolio's assets via efficient-frontier analysis (using the tools of modern portfolio theory).

Rather than cause readers' eyes to glaze over with mathematics beyond the scope of this chapter, we provide references to a number of useful sources (see especially Markowitz, Rom and Ferguson, and Balzer).

Analyzing the Trades

As we noted above, in our view both macro and micro analyses of a trader's performance are essential. The sample report in Exhibit 10–12 illustrates one way of looking at the details of trading profitability by market. While raw dollar figures are clearly not sufficient by themselves, they still are necessary. For example, it is very useful to know where (and when, for that matter) a trader is earning the bulk of profits, and with what degree of consistency. These figures also lend themselves very readily to bar chart and similar graphical views.

If you are considering hiring a trader for specific market expertise, it might not be a bad idea to review this level of detail. In addition, it is imperative that this analysis be continual, to ensure that the trader remains true to his or her trading style and philosophy.

Ongoing Monitoring of Traders

Even more important than the initial analysis of a trader is the ongoing monitoring. It is vital to continually reassess a decision to use a trader. You must keep monitoring the risk exposure of each trader—and of course, of the portfolio as a whole.

The daily monitoring of trading activity for each trader should attempt to ensure consistency with expectations in areas such as:

- Volatility (both upside and downside).
- Trading size (e.g., number of contracts).
- Margin usage (i.e., leverage or gearing).
- Velocity (transaction turnover).
- Performance per market environment.
- Overall adherence to trading strategy.

In cases where the trader has multiple accounts, due diligence dictates that one checks for parallel performance across accounts. In other words, make sure that all the good or bad trades are not going into one account. Likewise, it is important to periodically talk with the traders, find out what they are thinking, and keep tabs on their emotional stability. For example, during losing periods it is

EXHIBIT 10–12

Analysis of Trades by Market (1993-1994)

Market	$ Profit	$ Loss	Net	Ratio	Average Trade Size	Largest Single-Traded Profit	Contracts Traded (#)	Largest Single-Traded Loss	Contracts Traded (#)	Trades Profit	Trades Loss	Percent of Trades Profit	Percent of Trades Loss	Average Net Profit ($)	Average Net Loss ($)
German Bund	376,167	272,607	103,560	1.38	17	126,963	39	(48,120)	26	15	15	50	50	25,078	(18,174)
Aussie Bill	124,608	142,023	-17,419	0.88	41	69,327	30	(22,341)	52	13	27	33	68	9,585	(5,260)
Eurodollar	136,658	154,594	-17,936	0.88	26	88,119	77	(27,125)	49	7	20	26	74	19,523	(7,730)
EuroYen	219,747	308,012	-88,265	0.17	50	67,303	104	(61,391)	147	16	21	43	57	13,734	(14,667)
EuroSwiss	34,815	35,507	-692	0.98	9	23,447	24	(6,192)	24	11	22	33	67	3,165	(1,614)
Long Gilt	367,909	221,481	146,428	1.66	13	86,064	33	(46,967)	20	13	22	37	63	28,301	(10,067)
Italian Bond	336,611	138,104	198,507	2.44	6	70,373	15	(20,264)	10	17	16	52	48	19,804	(8,632)
JapaneseBond	719,555	417,644	301,911	1.44	3	102,426	8	(57,323)	4	15	16	48	52	47,970	(26,103)
Short Sterling	25,692	158,147	-132,455	0.16	13	17,170	39	(11,565)	14	8	49	14	86	3,212	(3,227)
Notional Bond	1,152,669	542,512	610,157	2.12	30	261,936	78	(144,792)	78	17	17	50	50	67,804	(31,912)
Pibor	286,440	201,667	84,773	1.42	27	67,401	80	(31,590)	42	17	20	46	54	16,849	(10,083)
Aussie Bond	547,537	391,314	156,223	1.40	13	221,692	42	(64,319)	42	19	26	42	58	28,818	(15,051)
Aussie 3yr	181,033	158,189	22,844	1.14	21	5,124	18	(17,366)	30	16	17	48	52	11,315	(9,305)
Euro/DM	76,616	80,373	-3,757	0.95	23	47,413	88	(13,229)	8	11	28	28	72	6,965	(2,870)
Tbonds	390,844	483,817	-92,973	0.81	14	115,154	18	(72,773)	28	16	21	43	57	24,428	(23,039)
Tnotes	10,117	43,886	-33,769	0.23	7	47,175	14	(26,324)	14	2	4	33	67	5,059	(10,972)
Interest rates	**4,987,018**	**3,749,877**	**1,237,141**	**1.33**	**20**	**261,936**	**Notional**	**(144,792)**	**Notional**	**213**	**341**	**38**	**62**	**23,413**	**(10,997)**

Source: Kenmar Asset Allocation Inc.

important to ensure that the trader is taking the losses in stride, that he or she is not altering the trading strategy and risk-management rules that made that trader successful (successful enough to have been selected to manage money for you). You certainly don't want a trader to *increase* exposure during losing periods in order to more quickly recover.

It is important to ensure that your traders employ their trading and risk-management strategies *consistently* over time. That doesn't mean they shouldn't modify their strategies over time as a result of ongoing research. It means that modifications should not be hastily made as an emotional response to excessive profits or losses.

Portfolio Monitoring

There is no substitute for knowing where your traders and portfolios are now, including their positions, latest market prices, and change from the previous close. Exhibit 10–13 is a subset of a sample report that shows this information updated on-screen in real time.

The overall portfolio must also be monitored for risk exposures in each market and market sector. This is important, since even if each trader is meticulously and successfully following his or her strategy, you could very well end up with too much exposure in a market on the portfolio level.

One must also constantly monitor portfolio exposure relative to market environment and opportunity. You can alter exposure by removing traders, adding or taking some money away from one or more traders, and by adding new traders who may concentrate in those sectors to which you want greater exposure.

Another view of portfolio diversification by market sector is presented in Exhibit 10–14. Note how the exposure changes over time to reflect expected relative market opportunities.

The most important message here is that, like it or not, the monitoring function is enormously time- and labor-intensive for all, and must involve everyone in the firm from the lowest-level clerk on up to the portfolio manager. It cannot be done part time or halfheartedly. Knowledge and experience are indispensable. You might get away without it for years, but the one time that you miss something, there may be no second chance to correct the error.

E X H I B I T   10–13

Real-Time Analysis of Exposure

Today's Performance: 0.6459%		Last Month's Ending Equity: $142,452,177.42	
Commodity	Equity Change	Current Position	Previous Settlement	Current Price
Financial Instruments				
Aussie 3-yr bond	0.0110%	198	90.2900	90.3300
Aussie 10-yr bond	−0.0302	156	89.9650	89.9100
Aussie 90-day bill	−0.0003	−5	91.0300	91.1300
German bund	0.5495	493	91.1200	92.0000
Canadian 3-mth bill	−0.0009	37	92.1400	92.1200
Canadian govt. bond	−0.0023	47	102.8100	102.7100
Metals				
Interbank lead	0.0000	29	619.2500	625.0000
Interbank nickel	−0.0000	−8	7,300.4000	7,460.0000
Gold, comex	−0.0793	706	387.2000	385.6000
Platinum	−0.0004	6	423.6000	421.7000
Silver, comex	−0.0030	433	476.2000	476.0000
Currencies				
Interbank b-pound	0.0100	34	1,613.2680	1,618.3680
British pound option	0.0263	200	2.5000	2.8000
British pound	−0.0055	14	159.5800	158.6800
Canadian dollar	0.0154	−274	70.4300	70.3500
Interbank deutsche	−0.0386	157	7,194.2450	7,166.2450
Softs				
LDN cocoa	0.0203	−200	99.200	98.300
Coffee	−0.3521	176	178.2000	171.2000
Coffee option	0.0000	20	13.0000	13.0000
Cocoa	−0.0007	8	13.5800	13.4600
Cocoa options	−0.0000	−27	0.1200	0.1200
Agriculturals				
Corn	−0.0485	922	248.5000	247.0000
Corn options	0.0175	−995	6.7500	6.2500
Cotton	−0.0089	283	109.0900	109.0000
Cotton options	0.0000	40	1.8600	1.8600
Soybeans	−0.0243	198	585.7500	582.2500

Source: Kenmar Asset Allocation Inc.

EXHIBIT 10-14

Portfolio Diversification by Market Exposure over Time

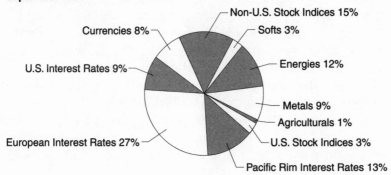

September 1994

Non-U.S. Stock Indices 15%
Currencies 8%
Softs 3%
U.S. Interest Rates 9%
Energies 12%
Metals 9%
Agriculturals 1%
European Interest Rates 27%
U.S. Stock Indices 3%
Pacific Rim Interest Rates 13%

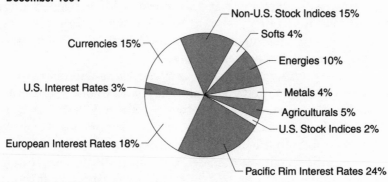

December 1994

Non-U.S. Stock Indices 15%
Currencies 15%
Softs 4%
Energies 10%
U.S. Interest Rates 3%
Metals 4%
Agriculturals 5%
U.S. Stock Indices 2%
European Interest Rates 18%
Pacific Rim Interest Rates 24%

Source: Kenmar Asset Allocation Inc.

Qualitative Side

Qualitative input and evaluation is just as important as quantitative input, if not more so. In fact, the two must often be used in tandem for best effect. You must know which statistical measures are most meaningful for different types of traders, and what is normal for each. For example, it is vital to understand the rebound/recovery capabilities (from a drawdown) for technical trend-followers, since their downside can be more extreme. Their ability to recover quickly is critical in making them good traders. One should also know that these types of traders usually lose on a majority of their trades, as opposed to discretionary traders, whose percentage of winning trades is generally much higher.

It is important for an analyst to have the judgment to know how and when to go from absolute and quantitative measures of performance to relative measures and analyses. For example, in evaluating a bond trader, it is key for an analyst to understand the market's past movement and to have an idea of the potential future movement in that market. Have there been opportunities in the bond market that the trader's style should have captured? Have others with similar styles captured additional profits or controlled risks more effectively? In addition, when comparing this bond trader against benchmarks and other traders, it is more relevant to compare the results against a benchmark that either consists of bond traders or the bond market.

A trader who is up 5 percent for a month may appear to be performing well. However, if the markets have been strongly trending, perhaps he or she should be doing two or three times better, based on our assessment of the trader's strategy and analysis of how and when he or she makes money.

Reliance on pure quantitative analysis alone will not help you here. Likewise, it can't tell you that a U.S. bond trader, for example, who made 50 percent per year between 1991 and 1993 was in the middle of a bull market of unprecedented proportions. What will or should happen to this trader's performance when interest rates start to climb? What happens if the interest-rate markets are volatile and trendless? Can this trader still make money? It is qualitative assessment and judgment that gives rise to these sorts of questions—as well as helping to find some of the answers.

Part of risk assessment and management can be called human risk. Due diligence warrants knowing your trader! There is no excuse for not fully investigating his or her educational and professional background, as well as outside interests. In addition, you should look into his or her moral character, emotional stability, and relationships with other people.

Knowing your traders means also investigating their administrative/operational/back-office capabilities. This is obviously especially important for external traders. You must visit their office, since one cannot measure a trader's ability to administer and operate a business with performance statistics. And as we all know too

EXHIBIT 10–15

Qualitative Factors in Portfolio Diversification

		Trader A	Trader B	Trader C	Trader D	Trader E	Trader F	Trader G	Trader H	Trader I
Style	Discretionary	✔		✔				✔		✔
	Computerized			✔	✔					
	Systematized		✔				✔		✔	
	Discretionary Overlay		✔				✔			
Analytical Tools	Technical	✔	✔	✔	✔	✔	✔		✔	✔
	Fundamental	✔		✔				✔		
Markets Traded	Diversified	✔	✔		✔		✔			
	Specialized		✔		✔			✔	✔	✔
	U.S. Markets	✔	✔		✔		✔	✔		✔
	Non-U.S. Markets	✔	✔	✔	✔	✔	✔		✔	

Source: Kenmar Asset Allocation Inc.

well, a failure to manage operational risk could just as easily be a trader's downfall as any trading loss.

The chart of trader attributes listed in Exhibit 10–15 illustrates another type of portfolio diversification that is very much qualitative in nature. Note that the nine traders in this portfolio are diversified not only by markets traded, but also by trading style and methodology.

MANAGING THE RISKS IN A PORTFOLIO OF TRADERS

In this section we put the various concepts and methodologies discussed in this chapter to work in a portfolio context. Much of the discussion that follows involves modern portfolio theory (MPT) and its offshoots. For those readers desiring some review, we recommend either Edwin Elton and Martin Gruber or Harry Markowitz. The essence though, is how and why to manage portfolio performance and risk via diversification, using an analytical technique called efficient frontiers (which we touch on below).

We start with a number of illustrations that show a high-level, more-theoretical view of MPT and the role of derivatives traders. Following this, we drill down to *real* examples of MPT in action, and how its concepts can be (and are) applied profitably via multiadvisor, multisector portfolios of external traders. It is hoped that this analysis will also help to ameliorate the concern among some readers over the utility of using derivatives traders for their portfolios.

MPT in Theory

Exhibits 10–16 through 10–18 help demonstrate the raison d'etre for managed futures and the whole concept of using derivatives traders, such as CTAs. Exhibits 10–16 and 10–17 illustrate graphically and via table, respectively, how a representative portfolio comprised of 50 percent stocks and 50 percent bonds benefits from both increased returns and lower risk as varying allocations to

E X H I B I T   10–16

Portfolio Optimization—Managed Futures with Stocks and Bonds

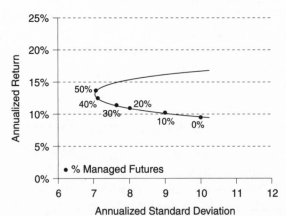

Portfolio Return/Risk Relationships
Stocks, Bonds, and Managed Futures
January 1961 – December 1995

Past performance is not necessarily indicative of future results.

Managed Futures: MLM Index
Stocks: S&P 500 with dividends reinvested
Bonds: U.S. Long-Term Bonds

Source: Kenmar Asset Allocation Inc.

EXHIBIT 10–17

Effect of Introducing Managed Futures

Balanced Portfolio (50% Stocks/50% LT Bonds) Optimized with Managed Futures (1/61–12/95)					
Portfolio % MF	Annualized Return	Annualized Standard Deviation	Return/ Std. Dev. Ratio	Total Return	Maximum Drawdown
0%	9.3%	10.0	0.93	2166.2%	−25.6%
10	10.2	9.0	1.13	2882.1	−17.4
20	11.0	8.2	1.34	3744.2	−14.3
30	11.7	7.6	1.54	4767.0	−12.9
40	12.4	7.3	1.70	5963.6	−12.3
50	13.1	7.3	1.79	7345.4	−11.8

Past performance is not necessarily indicative of future results.

Managed Futures: MLM Index

Stocks: S&P 500 with dividends reinvested

Bonds: U.S. Long-Term Bond

Source: Kenmar Asset Allocation Inc.

managed futures are added. The efficient frontier depicted in Exhibit 10–16 plots annualized return on the Y axis and annualized standard deviation on the X axis.

For example, going from a zero allocation of managed futures to 50 percent not only raises the return by nearly half—from 9.3 percent to 13.1 percent—but also decreases the portfolio risk as measured in a number of ways. We should also point out that replacing standard deviation with better risk measures, such as downside risk, does not change this effect.

Next, Exhibit 10–18 illustrates in a real-world context, and graphically, the heart of MPT as it pertains to derivatives and the really simple meaning of diversification. It shows the noncorrelation of derivatives in general and managed futures in particular to the equity market.

As the numbers and charts show, during the five worst periods for equities over the last three decades—as measured by the S&P 500—managed futures indeed provided a very attractive and positive return.

E X H I B I T   10–18

Analysis of Bear Equity Markets

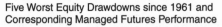

Five Worst Equity Drawdowns since 1961 and
Corresponding Managed Futures Performance

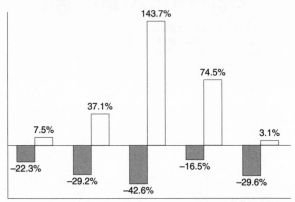

[1/62 – 6/62] [12/68 – 6/70] [1/73 – 9/74] [12/80 – 7/82] [9/87 – 11/87]

Past performance is not necessarily indicative of future results.

■ S&P 500   □ Managed Futures

Source: Kenmar Asset Allocation Inc.

MPT for Real

Now that we have set the stage with some real-world, but still general, examples, we can proceed to illustrate a specific portfolio application of MPT for derivatives-trading risk management. Our last exhibit is based on real data from a Kenmar portfolio and shows diversification from various perspectives.

The various market-sector returns depicted in Exhibit 10–19 clearly demonstrate the benefits of portfolio diversification—the tendency for some markets to be up while others are down. Sounds easy in theory, doesn't it?

In summary, effective measurement and management of risk in a derivative trader's and portfolio's performance have both quantitative as well as qualitative components, which must work together. You must know your traders in every sense, continue to monitor them, and understand what they are thinking about and how they tick.

It is critical to know how to use which measures and when, and to whom they should be compared—to which "like-style"

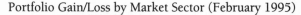

EXHIBIT 10-19

Portfolio Gain/Loss by Market Sector (February 1995)

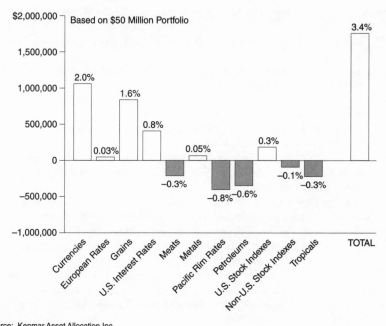

Source: Kenmar Asset Allocation Inc.

traders and/or market benchmarks/indices. You must also realize that there does not exist a single, perfect measure with which to slay the risk dragon. Rather, what is called for is a series of complementary approaches and techniques, a number of which we have tried to illustrate in this chapter.

Finally, one must always keep in mind that these are *only tools*, and cannot replace human thought, judgment, and a good dose of common sense.

ADDITIONAL READINGS*

Derivatives

"A Risky Old World: Financial "Derivatives" Can Make It Safer, But the Word Itself Is a Suitable Candidate for Banning." *The Economist*, October 1, 1994.

"Derivatives." *Financial Times Survey*, November 16, 1994.

---

*For those readers interested in any of these publications and unable to locate them, please feel free to contact the authors.

Figlewski, Stephen. "Innovations: How to Lose Money in Derivatives." *The Journal of Derivatives*, Winter 1994.

Loomis, Carol J. "Cracking the Derivatives Case." *Fortune*, March 20, 1995.

Monroe, Ann. "Derivatives Disclosure: What the SEC Really Wants." *CFO*, March 1995.

Pfabe, Peter K. "Making America's Derivative Markets Work." *Investor's Business Daily*, April 24, 1995.

"Using Derivatives: What Senior Managers Must Know." *Harvard Business Review*, January-February 1995.

Managed Futures

Baratz, Morton S. *The Investor's Guide to Futures Money Management.* Columbia, MD: LJR Communications, 1989.

Chance, Don M. *Managed Futures Investing for Institutional Portfolios.* Charlottesville, VA: The Research Foundation of the Institute of Chartered Financial Analysts, 1994.

Lapper, Richard. "Appeal of Derivatives Widens: There Is Growing Interest in Managed Futures Funds in Europe." *Financial Times*, April 18, 1995.

Lintner, John. "The Potential Role of Managed Commodity-Financial Futures Accounts and Funds in Portfolios of Stocks and Bonds." *Financial Analysts Federation Annual Conference*, May 16, 1983.

Peters, Carl C. *Managed Futures—Performance, Evaluation and Analysis of Commodity Funds, Pools and Accounts.* Chicago: Probus Publishing Company, 1992.

Rock, Mitchell S., and Joseph Rosen. "Does Money 'Barrier' Alter Trading Style, Returns?" *Futures*, April 1990.

Managing Traders

Acker, Bill. "Another Fine Mess." *The Banker*, April 1995.

Eichenwald, Kurt. "Learning the Hard Way How to Monitor Traders." *The New York Times*, March 9, 1995.

"Footloose Traders." *Financial Times*, April 26, 1995.

Gallo, Donald D. "How to Succeed in Business Without Betting the Bank." *The New York Times*, April 9, 1995.

Goodhart, Charles. "Why Bonus Payments Are Dangerous." *Financial Times*, March 23, 1995.

Krantz, Matt. "Brokers Find Reforming Traders' Pay to Be a Difficult Proposition." *Investor's Business Daily*, April 24,1995.

"Pay and Performance: Bonus Points." *The Economist*, April 15, 1995.

"Rethinking Remuneration." *Financial Times*, April 11, 1995.

"Taming the Masters of the Universe." *The Economist*, July 23, 1994.

Modern Portfolio Theory

Elton, Edwin J., and Martin J. Gruber. *Modern Portfolio Theory and Investment Analysis.* New York: John Wiley & Sons, 1991.

Markowitz, Harry M. *Portfolio Selection.* New Haven, CT: Yale University Press, 1959.

Rom, Brian, and Kathleen W. Ferguson. "Post-Modern Portfolio Theory Comes of Age." *Journal of Investing,* Winter 1993.

Rock, Mitchell, Joseph Rosen, et al. "The Right Multi-Advisor Mix or How Much Is Too Much?" *Futures,* April 1991.

Sortino, F., and R. vander Meer. "Downside Risk." *Journal of Portfolio Management,* Summer 1991.

Performance Measurement

Balzer, Leslie A. "Measuring Investment Risk: A Review." *Journal of Investing,* Fall 1994.

Essinger, James, and Joseph Rosen. *Advanced Computer Applications for Investment Managers.* Oxford, England: Elsevier Science Publishers, 1989.

"Pension Fund Investment." *Financial Times Survey,* April 27, 1995.

Sortino, F., and L. Price. "Performance Measurement in a Downside Risk Framework." *Journal of Investing,* Fall 1994.

Risk Management

Arterian, Susan. "Lessons of Barings: Understanding Your Broker's Appetite for Risk Is Not Enough." *Plan Sponsor,* April 1995.

Carey, David. "Getting Risk's Number." *Institutional Investor,* February 1995.

Davis, Stephen. "It's 4:15. Do You Know Where Your Risks Are?" *Institutional Investor,* December 1994.

Essinger, James, and Joseph Rosen. *Using Technology for Risk Management.* Cambridge, England: Simon Schuster International, 1991.

MacRae, Desmond. "In Search of Risk Sensitivity." *FW's Corporate Finance,* Winter 1994.

"Risk Management: Contracting Out." *The Economist,* October 1, 1994.

Rosen, Joseph. "Managing Risk Through Multi-Advisor, Multi-Sector Portfolios." Computers in The City 8. Proceedings of the conference held in London, November 1989, Blenheim Online Publications.

Technology

Essinger, James, and Joseph Rosen. Advanced Computer Applications for Investment Managers. Oxford, England: Elsevier Advanced Technology, 1989.

"Information Technology." *Financial Times Review,* April 5, 1995.

"Waste Not, want Not." *USBanker,* March 1995.

11

ⓖ ELECTRONIC
MESSAGING STANDARDS
AND STANDARDS
DEVELOPMENT
ORGANIZATIONS

Claire Frankel
Vice President
National Securities Clearing Corporation

The adoption of specific international messaging standards—format, syntax, and semantics—provides the worldwide securities industry with a uniform way of presenting and transmitting all varieties of securities information in electronic format that can be easily read and interpreted by automated systems. Messaging standards contribute to an important long-term goal of the securities industry, that of a paperless, automatic, and electronic trading and settlement environment. Standards enable the industry to employ faster and smarter technology, which ultimately leads to shorter and shorter settlement windows, thus reducing risk to both the participants in a trade and to the industry as a whole.

In the last 10 years, the securities industry has seen exponential growth in the use of automated systems and networks, and in the last 5 years global cross-border trading has also grown tremendously, facilitated by these systems. Given these two phenomena, there is a corresponding need for greater compatibility among the industry's systems and networks. Prior to the adoption of messaging standards, custodians and clearinghouses would receive hundreds of messages, all incompatible with each other and with the receivers' own systems; translating and rekeying the messages required time and labor. The need for greater compatibility highlighted the fundamental benefit of devising a uniform but versatile structure and common language for electronic information flows worldwide. There can be seen, therefore, an intensifying focus on setting standards related to the automated information flows among investors, their agents, and market/settlement systems and services. By offering more compatible information flows between these four groups worldwide, the potential benefits of international standards include raising productivity, improving accuracy, minimizing error and confusion, reducing costs and risks, and enlarging comprehension across language and systems barriers worldwide.

INDUSTRY STANDARDS
GROUPS AND THEIR FUNCTIONS

The trend toward standardization in the securities industry centers on activities coordinated within the International Organization for Standardization (ISO), one of the world's preeminent standards federations, headquartered in Geneva, Switzerland. Founded in 1949, ISO promotes a wide range of industry-derived technical standards ranging from film speed to product/service quality. ISO is organized into committee structures that address each industry, and subcommittees that address the various areas of concern for each industry. ISO has been officially involved in securities industry standardization efforts since 1975, when a securities subcommittee was formed within the Financial Technical Committee 68. For ratifying standards and for recruiting the technically expert groups that develop them, the ISO TC 68/ SC4 subcommittee is structured around national affiliated committees in a number of countries; typically these committees focus on national standards as well. In the United States, for example, ISO's affiliate is the American National Standards Institute, (ANSI). It is ANSI's Accredited Committee X9 that serves the financial industry. The ANSI Accredited Subcommittee X9D deals with securities industry standards, U.S. domestic securities standards, and through secondment to ISO committees, international securities standards.

Over the past 20 years, the ISO securities committee has sponsored the adoption of two major securities industry standards, ISO 6166, the International Securities Numbering System (ISIN), and

ISO 7775, International Securities Messages. Much of the impetus for the greater use of these two ISO standards stems from the Group of Thirty's recommendations related to more efficient and effective clearance and settlement systems around the world.[1] Among the nine recommendations made by the 1989 Group of Thirty (G30) Working Committee on reducing risk, were recommendations calling for each country to adopt the standard for securities messages developed by the International Organization for Standardization (ISO Standard 7775).[2] In addition, it recommended that countries adopt the ISIN numbering system for securities issues as defined in the ISO Standard 6166, at least for cross-border transactions.

The ISO 6166 standard, published in 1981, provides a unique number, known as the International Securities Identification Number (ISIN), for the identification of each issue of securities. This code is particularly important for cross-border trades because it mandates a single, unique code to identify any international or domestic security, reducing confusion when an issue is traded in multiple markets. The ISIN is a 12-digit code consisting of a 2-digit country code, 9 digits available for the national identification code, and a 1-digit check code. Because the longest national securities identification number is the U.S. CUSIP, the middle field was assigned a maximum length of nine digits. Countries with national securities numbering systems of less than nine digits insert their number into the middle field, right justify, and fill in zeros to the left.

In 1992, the responsibility for maintaining the ISO 6166 standard was delegated to the Association of National Numbering agencies (ANNA). ANNA's membership consists of all the ISIN numbering agencies, generally national numbering associations (NNAs). The U.S. NNA representative to ANNA is the CUSIP Service Bureau. The CUSIP Service Bureau, operated by Standard & Poor's for the American Bankers Association, was initially created

---

1. The Group of Thirty (G30) is an independent, nonpartisan, nonprofit organization established in 1978 to deepen understanding of international economic and financial issues, to explore the international repercussions of decisions taken in public and private sectors and to examine the choices available to policy makers.
2. These recommendations called for comparison of trades by T + 1, membership of indirect market participants in a confirmation/comparison system, a central securities depository, review of a trade netting system to determine its appropriateness, delivery-versus-payment, same-day funds settlement, rolling settlement on T + 3, encouragement of securities lending and borrowing, and adoption of an international standard for securities numbering and messages.

for the primary domestic purpose of uniquely identifying U.S. issuers and issues of securities and financial instruments within a standard framework, and disseminating this data to the financial marketplace via various media. CUSIP numbers and standardized descriptions are used by virtually all sectors of the U.S. financial industry to facilitate cross-border activities in U.S. securities. The CUSIP Service Bureau has created ISINs based on the U.S. CUSIP numbers, and participates in ANNA's cooperative network which circulates the ISINs assigned by each NNA to the other NNAs and interested parties.

The ISO 7775 International Securities Messages standard was developed in close cooperation with SWIFT, the financial electronic network provider, best known in the world of interbank payments.[3] Nearly 20 years ago, SWIFT decided to adapt its payment-related banking instruction, notification, and reporting messages to securities custody and settlement. In 1984, an ISO international ballot raised the status of a group of 35 SWIFT securities messages, grouped together as ISO 7775, to international standard. Several editions have been published since then, updating and improving on the standard messages in line with the industry's experience in using them.

For a long time, the only large-scale implementation of financial messaging was on the SWIFT network, although many banks individually adopted the ISO 7775 approach on their internal or proprietary networks. Since these were SWIFT's own network messages, SWIFT's technical experience was relied on along with an ISO working group that regularly reviewed suggestions for revisions, additions, and updating. For example, as broker-dealers gained access to SWIFT, which was a bank-only network until the late 1980s, their business required some changes in the messages. The need for brokerage industry expertise as input to the message-design process, in conjunction with the actions of the Group of Thirty, stimulated the formation of industry standards groups,

---

3. SWIFT—Society for Worldwide Interbank Financial Telecommunication. Historically, SWIFT provided and continues to provide a banking/brokerage worldwide proprietary electronic communications network with its own security, protocol, and a message structure based on ISO 7775. Since 1994, SWIFT has introduced some commercial ventures of their own, available over the network that in some instances place them in competition with the banks and securities businesses they are serving.

ISITC and SSAB, whose purpose was and is to advise ISO, ANSI X9, SWIFT, and other standards organizations and standards vendors around the world. The Industry Standardization of Institutional Trade Communications (ISITC) focuses on standardizing and automating information flows between investment managers and custodian banks in the United States, Europe, and Asia. From its inception in 1992, as investment managers increased their automation, including gaining access to the SWIFT network, ISITC has focused its attention and recommendations on the message structure and content, as opposed to the delivery mechanism, for trade settlement and reconciliation instructions and advices between fund managers and custodian banks. For example, ISITC-recommended code words have been developed to fit within several of the ISO 7775 messages on the SWIFT network.

As a result of this growth and cooperation, by 1993 applications of ISO 7775 were growing much wider than the SWIFT network. While this was ISO 7775's great success, SWIFT itself acknowledged the need for wider industry involvement in updating the ISO 7775 messages, and the need to pursue new standards for the industry's information flows. SWIFT, therefore, proposed the formation of the Securities Standards Advisory Board (SSAB) as a means of reaching all users and service providers, including the SWIFT network, and going beyond it.

The SSAB is an independent industrywide forum founded on the idea that the industry's willingness to use new standards is directly proportional to how much the users have participated in defining them or trust others who did.

The SSAB has represented a coordinated effort by major international organizations ranging from the International Federation of Stock Exchanges to the Securities Industry Association in the United States to work together to support standards and to ensure their effectiveness and independence. Whether in encouraging the adoption of standards, or supporting the appropriate ISO-appointed groups in articulating ISO 7775 and related standards, the SSAB's primary aims have been to enable the industry to articulate the business needs of all sectors of the market, and to determine the strategic direction of standardization efforts. The SSAB also has assisted users and service providers in implementing securities standards around the world.

THE TRADING CYCLE AND ITS ASSOCIATED STANDARDS

Trade Routing and Trade Execution

When a dealing firm receives a securities buy or a sell order from a client, the order is usually required to be transmitted to a stock exchange for execution. The U.S. national exchanges for equity and fixed income trading, the New York Stock Exchange (NYSE), the American Stock Exchange (Amex), and the National Association of Securities Dealers (NASD), allow a variety of mechanisms for submitting trades but the trading message protocol must be compatible with the Common Message Switch protocol (CMS) developed by the NYSE. In 1993, a group of brokerage and investment management firms including Fidelity Management and Research Co.; Fidelity Capital Markets; Alliance Capital; State Street Global Advisors; Morgan Stanley; Paine Webber; Salomon Brothers, Inc.; Scudder, Stevens and Clark; and Goldman Sachs & Co. designed a messaging standard that would allow dealers to exchange real-time financial data with their counterparties and with their investment manager clients. The standard, Financial Information Exchange, (FIX), allows investment management firms to place orders for stocks and bonds with the brokers. FIX also enables these investment managers to receive marketing materials prior to trade, trade confirmations, and reports on their market positions. FIX is somewhat compatible with SWIFT and much of the data content is based on the NYSE's CMS transaction data content.

However, SWIFT messages and the business sector's electronic data interchange (EDI) standards are so far not utilized to submit trades to the exchanges. Where a firm is submitting trades to the exchanges, if they are not using the FIX data standard, the message standard being utilized will be an exchange proprietary standard, and compatible with the CMS protocol.

Trade Settlement and Confirmation (Post-Trade)

The exchanges currently lock-in or automatically match an average of 92 percent of the buy and sell sides of all trades submitted to them. The other 8 percent are matched through separate comparison of the buy and sell side data. All trades are then transmitted to the National Securities Clearing Corporation's (NSCC) proprietary

Datatrak System for clearance and settlement on the accounts of NSCC's member firms. In 1994, the NSCC began an evolutionary transition in its United States securities applications, committing that future systems development will seek to apply the ISO messaging standards, so as to bring domestic and international business formats into closer compliance with each other. Since then, ISO/SWIFT messaging standards have been applied to NSCC's New York Window application; this electronic facility provides local New York services for accounting as well as physical securities handling for NSCC participants located outside the New York financial district. NSCC's Money Settlement application, which settles the cash portion of trades, and NSCC's Mutual Fund Profile, which provides price and account information for the mutual fund industry, have recently begun to use SWIFT message formats as well.

Instructions, confirmations, and statements of international trades are transmitted to the International Securities Clearing Corporation (ISCC), a subsidiary of the NSCC. International trades cleared by ISCC are in compliance with ISO 7775; that is, the messages submitted to ISCC by ISCC's broker-dealer participants and also ISCC's communications with the agents supporting its Global Clearing Network.

Securities industry messages are designated on the SWIFT network as the MT5xx or MT 500s series of messages. The MT5xx header is followed by a number of mandatory and optional fields of information. Reference Appendix A of this chapter for the list of MT5xx message types and Appendix B of this chapter for an example message format, the MT 520, Receive Free.

THE NEAR FUTURE

ISO 15022—The Data Field Dictionary

The SWIFT implementation of ISO 7775 message standards is currently available throughout the banking and brokerage communities. The existing message standards, however, were designed with the goal of automating the earlier paper-based procedures. Additionally, the message types have little adaptability, limited expressive power, and contain too much unstructured text. The meaning of a data element is sometimes implied by a field tag, sometimes through its position within a message, and sometimes by a preceding code word. Primed by the SSAB's work, ISO in late 1995 began a new initiative that furthers the evolution of securities information standards. Entitled the Data Field Dictionary (ISO 15022), it will consist of syntax rules for data fields and messages, a data field dictionary structure, a catalog of message, and search criteria for identifying and retrieving messages. Thus, authorized financial and nonfinancial data fields (parts of messages), in addition to full financial message types will be stored, administered, and made readily available to the industry. Its approach is not the substitution of an electronic mechanism for the old paper-based approach, but rather a basic message and data structure that can be more easily utilized by the newer technologies of relational databases and object-oriented programming. The data dictionary will be administered by SWIFT, as the registration authority for data fields and financial messages included in the dictionary. Development work on the structure and content of the dictionary, supported by subcommittees of ISO and ISITC, is proceeding with initial implementation planned for the end of 1997.

THE INTERNET

In spite of the Internet's current vulnerability to hackers, some Wall Street firms are preparing to use it to send financial data. Among other industry organizations, the FIX executive committee has called for open communications between firms and the protocol has been written to allow messages—including equity trade orders—to be sent over the Internet. Current available technology, including firewalls and encryption, is being utilized to protect messages, with the anticipation that the Internet user/vendor community will develop more sophisticated protections in the near term. Internet addresses that are of interest to the brokerage community can be found in Appendix C of this chapter.

In conclusion, as the financial services industry has grown, worldwide organizations, including ISO, SWIFT, ISITC, and SSAB, have been established to consider, analyze, and respond to the business communications needs of the industry as a whole. International standards, such as ISO 6166 and ISO 7775, are now widely implemented; and new standards, such as ISO 15022 (the Data Field Dictionary), necessary to meet today's and tomorrow's financial needs, are actively being developed, along with new delivery mechanisms that will ride the Internet and the networks of the future.

Securities Industry Swift Message Types

CATEGORY 5: SECURITIES MESSAGES

Trading Instructions and Confirmations

MT 500   Order to Buy
MT 501   Order to Sell
MT 510   Confirmation of Purchase or Sale
MT 512   Securities Trade Confirmation

New Messages for Message User Groups

MT 502   Order to Buy or Sell
MT 513   Client Advice of Execution
MT 514   Trade Allocation Instruction
MT 515   Client Confirmation of Purchase or Sale
MT 517   Trade Confirmation Affirmation
MT 518   Market-Side Securities Trade Confirmation
MT 519   Advice of Execution

Settlement Instructions and Confirmations

MT 520   Receive Free
MT 521   Receive Against Payment
MT 522   Deliver Free
MT 523   Deliver Against Payment
MT 530   Confirmation of Receipt Free
MT 531   Confirmation of Receipt Against Payment
MT 532   Confirmation of Delivery Free
MT 533   Confirmation of Delivery Against Payment
MT 534   Notice of Settlement Problem
MT 539   Advice of Receipt/Delivery
MT 580   Instruction to International Clearers
MT 583   Depot Management Advice

Corporate Action and Events Notice

MT 550   Notice of Rights
MT 551   Notice of Event
MT 552   Notice of Offering or Privilege
MT 553   Instruction to a Custodian
MT 560   Notice of Bond or Shareholders' Meeting
MT 561   Proxy or Authorization and Instructions to Vote

MT 562   Corporate Action Status Report
MT 563   Corporate Action Confirmation

Capital and Income Advices
MT 554   Advice of Money Income
MT 555   Advice of Income in the Form of Securities
MT 556   Advice of Redemption
MT 557   Advice of Securities Proceeds
MT 559   Paying Agent's Claim

Statements
MT 570   Request for Statement
MT 571   Statement of Holdings
MT 572   Statement of Transactions
MT 573   Statement of Pending Transactions
MT 574   Statement of Open Orders
MT 576*   Statement of Open Orders
MT 577   Statement of Numbers
MT 579   Certificate Numbers

Securities Lending/Borrowing
MT 516   Securities Loan Confirmation
MT 526   General Securities Lending/Borrowing
MT 581   Collateral Adjustment Message
MT 582   Reimbursement Claim or Advice

Inter-Depository Clearing Systems
MT 525   Inter-Depository/Clearing System
          Receive/Deliver Transactions
MT 585   Inter-Depository/Clearing System Administration

Common Group Messages
MT 590   Advice of Charges, Interest and Other Adjustments
MT 591   Request for Payment of Charges, Interest
          and Other Expenses
MT 592   Request for Cancellation
MT 595   Queries
MT 596   Answers
MT 598   Proprietary Message
MT 599   Free Format Message

---

*New Message for Message User Groups

Swift Message Layout Sample

MT 520 RECEIVE FREE

Scope

This message is sent from one financial institution to another to instruct the Receiver to receive specified securities, physically or by book-entry, from a specified party, without paying an amount of money.

Format specifications

MT 520 Receive Free

M/O	Tag	Field name
Sequence A		
O	30	Delivery Date
M	20	Transaction Reference Number
O	21	Related Reference
O	31P	Date and Place of Trade
M	35B	Identification of Securities
O	35a	Next Coupon
O	35V	Book Value
O	82A	Instructing Party
Sequence B		
M	35A	Quantity of Securities
O	83a	Safekeeping Account
O	35E	Certificate Numbers
Sequence C		
M	87a	Deliverer of Securities
O	88a	Beneficiary of Securities
O	85a	Deliverer's Instructing Party
O	77D	Registration Details
O	77R	Declaration Details
O	72	Sender to Receiver Information

M = Mandatory   O = Optional

APPENDIX C

Internet Addresses of Interest to the Brokerage Standards Community

http://www.geocities.com/ Wall Street/
   A variety of Wall Street information

http://www.ansi.org
   The American National Standards Institute home page

http://www.iso.ch
   The International Standards Organization home page

http://www.sec.gov
   The Securities and Exchange Commission home page

http://www.sec.gov/ edgarhp.htm
   The SEC's Edgar database home page

http://www.cusip.com
   Standard & Poor's CUSIP/ CUSIP International home page

Database home page FIX information can be obtained from the Internet at fix@world.std.com. Included at this address are the FIX protocol spec latest, FIX protocol spec ascii, agendas, FIX committee meeting minutes, application notes, and FAQ (frequently asked questions).

12

⑥ PAYMENT, CLEARANCE, AND SETTLEMENT SYSTEMS

Robert F. Gartland
Managing Director
Morgan Stanley & Co., Incorporated

In recent years, payment, clearance, and settlement systems have received increasing focus from market participants and regulatory bodies as they have come to recognize that the soundness and security of such systems are vital to the health of the world's financial markets.

Payment, clearance, and settlement systems comprise the infrastructure supporting the means for global economic growth. Flows of securities and cash in the global capital markets total in the trillions of dollars per day, and are supported by a complex web of technology. The payment, clearance, and settlement activities of investment managers, broker/dealers, clearing brokers, custodian banks, and clearing and depository institutions employ tens of thousands of people on a global scale and require ongoing investment in systems and technology to support ever-increasing volumes and complexity. Electronic information technology and deregulation have been fundamental factors in the rapid growth of cross-border investing and the development of sophisticated new investment products.

The adoption of free market policies by most countries has resulted in expansion in the number of stock markets to more than 150 in over 90 countries and the transfer of wealth from private ownership to the public securities markets. The convertibility of currencies, financial engineering capabilities, and the sophistication of investors assisted by new technologies are resulting in ever-increasing size and velocity of cash and securities transactions.

At the end of 1994, the capitalization of the public securities markets was estimated at $34 trillion. Supported by the trends mentioned earlier, a recent study by McKinsey Global Institute suggested that this market would grow to over $80 trillion by the turn of the century.[1] According to data published by the Bank for International Settlements (BIS), daily turnover in the foreign exchange markets has grown from some $60 billion in 1983 to over $1.3 trillion in 1995. The primary driver of these flows is no longer imports and exports but cross- border financial transactions. Cross-border investment exceeded $150 billion in 1994 and is expected to more than triple by 1997. The notional value of the derivatives market is estimated at $37 trillion, larger than the cash market. Daily share volume on the New York Stock Exchange (NYSE) has grown from 45 million in 1980 to over 400 million in 1996. These powerful growth trends in the financial markets could not have been achieved without electronic information technology.

THE ROLE OF TECHNOLOGY

Billions of dollars have been invested by market participants, vendors, and industry utilities in the development of electronic systems to support the investment and management of capital. Technology has improved the timeliness and expanded the availability of market information to investors, and has reduced the cost and increased the capacity and efficiency of executing and processing cash and securities transactions. Electronic information technology is also converting financial assets to electronic records. Some examples of this phenomenon include electronic funds transfer replacing paper cash and paper checks, and book entry securities replacing physical certificates. Many retail investors have resisted this conversion due to concerns over security and soundness. The transition to electronic commerce in financial markets is an evolutionary one that is likely to span many generations.

In addition to basic hardware, technology supporting payment, clearance, and settlement processes can generally be classified into

---

1. "The Global Capital Market: Supply, Demand, Pricing and Allocations," McKinsey Global Institute, November 1994.

proprietary software systems developed by market participants and customized to their own needs, vendor-developed software systems with general capabilities available to market participants, and systems developed by utilities such as clearing corporations and depositories to service banks, broker-dealers, investment managers, and other market participants.

For example, Morgan Stanley's Trade Analysis and Processing System (TAPS) is a proprietary system developed to support the firm's trading, market making, brokerage, clearing, settlement, and custody activities on a global scale. Many other broker/dealers and custody banks employ self-developed proprietary software to support their business activities.

Sunguard's Invest-One product for fund accounting is an example of a vendor-developed software system used by investment managers and custody banks such as the Chase Manhattan Bank to support their business requirements. Such systems are electronically connected to or integrated with other vendor-developed systems, proprietary systems, and utilities to complete the functionality required to support the investment and management of capital. (See Exhibit 12–1.)

The Euroclear Euclid system and Cedel's Cedcom system are examples of utilities that provide a telecommunications network supporting trade capture, matching, settlement, custody, and information flow to participants for Eurobonds, domestic government bonds, convertible bonds, warrants and international equities.

Many of these systems are targeted to particular asset classes (e.g., equities), geographic sectors (e.g., UK equities), or process steps (e.g., trade matching for UK equities). There is a general lack of integration in systems across asset classes, geographical sectors, and process steps; this is an area for further opportunity.

A major challenge facing market participants is the interconnection and integration of proprietary, vendor-developed, and utility systems to maximize efficiency, while meeting economic considerations and insuring security and soundness.

THE PLAYERS

Payment, clearance, and settlement processes span multiple institutional parties who play important roles supporting the investment and management of capital. Such parties include investment

E X H I B I T   12–1

Examples of Electronic Information Technology Supporting
Payment, Clearance, and Settlement Systems

Process Step	Vendor Developed	Utilities
• Trade capture and/or execution	• Merrin (U.S.) • Brass (U.S.) • Longview Landmark (U.S.) • Tradepoint (U.K.)	• NYSE Dot System (U.S.) • Int'l Stock Exchange SEAQ (U.K.) • Toronto Stock Exchange—CATS (Canada, France)
• Confirmation or affirmation or matching • Clearance or netting	• Thomson Financial—OASYS	• DTC ID System • ISMA - Trax
• Settlement or continuous net settlement or DVP–RVP	• ADP Brokerage System (U.S.) • Wilco-Gloss (Europe) • Sunguard Phase III (U.S.) • Thomson Financial Beta (U.S.)	• NSCC CNS System (U.S.) • Euroclear, Cedel
• Custody, post-settlement functions	• Financial Technologies (FTI) • VISTA Concepts	• DTC • Euroclear, Cedel
• Payments	• Citibank • First Chicago • Chase	• CHIPS • SWIFT • Fedwire
• Margin or mark-to-market	• ADP Brokerage System (U.S.) • Sunguard Phase III (U.S.) • Thomson Financial Beta	
• Portfolio valuation	• HI-Portfolio (Australia, U.K.) • Advent (U.S.) • Thomson Financial—Portia • Sunguard Invest One (U.S.) • Princeton Financial-PAM (U.S.)	

banks and broker/dealers, clearing brokers, global custodians, local (domestic and regional) bank custodians, clearing corporations, depositories, and other utilities such as SWIFT, the Society for Worldwide Interbank Financial Telecommunication.

Investment Banks and Broker/Dealers serve as intermediaries between the providers and users of capital. They assist institutions and corporations in raising capital in the public and private securities markets, provide quantitative and qualitative research, facilitate the purchase and sale of assets through principal market-making and agency broker activities, provide financing and collateral to market participants, clear and settle transactions for institutional and private clients, and sometimes custody and safekeep securities for their clients. Most large institutional broker/dealers employ proprietary software systems to support trade processing, clearance and settlement, custody, and other postsettlement processes. For example, CS First Boston has developed the New Arc system, investing several hundred million dollars over 10 years. Morgan Stanley developed the Trade Analysis and Processing System (TAPS), investing more than $500 million on development and maintenance over a 15-year period. Small and medium-size broker/dealers use vendor systems for trade processing such as ADP's brokerage system, Sunguard's Phase III, or Thomson Financial's Beta System.

Global Custodians service large institutional cross-border investors such as pension funds, mutual funds, insurance companies, investment managers, and other intermediaries. There are about 20 credible global custodians in the world today. It is estimated that they collectively held in custody approximately $16 trillion of the $34 trillion in public securities at the end of 1994. Global custodians provide their clients with transaction-capture systems, payment and settlement services; custody, safekeeping, and other postsettlement functions; portfolio valuation; and accounting and performance measurement for cross-border investments. They generally employ domestic (local) custodian agents in each geographic sector to process and provide custody in the local market. Global custodians require huge investments in systems to provide multicurrency- and multiasset-class trade processing and accounting services and to link electronically to plan sponsors, investment managers, domestic custodian agents, and industry utilities. State Street Bank's Horizon system is a proprietary product supporting its trade processing, global custody, and accounting business requirements. The system took 10 years to develop and implement. The Royal Bank of Scotland, on the other hand, has selected, modified, and implemented a vendor-developed system, VISTA Concepts, to provide these capabilities to its clients.

Local (Domestic) Bank Custodians are employed by broker/dealers, global custodians, and depositories such as Euroclear and

Cedel as agents in each geographic market for payment, clearance, and settlement services. Information and instructions are exchanged by way of electronic networks such as SWIFT. Even when a local market has a clearing corporation and/or depository, local bank custodians play an important role in the investment and management of capital by providing payment services and postsettlement services such as corporate events and income collection.

Local custodians, like global custodians, employ vendor-developed and proprietary systems for trade processing and custody. Paribas, a large regional/custodian in Europe, uses the Automated Banking System (ABS), a proprietary system specifically developed to support their local custody businesses. ABS has been in production for five years and cost more than $125 million to develop and implement.

Clearing Corporations and Depositories service institutional market participants by providing matching, clearance and netting services, settlement capabilities, and custody and safekeeping of assets. Not every market is yet supported by such entities and there is great potential for the expansion of services by these utilities to bring greater efficiency and security to the payment, clearance, and settlement process.

These institutions invest substantial sums in proprietary utility systems to provide services to their participants. For example, CEDEL and Euroclear have substantially upgraded their systems in recent years to provide computer-to-computer trade reporting, matching, and settlement, for the most part in a fungible (book entry) environment. Euroclear has recently announced that it will develop on-line settlement capabilities that will provide the basis to trade and settle on a same-day basis.

SWIFT and Other Utilities support the investment and management of capital by providing important intermediary services. SWIFT is an organization owned collectively by a large group of international banks to facilitate electronic payments and messaging. In the mid-1980s SWIFT opened its membership to broker/dealers and later to investment managers and other securities market participants. In addition, SWIFT began developing products and services to support the clearance and settlement process for cross-border investment based on electronic information technology. These products and services collectively are known as Straight-Through Processing (STP) and will be evolving into a significant core utility for the global investment and management of capital. Today, the SWIFT network connects more than 5,000 institutions in 130 countries and processes over 200,000 securities-related messages per day. Other important utility systems include the Depository Trust Company's ID trade affirmation system, and the U.S. Fed Wire System.

SETTING STANDARDS

In March of 1988, the Group of Thirty, a private sector group concerned with the working of the international financial system, took the initiative to conduct a symposium in London focusing on clearance and settlement systems in the world's securities markets. The session was attended by approximately 100 invited participants including investors, traders, exchange officials, bankers, and regulators. After a full day of presentations and discussion, the symposium concluded that while the development of a single global clearing facility was not practicable, agreement on a set of practices and standards that could be embraced by each of the many markets that make up the world securities system was highly desirable. The participants also concluded that existing standards of clearance and settlement systems were not acceptable: They were inefficient and generated excessive cost and overt, hidden, and undue risks for participants. By March of 1989, the Group of Thirty initiative resulted in the adoption of nine recommended standards for securities clearance and settlement systems; see Exhibit 12–2.

RISK REDUCTION

A major objective of the Group of Thirty was to reduce risk to market participants. Risk is introduced most fundamentally by the time lag between trade execution and final settlement, including any delay between the contractual settlement date, the delivery of securities, and the final payment for them. For example, the market value of a security could decrease over this period, resulting in a

E X H I B I T   12-2

Group of Thirty Recommendations for Clearance and Settlement Standards in the World's Securities Markets—March 1989

1. By 1990, all comparisons of trades between direct market participants (i.e., brokers, broker/dealers, and other exchange members) should be accomplished by T + 1.
2. Indirect market participants (such as institutional investors, or any trading counterparties that are not broker/dealers) should, by 1992, be members of a trade comparison system that achieves positive affirmation of trade details.
3. Each country should have an effective and fully developed central securities depository, organized and managed to encourage the broadest possible industry participation (directly and indirectly), in place by 1992.
4. Each country should study its market volumes and participation to determine whether a trade netting system would be beneficial in terms of reducing risk and promoting efficiency. If a netting system would be appropriate, it should be implemented by 1992.
5. Delivery versus payment (DVP) should be employed as the method of settling all securities transactions. A DVP system should be in place by 1992.
6. Payments associated with the settlement of securities transactions and the servicing of securities portfolios should be made consistent across all instruments and markets by adopting the "same day" funds convention.
7. A rolling settlement system should be adopted by all markets. Final settlement should occur on T + 3 by 1992. As an interim target, final settlement should occur on T + 5 by 1990 at the latest, save only where it hinders the achievement of T + 3 by 1992.
8. Securities lending and borrowing should be encouraged as a method of expediting the settlement of securities transactions. Existing regulatory and taxation barriers that inhibit the practice of lending securities should be removed by 1990.
9. Each country should adopt the standard for securities messages developed by the International Organization for Standardization [ISO Standard 7775]. In particular, countries should adopt the ISIN numbering system for securities issues as defined in the ISO Standard 6166, at least for cross-border transactions. These standards should be universally applied by 1992.

loss to a seller should the buyer default. The time lag between trade date and settlement date varies by asset class and geographic sector.

In cross-border investment, the trade-date/settlement-date lag contributes to further risks including exchange rate risk, market risk, credit risk, counterparty risk, liquidity risk, legal risk, operational risk, and systems risk. As a result, one goal of the Group of Thirty was the reduction and eventual elimination in the trade-date/settlement-date time lag.

While few, if any, countries complied with the Group of Thirty recommendations in the targeted time frames, numerous improvements have been implemented in clearance and settlement systems around the world. In 1989, the Hong Kong Securities Clearing Co. Ltd. (HKSCC) was formed to design and operate a Central Clearing and Settlement System (CCASS). CCASS was successfully implemented in 1992 based on the principles outlined by the Group of Thirty and includes the following capabilities for clearance and settlement in the Hong Kong market:

- A full service Central Securities Depository (CSD).
- A computerized system of book-entry transfer between participants (brokers, custodians, securities lenders, and pledgees).
- Immobilization of securities within the CSD, with optional physical withdrawal and registration.
- A continuous net settlement system (CNS) with guaranteed settlement by HKSCC for most broker-broker trades.
- A delivery versus payment system for money settlement utilizing the clearing system of the Hong Kong Association of Banks.
- A comprehensive risk management and guarantee system to minimize and manage the risk incurred by HKSCC and other CCASS broker participants with respect to CNS transactions.
- Electronic communication and data interface between HKSCC and CCASS participants.

Since 1994, the U.K. equity market has moved from a biweekly fixed settlement standard to a five-day rolling settlement. In June 1995, the International Securities Market Association (ISMA), which oversees the Eurobond market, reduced the settlement period from trade date plus seven days (T + 7) to trade date plus three days (T + 3), and in the United States the SEC changed the settlement of equity and corporate debt securities from trade date plus five business days (T + 5) to trade date plus three business days (T + 3) in 1995 and adopted payment in same day funds in early 1996. While it is generally recognized that it is impossible to eliminate this time lag entirely, advances in electronic information technology and the development of communications standards are facilitating progress toward the industry's acknowledged long-term goal of continuous settlement and real-time reporting for market participants.

Real-time clearance and settlement will require the players to be electronically networked and maintain relational databases of proprietary and client positions and balances. (See Exhibit 12–3.) The technology to support such an environment exists today, as evidenced by market data and trade execution systems. However, hundreds of millions of dollars in software development will be required by broker/dealers, global and local custodians banks, clearing corporations, and depositories to replace legacy batch-oriented trade processing systems with real-time capabilities.

NEW RISKS

Recently, the focus on risk reduction in payment, clearance, and settlement systems has increased. Electronic information technology, while facilitating reduction in the types of risks mentioned previously, has introduced new risks to the operation of payment, clearance, and settlement systems. Such risks include fraud related to unauthorized access and authentication, system disruption due to computer viruses or hardware and software failures, the adverse response of such systems to stress caused by periods of high volume and other general business continuity issues. At a Goldman Sachs & Co. conference on risk reduction in payment, clearance, and settlements in January 1996, John Reed, chairman of Citicorp, stated: "Technology applied to payment, clearance, and settlement systems creates risk that is not well understood." Market participants are responding to this issue by assigning more resources to the identification, control, and management of risk. For example, Morgan Stanley established a firmwide operational risk department and steering committee in 1996 as part of the central risk management division established in 1993.

THE FUTURE

The investment management industry is experiencing a period of in-tense competition for gathering and retaining assets, facing increasing pressure to lower fees from customers who are nonetheless demanding exceptional performance, and is incurring increasing costs for technology to process and deliver information and to cope with complexity. These factors are the basis for the rapid consolidation occurring in the industry, evidenced by Swiss Bank Corp.'s acquisition of Brinson Partners; Franklin Resource's acquisition of Templeton; CS First Boston's acquisition of BEA Associates; Barclay's acquisition of Wells Fargo Nikko Investment Advisors; Morgan Stanley's acquisition of Miller, Anderson, Sherrerd; Mellon's acquisition of Dreyfus and the Boston Company; and Alliance Capital's acquisition of Cursitor-Eaton. These transactions alone collectively affected more than a half trillion dollars in client assets.

While the broker/dealer community has traditionally been in a strong position in dealing with their investment clients, electronic information technology is enabling the buy-side to level the playing field. Pressure is clearly on the service providers to the investment management industry, namely broker-dealers, clearing brokers, global and local custodians, clearing corporations, depositories, and other utilities, to lower costs; increase efficiency; and reduce risk in payment, clearance, and settlement processes and systems. Technology will continue to play a key role in this evolution. Some of the likely trends in the future of payment, clearance, and settlement systems are described below.

Standardization and Reduction in the Trade-Date/Settlement-Date Time Lag

Countries will continue to strive to meet or exceed the nine recommendations of the Group of Thirty. The adoption of security numbering standards and SWIFT/ISO message standards will facilitate the automation of security transaction communications. In the United States, a standard trade order delivery protocol called the Financial Information Exchange (FIX) was recently developed and adopted by Salomon Brothers, Fidelity Capital Markets, State Street Global Research, Alliance Capital, and others. While FIX is a step forward, it has limitations with regard to cross-border trades. Standards such as FIX are important elements in increasing efficiency and timeliness. As standards for messaging, information exchange, and clearance and settlement terms are adopted globally and legacy batch systems are reengineered in real time, the lag time between trade date and settlement date will be eliminated for all securities transactions.

Growing Role of Clearing Corporations, Depositories, and Utilities

Industry intermediaries will continue to take on additional services to reduce risk, achieve economies of scale, and support new products. For example, the National Securities Clearing Corporation and the Depository Trust Company are working cooperatively on a plan to support the clearance, settlement, and custody of international securities. Euroclear and Cedel in recent years have expanded their services to the equity markets and to trade-matching and confirmation. It is likely that some utilities will merge, creating more efficient and uniform services such as the recent acquisition of the Midwest Clearing Corporation by the National Securities Clearing Corporation in the United States.

Outsourcing to Reduce Costs

Some custodian banks and broker/dealers are outsourcing major processes to specialized vendors to improve service and reduce costs. Swiss Bank Corporation outsourced its data center operations to Perot Systems. Salomon Brothers outsourced the maintenance of its mainframe trade processing systems to Andersen Consulting. Several broker/dealers, including Bear Stearns, Morgan Stanley, and PaineWebber, outsourced the receipt and delivery of physical transactions to the National Securities Clearing Corporation. Outsourcing is likely to gain momentum in future years in response to economic pressures and the allocation of scarce resources to value-added services.

Alliances, Joint Ventures, and Cost Sharing

The ever-increasing cost and demand for technology is causing market participants to form alliances and joint ventures to share these expenses in the face of growing queues of technology requirements.

Interbank On-Line System Limited (IBOS) is an example of a joint venture that has been successfully implemented in the field of transaction and information processing. IBOS was established in 1991 as a joint venture between the Royal Bank of Scotland and Banco Santander to deepen their reciprocal banking agreement. In 1992, the group was expanded to include Crédit Commercial de

France and Banco de Comércio e Industrial of Portugal. The resulting network totals 2,500 branches of four banks in Europe; on this base, they have formed the Euro Banking Services Association for business cooperation. In January 1994, ownership of the IBOS network and operation was transferred to an independent company, allowing banks from around the world to buy into the network. The shareholders of the new company are the Royal Bank of Scotland, Banco Santander, and EDS, each with 31.7 percent of the equity; the remaining 5 percent is held by Goldman Sachs. Of the three principal shareholders, the two banks view IBOS as a part of their banking business. For EDS, with a large funds-transfer services business providing for thousands of financial institutions, IBOS is a natural extension.

Intersettle is a joint undertaking of the major Swiss banks that provide its members with cross-border clearance and settlement. The Intersettle system provides a common communication network to subcustodian (local) banks in 26 countries. As of December 1995, Intersettle had 82 participants and processed more than 40,000 transactions per month.

Eight regional broker/dealers in the United States formed Comprehensive Software Systems in 1994 to share the design and development of a trade processing system utilizing a client/server architecture. The founding group included Raymond James & Associates, Legg Mason, Ameritrade, BHC Securities, Hanifen Imhoff, McDonald & Co., Southwest Securities, and Stephens and Company. The group was joined by Morgan Stanley in 1995. Designed in object-oriented methodology, the system will include a broker workstation, order management and routing, documentation scanning and management, multicurrency- and multiasset-class trade processing, postsettlement functions, and margin, custody, and portfolio valuation functionality. The nine participating firms will each receive the source code when completed and the system will be marketed to the general broker/dealer community. Modules of the system were delivered in early 1996 and completion is scheduled for 1997.

Other Challenges

The continued growth of cross-border investing and the development of new channels for trade execution such as the Internet, crossing networks, direct registration, and dividend reinvestment programs, will challenge service providers and payment, clearance, and settlement systems to be flexible and responsive. Continuing deregulation and other macroforces are likely to change the competitive landscape of the players, resulting in new roles and institutional paradigms. For example, broker/dealers and banks in the United States are likely to evolve into the universal bank model as Glass-Steagall legislation is dissolved. Large mutual funds are starting broker/dealers and trust companies to internalize services and diversify their revenues. During the few remaining years preceding the new millennium, we are likely to see and experience more change than in the preceding two decades.

E X H I B I T 12–3

Interaction of the Players in the Investment and Management of Capital

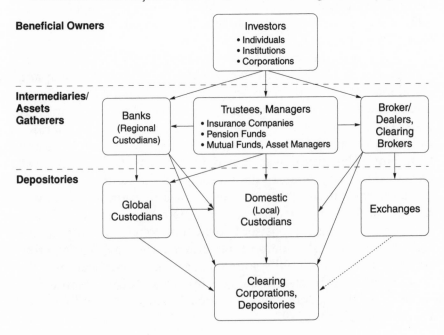

The Process: Payment, Clearance, and Settlement

Supporting the investment of capital is a complex process that varies depending upon asset class and geography. Irrespective of those two factors, almost all securities transactions are completed by the sequence of some or all of the following steps:

1. **Trade Execution**—the agreement between two parties to purchase or sell an asset at mutually agreeable terms.
2. **Confirmation**—the notification to a counterparty of the terms of a trade, including the specific asset description, quantity, prices, any additional fees, settlement terms, and delivery instructions.
3. **Matching**—the comparison of trade records to ensure that both sides of a trade correspond.
4. **Affirmation**—when used in the context of a comparison or matching system, affirmation refers to the counterparty's agreement with the terms of the trade as communicated.
5. **Clearance**—the process of determining accountability for the exchange of money and securities between counterparties to a trade; clearance creates statements of obligation for securities and/or funds due.
6. **Netting**—a process whereby securities transactions are pooled and buys and sells are offset with each other, resulting in one final long or short position for each participant.
7. **Settlement**—the completion of a transaction, wherein securities and corresponding funds are delivered and credited to the appropriate accounts.
8. **Continuous Net Settlement**—a system whereby all trades in a given security are continuously pooled by issue to arrive at the smallest number of (net) deliveries at the end of a given period. The term *continuous* means that once trades are reduced during a trading period to a net receive

or deliver position, any net unsettled (failed) position is carried over and offset against the next day's trades.

9. **Mark-to-market**—the practice of daily repricing of securities against an open settlement position. In general, whenever a party owes securities to another (counterparty), mark-to-market is the practice of pricing those securities periodically so as to have a current value of the exposure to the delivering party.

10. **Delivery versus Payment (DVP)/Receive versus Payment (RVP)**—the simultaneous exchange of securities and cash value (payment) to settle a transaction.

11. **Finality of Payment**—the certainty that funds presented have cleared, are irrevocable, and are credited to the appropriate account.

12. **Postsettlement Functions**—administrative functions connected with the custody and safekeeping of securities, such as income collection, processing of stock dividends, warrant and bonus share processing, notification of rights and tender offers, redemptions, and other corporate events.

13. **Margin**—the computation and collection of collateral to support open financial obligations such as margin loans, short sales, derivative positions, and repurchase agreements

14. **Portfolio Valuation**—the computation of the aggregate value of a portfolio of securities using market prices at a point in time.

NEW TECHNOLOGIES
AND THEIR APPLICATIONS

13

⑥ STRATEGIC SYSTEMS TECHNOLOGY: IGNORE AT YOUR OWN RISK

Lance J. Naber
Vice President
Enterprise Technology Corporation

Strategic systems technologies represent one way of improving a corporation's competitive posture relative to larger competitors or competitors with deeper pockets. To successfully compete, a corporation needs to maintain an advantage in one or more aspects of its business: marketing, operations, advertising, product quality, and/or customer service, to name a few. Technology offers significant advantages in cost savings, quality improvement, communications, and timeliness of product delivery that apply directly to the bottom line.

Trends in computer technology suggest that computing power doubles in performance and halves in cost every three years. Unfortunately, it hasn't effectively changed the average cost of ownership of computers because new software demands more powerful hardware. However, one trend to follow is the downsizing of strategic technology. Many technologies are previewed in enormously expensive, customized forms, but emerge a few years later in prepackaged, commoditized forms that become available and cost effective for much smaller firms.

The lesson to be learned is that if you identify and implement strategic technologies ahead of your competitors, you will enjoy a competitive advantage and earn significant rewards. This chapter introduces various strategic technologies and explains what competitive advantages they offer. Many of these technologies were unattainable only a few years ago and now have become more common and affordable—both to you and your competition. Each has its associated risks. Each offers a competitive advantage at the present and stands to become commonplace and ordinary in the future. Either way, each offers significant cost savings, quality improvement, and/or revolutionary productivity benefit. Let's look at what makes technologies risky and how those risks may be minimized. Remember, there is a significant downside risk if you ignore technologies that improve your competitors.

This chapter describes the following technologies: electronic mail, groupware, Intranets, Internet, desktop publishing, videoconferencing, multimedia, telephony, voice recognition, voice synthesis, data warehouses, document imaging, and ISDN.

STRATEGIC TECHNOLOGY RISKS

Implementation of strategic technologies has its own set of associated risks. Most risks are overshadowed by the benefits, but the risks are still real and cannot be ignored. Let's examine the various kinds of risks:

• **Acceptance Risk**—Acceptance risk describes the risk associated with the corporate staff deciding whether or not to cooperate with the implementation. At one end of the spectrum is the staff that embraces and propels the new technology. At the other end of the spectrum is the staff that ignores the technology and does things the old way. Another element of acceptance risk is associated with management. If management perceives the technology negatively, then it is going to transfer this doubt to the staff and undermine the implementation. Appropriate management participation and support are crucial to minimizing the acceptance risk.

• **Maturity of the Technology Risk**—Maturity of the technology risk describes the risk associated with how new the technology is and how likely it is to succeed or fail. Many great ideas have failed for lack of consumer and/or business acceptance, or due to introduction before their time. A mature technology has had enough time in the marketplace to establish its presence for the longer term. An old saying in technology is "pioneers get arrows in the back." It highlights the additional risk associated with being too far on the leading edge in technology.

• **Critical Mass Risk**—A technology sponsored by and available from a single source has significantly more risk than a technology widely available from multiple sources. A technology has achieved critical mass when its viability is not significantly compromised by the loss of a major vendor. PCs are an example of this phenomenon. Even though PC manufacturers come and go, the viability of the technology is no doubt due to sufficient critical mass.

• **Appropriateness Risk**—Appropriateness risk describes the degree of appropriateness of a technology to a specific application and environment. A perfectly mature technology that has achieved critical mass can be incredibly risky if it is inappropriately applied to an environment. Some factors that affect appropriateness include education level of staff, ability to adapt, management acceptance and support, and the number of implemented technologies of similar sophistication.

• **Ability to Support Risk**—Ability to support risk describes an organization's capacity to provide support to users of a technology. Lack of ability to support the technology is a killer to its success. Sometimes support is easily provided by an outside vendor; other technologies are supported by both inside staff and an outside vendor. One example is copier technology. In-house staff needs to be able to load paper and replace supplies such as toner. An outside vendor may provide preventive maintenance and support for breakdowns. Firms must consider all aspects of support to ensure the success of new technology implementation.

• **Inflated Claims Risk**—A little tongue-in-cheek accompanies this discussion. An anecdote illustrates the point: A few years ago I was asked to evaluate vendor claims for a new technology that a major corporation was considering implementing. After significant preparation in studying the product, I attended a marketing presentation by the vendor. When particularly glaring over-representation of capability and function left me shaking my head, the vendor stopped the presentation. I compared the tech-nical specifications to the presentation and the vendor retracted the statement. After several more of these incidents, the marketing person began to pause after each statement, waiting for the clarification of the overstatement. The stretching of the truth by the marketing person attempted to qualify a product for a situation for which it clearly was not appropriate. The client decided to pursue other alternatives.

Truth in advertising is particularly important to a firm's success in implementing technology. When truth is absent, it can even present a paradox: Technology that is successfully implemented can fall short because the benefits were overstated; thus, it fails to fulfill its promises to management.

Nothing Up My Sleeve Risk—Nothing up my sleeve risk is associated with an incredibly slick presentation of what is essentially content-free information. One example of this phenomenon was a presentation by a major vendor of PBX systems. I was spearheading an effort to purchase a new PBX and had compiled a list of important criteria I expected each vendor to address. When I reminded the vendor that I was not interested in soft information but needed to have technical features and capabilities addressed, the marketing person remarked that they would have to return another day, since no one on the five-person presentation team was capable of having a technical discussion. Apparently, no one had ever asked them to present their system based on its technical merits. Most soft presentations include some factual information regarding the company's strengths, customer service, and the technical merits of a product. Beware of junk-food presentations that offer empty information calories and leave you hungry for substantive data.

Other Factors

Other factors affecting the successful implementation of strategic technology include planning, presentation, lead time, training, and adaptation. Let's look at each in context.

Planning can create a successful implementation by making sure tasks are carried out in the necessary order and tasks on the critical path receive appropriate attention and resources. Proper management of the implementation of strategic technology frequently requires composition of teams across lines of responsibility and departments. Planning helps to identify responsibility and accountability; both are required for successful implementation.

Presentation is critical to the acceptance of the strategic technology. Your staff may need lead time to absorb the impact and import of new technology, time to ask questions and provide feedback.

Inappropriate presentation creates bad feelings and undermines employee morale. Since implementation of new technology creates a significant upheaval associated with change, proper presentation is critical to helping management and staff accept the hardships associated with initial changes.

Lead time can make or break an implementation. Proper lead time assures that all bases are covered and that no loose ends remain. Rushing an implementation can be disastrous. Even the appearance of being behind schedule can have a significant negative impact. Too much lead time results in too much lag between presentation and implementation. Technology projects succeed best with momentum. Acquiring and achieving momentum can be enhanced by skillful timing.

No new technology is successfully implemented without careful consideration of training needs. Training provides the skill sets needed to maintain implementation momentum. New technology implementation creates some frustration as new procedures need to be created and tested and new habits need to be formed. Proper training assures that the staff is ready to use the new technology both emotionally and procedurally.

Adaptation is not frequently mentioned in new technology implementations. It describes the ability of the implementation team to modify its approach or result to adapt to new information or new situations that arise. Not everything can be perfectly forecast; some reacting will be needed. In addition not every technology can be successfully applied with a formula. Some on-the-fly changes and adaptations are needed and will be crucial to success.

STRATEGIC TECHNOLOGIES

Electronic Mail

Electronic mail (E-mail) is increasingly becoming the vehicle of choice for communicating with suppliers, clients, research institutes, universities, and even magazine writers. Most software and hardware vendors now maintain E-mail as a preferred support mechanism. E-mail may be accessed through individual accounts with vendors, a network gateway to a service provider, or as part of an overall Internet offering.

Description

Electronic mail is a strategic technology taken for granted in technologically forward companies. It is no longer leading edge, in fact, in many industries it is critical to maintaining a competitive posture. Integrated scheduling frequently accompanies E-mail implementations and enables companies to waste less time setting up meetings and booking resources such as conference rooms.

E-mail can be made more useful by a gateway to an external mail source, such as a common carrier or the Internet. A common carrier utilized by a common circle of communications can provide a secure and private vehicle for E-mail. While the Internet is less private, it too can be used for communications that are not sensitive in nature and have no consequences if anyone looks at them. One example is reporting a bug in a software package to a vendor. Such E-mail contains no proprietary company data, and it is beneficial to communicate in this manner as opposed to waiting in a phone queue for support that is frequently charged for.

Costs/Benefits

E-mail costs are quoted as cost-per-seat for implementation. The cost for each software license is minimal (around $20 per seat or less). The cost for installing and training is probably twice the per-seat cost. All in all, the associated costs are so minimal and the benefits are so great that E-mail is easy to justify. E-mail requires training and an etiquette, but offers clarity, a written record of communications, easy distribution, a simplified way to maintain a dialogue, and less time to communicate than a phone call.

Implementation Risks

E-mail has become a commodity, and implementation risks associated with the technology are minimal. E-mail is not leading edge, it is strategic, and there are many different viable commercial offerings, most of which offer a common set of features. Acceptance risk is becoming minimal as employees are beginning to see E-mail as being as ubiquitous as the telephone.

Groupware

Groupware is a term coined to describe a group of software applications used to support collaboration and enhance the productivity of a group of people. As a separate category of software it is a relatively new concept, coming to fruition in 1984 with the introduction of Lotus Notes. The marketplace now has other products sharing the spotlight, vying for interest. No attempt will be made here to select or endorse a product. I am introducing the concept as a type of strategic software that can reap major benefits. Lately, groupware has been made attainable to smaller entities by the revolution in computing and networking.

Description
Different kinds of groupware include:

- **Communications**—Information is communicated to people and applications. E-mail describes the people part of the communications.
- **Information sharing**—Information is shared through the creation of an organizational knowledge base. Conferencing facilitation is included here.
- **Document and image sharing**—Storage and management of shared documents provides a facility for organization images and other information not generally collected in databases.
- **Scheduling**—Scheduling assists groups of people with meetings and calendar functions to coordinate individual and collaborative projects.
- **Work-flow management**—Managing the work flow provides for business process automation.

Groupware as a category of software assists an organization to increase the knowledge base of decision making, schedule people and resources to make a decision, and communicate that decision once made. It also provides facilitation for other multistep processes involving lots of dependencies, steps, and possibly sign-offs.

As described previously, E-mail and scheduling are first steps that can assist an organization to move toward a more comprehensive groupware implementation. But it is possible to reap benefits from groupware applications while implementing less than the complete set of applications.

Costs/Benefits

Groupware widely varies in costs and features. Because the current marketplace for groupware is still developing, products vary widely in maturity and support. Successful implementation requires considerable organizational commitment and management support. There are a lot of hidden costs; that is, costs not immediately apparent on purchase but incurred in the setup and continued use of these products.

All that said, why bother with groupware? Big paybacks are possible. For instance, groupware offers a hand in shortening product-development life cycles and decision-process times while increasing the quality of the decisions, facilitating better collaboration for higher-quality products in less time, or even helping to transform a corporate culture during a reengineering project.

Costs to keep in mind include hardware costs of increasing network bandwidth to support increased demand, more server power, application development costs of customizing groupware applications, training costs for successfully using the products, and increased personnel in systems to support the products.

Benefits are simple: Huge rewards await following successful implementation. These include improved quality, reduced costs and lead times, as well as eliminated waste, duplication of effort, and costs associated with communications problems.

Implementation Risks

Systems-management literature is littered with stories of failed groupware implementations due to unrealistic expectations, time frames that were too short, less than optimal resourcing, lack of management commitment, and/or failure of one or more vendors to deliver. Groupware is certainly in the class of software that should have a clearly worded warning label: "Do not attempt to implement this software without a highly skilled team of professionals working closely with and supported by senior corporate management." Stepwise implementation, specific milestones, and realistic time frames all are critical to minimizing implementation risks.

Given appropriate resources and commitment, the implementation risks are greater than the risks inherent in many individual technologies, because groupware covers a huge amount of territory and usually requires some changes in corporate culture. In this case, the higher risks are accompanied by the possibility of significantly higher rewards.

Intranets

Intranet is a term that describes tools used for Internet browsing and access, and which are used internally in a private corporate network. It may have the look and feel of the Internet, but because it is an internal system it does not carry the negative security issues raised by a public network like the Internet. Intranet tools do not currently have a separate market niche. Vendors today are marketing their Internet tools for Intranet use. It is reasonable to expect Intranet-only tools to emerge in the near future.

Description

Intranet tools offer many capabilities for presenting and sharing documents and information. In addition, E-mail (and scheduling) capabilities integrate fairly simply. The newness of the marketplace leaves a more do-it-yourself feel for assembling all of the components of a groupware Intranet. Since the Internet is becoming a more familiar paradigm for many people, Intranets carry with them fewer implementation training issues for companies whose users have some Internet experience.

Intranets can seamlessly connect to the Internet and provide all of the attendant Internet benefits (and risks; see the Internet discussion in a following section). Many companies benefit from using an Intranet as a simple way of disseminating information, such as company benefits and retirement plan options. As an information sharing vehicle, Intranets can be used in addition to groupware applications.

Should you want to use an Intranet instead of groupware, you need to be aware that the software lacks some groupware components and/or features. Some of the components less likely to be found in Intranet solutions include work-flow management and group-decision-making support. These tools are much less mature than groupware tools and at the present are not at a comparable level of functionality.

Costs/Benefits

Using Intranets as an information sharing and communications vehicle is a new, but not bleeding edge technology. Presentation vehicles are easy to use and low cost. Browser software is inexpensive as vendors try to give away the browsers to sell their own server software. The same browsers also may be used for the Internet, without any modifications. This technology is low cost, easy to administer, and high payback. A real winner!

The major benefit of an Intranet versus groupware is lower cost. You get less, you pay less. This can be significant to smaller companies needing some of the information sharing and document sharing benefits offered by Intranets and willing to forgo some of the missing features. Some companies have their Intranets side-by-side with their groupware, while others will have it instead of groupware, and other companies will have only groupware. The benefits for the features that both software technologies have in common are the same: high-impact sharing of information, better quality decision making, lower costs, fewer decisions made on incomplete or incorrect information, and more people informed for better discourse.

Implementation Risks
Intranets offer few implementation risks. Since the technology is relatively new, it accomplishes less than it will in the future. As the Intranet gets more complex, it will have more risks. The technical challenges of implementing an Intranet are well understood and manageable; the magnitude and cost of these projects tends to be easily manageable.

The bottom line is: If you have a need for an Intranet as an information-sharing vehicle, it is fairly low cost to set up and relatively simple to administer. Risks increase as the knowledge and experience level of the implementing staff goes down.

Desktop Publishing

The revolution in printing occurred several years ago. Companies now have the ability to produce published material that would have required a professional printer less than 10 years ago. If you haven't benefited from this technology yet, you have already been left behind. Corporate newsletters, marketing literature, and other items that once were professionally printed can now be created for each presentation in a custom fashion for a really special look.

Description
Desktop publishing software has become a commodity product, although specialized versions exist for high-end printing applica-

tions. Many different vendors offer competing products and even word processing programs offer rudimentary desktop publishing capabilities.

As with other specialized software, producing a professional result is not necessarily as easy as it looks. Many of the software products include templates for producing your own professional quality work. More complex applications require a creative and skilled individual. Results can be dazzling!

An increasingly common application for desktop publishing is the creation of customized marketing materials that have a professionally published look and feel. A professional look increases the readership of your company newsletter. Client and senior management presentations can be produced in-house with a really slick look.

Desktop publishing software is available for both PC and Macintosh computers running all of the popular operating systems. System requirements for desktop publishing software include a fast video card with extra memory, 16 Mb or more RAM, a large hard drive, a larger monitor, and a high-quality printer.

Costs/Benefits

As with all other computer equipment, a desktop publishing setup can now be assembled for under $10,000, and a credible setup for a small company can be done for under $5,000. Higher-end setups can cost more, depending on processing power and capacity. An additional cost is the cost for training or hiring a skilled person. A skilled and creative person can make an enormous difference in the final overall quality of a presentation.

The benefits of desktop publishing are the same as for any professionally created: lower cost and shorter lead time. High-quality and high-impact materials can be produced at a very cost-effective rate. Desktop publishing can help a business raise the quality of its presentation materials.

Implementation Risks

Minimal. Expectations risks and lack of adequately qualified staff are the main risks. Also, if desktop publishing becomes mission critical, then a backup set of hardware, software, and personnel will lower the risks associated with a failure of one component of the setup.

And remember, desktop publishing will not improve the content of your publications, although it can make content-free presentations simply beautiful (maybe no one will notice the content part).

Internet

Commerce on the Internet includes a wide variety of activities. Manufacturers place product catalogs on the Internet and accept orders that need to be confirmed by telephone or fax. Software companies offer support and assistance via E-mail. Service companies place descriptions of their services, case studies, and other marketing literature on the Internet. Other kinds of information available on the Internet come from sources as diverse as NASA, financial institutions, money managers, rock musicians, universities, the National Institute of Health, and others too numerous to mention. Having a plan for taking advantage of the Internet will become a crucial strategic weapon in the competitive wars.

The Gartner Group has defined commerce on the Internet as direct order placement, order confirmation, direct debit of funds, and acceptance of payment via credit card and other modes of payment. Players currently known to be looking at creating these vehicles include Microsoft, Visa, and Citibank.

Firms need to examine Internet uses for marketing, customer service, customer relations, market research, client communications, and research applications with an eye toward more revenue-oriented applications in the near future.

Description

The Internet is a public network whose usage has increased exponentially during the mid–1990s. Once used primarily by defense contractors and college students, the Internet today is used for a wide variety of information dissemination and communications uses. In addition, companies are beginning to use the Internet for generating orders, displaying catalogs, communicating with customers, and for other uses more consistent with commerce.

Although the Internet is a very hot topic, it is not anywhere near saturation or maturation. As use of the Internet starts to mature, commercial applications will abound and those early implementers will have a head start toward understanding how to make best use of this strategic resource. Early uses of the Internet are dominated by marketing, information dissemination, and com-munications applications.

The promise of low-cost Internet access devices as ubiquitous to consumers as televisions (and integrated into the televisions) should drive more and more commercial Internet applications.

Costs/Benefits

An Internet presence may be obtained for $200 per month for a modest web page after an initial set-up cost of up to $5,000 for the design and implementation of the page. In-house Internet web publishing costs can be upwards of $100,000 for the hardware, communications, and expertise needed to maintain an Internet presence. Of course, in-house Internet sites can also be Intranet sites (see prior discussion) although the trend is more to open Intranets to the Internet than vice versa.

Benefits may be difficult to quantify depending on the appli-cations. Marketing applications can measure hit ratios and pur-chasing decisions based on Internet usage. Other applications like communications can have major benefits of timeliness and quality of communications to improve decision making, but may be diffi-cult to express quantitatively.

Implementation Risks

The most highly publicized risk associated with the Internet is security. While Internet security is very important, it must be viewed in context. No site is 100 percent secure, but then neither is a home. If you relate Internet security to home security, you will see that while you can implement measures to make breaking in more difficult and less likely to succeed, a determined thief with time and resources can break into almost anything. Since most security breaches occur based on inside information—current employee, relative of current employee, or former employee—simply improv-ing the internal security of access codes and passwords will go a long way to improving security.

Internet security applications include a firewall. This special-ized piece of software (and frequently hardware) filters communi-cations and blocks inappropriate or unauthorized access, both inward and outward. Firewalls range in price and complexity; select one based on your budget and risk tolerance.

Other implementation risks relate to the unknowns of what audience an Internet site will attract and how you will measure the success of the site. Expectations risk and risk of the unknown are both manageable. Ultimately, the Internet in its current form represents very leading-edge technology with a promise of major benefits, but no guarantees. Even though it has a higher risk than other technologies, like a scalpel to a surgeon, it is a very important tool in the right hands.

Videoconferencing

The next best thing to being there, videoconferencing is currently at a crossroads where proprietary hardware is beginning to be challenged by open standards. The problem with proprietary hardware in a telephone application is the real potential that your caller will have different hardware from you. Imagine if the world had four different incompatible standards for telephones! As preposterous as that would seem, this is the current state of videoconferencing.

Videoconferencing is an excellent alternative to travel, wherever possible. Videoconferencing reduces wear and tear on important staff members and unproductive time in airports and taxis. Companies desiring to make use of videoconferencing may start with hourly rentals of off-site videoconferencing facilities until sufficient need is generated to purchase in-house equipment.

Description

Videoconferencing today resembles the early days of the railroad industry. There are plenty of ways to get from here to there, but the lack of a unified standard leaves plenty of room for not connecting and not communicating with owners of different vendors' hardware. Videoconferencing includes not only the telephone and video screen but frequently includes a white board or another device for sharing notes and drawings done in the course of the meeting.

The advantages of videoconferencing include the benefits of face-to-face meetings without the discomfort and inconvenience of travel. Videoconferencing ranges from single user units attached to a PC to whole room units capable of covering a meeting of 20 or more people. Of course, the costs increase with the capability, although the cost of the 20-person videoconferencing setup is more than the cost of 20 one-person setups.

Single person videoconferencing units work on either plain old telephone service (POTS) or Integrated Services Digital Network (ISDN), a digital technology discussed later in this chapter. The POTS units work with existing analog telephone service and suffer some quality deficits as a result. The ISDN units utilize dedicated digital bandwidth and provide a higher quality transmission at a corresponding higher cost.

Costs/Benefits
Single user videoconferencing units can be had for as little as $1,200 for a simple setup including a video camera, sound card, speakers, microphone, telephone interface, and software. Units that use ISDN cost as much as $5,000. Full room units can cost as much as $100,000. Of course, given the price drops that technology experiences as new technologies are introduced, if you don't like these prices, wait a year and they will be lower.

Videoconferencing pays for itself quite fast if you compare its cost to the cost of travel, especially for three or more people. Besides the cost of travel, you also save the time associated with travel, which for many executives costs far more than the actual trip.

Benefits besides cost include being able to bring multiple groups of people in disparate parts of the world together for meetings and presentations. Videoconferencing is also used more and more by companies to make major announcements. Customers from many cities are on-line, allowing the announcement to happen in many cities simultaneously. Videoconferencing will be widely used in the future and offers major benefits in the present.

Implementation Risks
The primary implementation risk is that you select a vendor with a proprietary technology that will talk to no one in the future. Otherwise, videoconferencing offers few risks and many rewards.

One risk to consider for a single-user system is your ability to comfortably operate the computer. Videoconferencing is no more difficult to operate than a spreadsheet, but that may be too difficult for some people.

One way to minimize implementation risk is to rent the videoconferencing equipment at a location operated by a service provider. That way, your only responsibility is to show up and participate in the call. This can be a very easy way for businesses to try out videoconferencing before making a major investment.

Voice Synthesis

Voice synthesis is a technology that should be subtitled the talking computer. It offers a way for computers to read text aloud; a real help for people who have difficulty reading a computer screen. Voice synthesis is no longer a product of science fiction. Purchase a low-cost sound card and there are various software programs that will use it as a vehicle for creating speech.

Description

Voice synthesis offers a way to reduce the ominous aspect of using a computer by supplying a familiar method of feedback to the user. Applications assisting handicapped individuals exist today and voice synthesis is ready to move into mainstream computing.

Use of voice synthesis requires some programming, since few applications can make use of it. Despite not having a list of applications to suggest its use, it is still presented because the technology has reached sufficient maturity to include it as something to watch in the future.

Costs/Benefits

Simple applications that use voice synthesis are shipped with a variety of sound cards sold today. Benefits include a way for people needing computer information to not have to take their eyes off what they are doing to read a computer screen. Other similar uses can have major benefits, especially when another technology cannot be substituted.

Implementation Risks

Implementation risks are minimal; for example, you might choose an application that doesn't lend itself too well to voice synthesis. Acceptance risk will diminish as the computer generated voices sound less artificial and more realistic.

Voice Recognition

Voice recognition is the cousin of voice synthesis. The same technological foundation that allows voice synthesis is the basis for voice recognition. Words are broken into syllables and compared to a dictionary for both homonyms and context. Despite the number of words in our language that sound alike, voice recognition software can be more than 90 percent accurate, albeit for one speaker for whom the software has been trained. Training is a process by which the speaker provides the software with a base vocabulary of words that represent most of the possible sounds of the language. Based on this input, the software calibrates itself for the speaker and increases its accuracy.

Description

Voice recognition is the ability of the computer to process spoken words and use them as commands or simply record them as a secretary taking dictation would. Dictation software is becoming commonplace and its cost is currently around $1,000 for a low-end package. Higher-end packages can cost considerably more, but even the low-end packages offer high accuracy and ease of use.

Voice recognition is increasingly being used for taking technical dictation. Law and medical libraries may be purchased with the software, allowing firms to replace very high-cost specialized administrative assistants for these tasks. For companies that can't afford administrative assistants, voice recognition offers one basic benefit that can save lots of time.

Voice recognition with a small vocabulary and wide group of speakers is now being used by telephone companies to confirm dialing instructions for directory assistance calls. Other future applications include appliances that respond to voice commands as well as manual controls.

Costs/Benefits

Voice recognition packages start around $1,000 and may range over $10,000 for sophisticated offerings. But even $10,000 pays for itself very fast if the package eliminates the need for an additional hire.

The other major benefit is the ability to take dictation any time of the day or night and have the results ready for use. Many slow typists would prefer to dictate if possible, rather than having to go through the time and expense of learning how to type faster.

Implementation Risks

The implementation risks are few. This is proven technology. Over time it will diminish in cost and greatly increase in capabilities. For now, a state-of-the-art voice recognition program requires training by each user. This takes time and increases acceptance risk.

The technology is reasonably mature and proper training reduces the error rates and makes the program more acceptable. Proper setup and training of the user are required to reduce general implementation risk. All told, this offers quite a bang for the buck.

Data Warehouses/Enterprisewide Databases

Data warehouses are the latest trend in enterprisewide systems architecture. These warehouses collect data across a corporation and across all its relevant systems while they maintain consistent and accurate views of the data. Data warehouses are used to correct problems caused by systems on different platforms, using different storage methods and different data views and summation levels. One set of tools then can access and correlate disparate data to everyone's benefit.

These collections of data were previously called executive information systems (EIS) or decision support systems (DSS). The main difference between these legacy concepts and data warehouses is that current data warehouses use more standardized technology and require less customized software development. EIS and DSS applications involved significant customized software development using proprietary tools that resulted in very high maintenance costs. Data warehousing addresses these costs by empowering users with end-user reporting and inquiry tools. In a way, self-service data.

Description

Why warehouse data? Warehousing arose out of the need to relate data from many different corporate sources in order to make intelligent decisions. In addition, the need to normalize data across different implementations, databases, or customized applications results in significant costs if a customized application needs to be written. And every information request cannot be fulfilled by a customized application. A better way is needed to answer questions and make decisions.

Data warehouses can significantly improve a company's competitive posture by facilitating more accurate decision making using more timely and accurate data. Side benefits include potential quality improvements and productivity enhancements in areas not necessarily envisioned in the initial implementation.

Tools to use data warehouses are becoming standardized and mature. Given the existence of database standards, query tools and databases are becoming more interchangeable. Applications written against a data warehouse do not have to be modified when underlying data structures change, since the warehouse provides a buffer between the underlying application and the warehouse-based application.

Resistance to data warehouses arises because of concerns about data redundancy and access. Turf issues and ego issues become important as individuals who see data as their private province now face the prospect of having a wider audience and more accountability. Warehouses require an interface from each system; the cost and time needed to produce these interfaces can add up.

Despite these objections, data warehouses offer significant cost savings, quality improvements, and improvements in timeliness. Warehouse load programs have the potential to spot inconsistencies in underlying data and can help overall data quality when appropriately conceived and implemented.

Costs/Benefits

Data warehousing costs are directly related to the ultimate size of the data warehouse, network configurations, number of interfaces, number of customized views and applications, and number of users. Sometimes the cost of a data warehouse is justified by the fact that the data warehouse is the only feasible method for relating and normalizing very different data. Some of the associated costs, such as data storage and networking, have dramatically dropped recently and can be expected to continue to decline.

The implication of dropping component costs is that data warehousing costs will diminish over time. Maturity of products and market penetration will also help prices decline. Furthermore, competition among vendors helps to move prices down.

The benefits of data warehousing are significant. Data in the warehouse frequently cannot be found or even created elsewhere without great effort and long lead times. The major benefit of a data warehouse is the timeliness and accuracy of the data. Normalized data (that is data with matching periodicity and summarization level) can be more easily related. Users have a better chance of understanding these data and making use of them.

Some of the benefits of data warehouses are not even known until after the implementation. The availability of previously unavailable data combined with powerful end-user tools lead to pleasant surprises and unanticipated benefits. While controlling expectations is very important, there are frequently hidden benefits that don't surface until the data warehouse has been implemented and used for a while.

Implementation Risks
Implementation risks associated with data warehouses are significant. This is not a project for part-time or amateur systems staff. These projects tend to have long lead times, wide-ranging effects, and require excellent project planning. In addition, a significant endorsement and commitment from senior management is critical to user acceptance and proper application of resources.

Phased implementations are usually the most successful. Keeping the project scope in small, easy-to-implement pieces is crucial to success. User involvement and active management of expectations also helps. Remember, a data warehouse is a living system. It will require active management and a team of tactical systems staff available for user training, assistance, and larger application development. Without some support, the success of a data warehouse will be minimal, because frustrated users will abandon efforts to use it and will seek other means to get their answers.

There are risks associated with the database and warehouse tools. Be sure to use tools that have shown some maturity and visit implementation sites that approximate your company's size and complexity. Use the information provided by others who have preceded you to help identify pitfalls and estimate shortfalls. Data warehouses require excellent project management and a top-notch technical staff along with excellent support from the tool vendor. Avoid scope creep, keep expectations and goals reasonable, and success will be attainable.

Document Imaging

Organizations are finding that as the retention and storage rate of documents continues to grow, no amount of storage will be sufficient. Document imaging offers the ability to store large amounts of documents in an organized fashion at relatively low cost. Immediate retrieval of critical documents will have a considerable productivity impact, especially if it supports collaboration and teamwork. Paper savings, cross-referencing possibilities, time savings, and cost savings all go directly to the bottom line. The future impli-cation of document imaging is that storage of paper should signi-ficantly diminish as electronic image storage becomes more commonplace.

Description
Document imaging is the use of a scanner to convert documents into digital images and store them on a high capacity storage device. It can also mean producing documents with a computer, and rather than printing them, passing them to the imaging system for storage, indexing, and retrieval. The key issue with document imaging is how easy is it for someone to access a document and how long will it take to accomplish that access? Successful document-imaging applications provide reasonable access time, ease, and enable sharing of documents without printing, faxing, and producing mounds of paper.

For some paper-intensive businesses, document imaging looms as a way to cut down on paper, printing, archiving, and retrieval from archives of documents. Medical offices, legal offices, and insurance companies have been leading implementers of document imaging. Financial-sector implementers also include brokerage firms and money managers who need to save huge amounts of paper for compliance and regulatory reasons.

From a technical perspective, document-imaging decisions involve how many scanners and how fast do they need to be, storage methodology and devices (optical jukeboxes have the early lead), and networking issues associated with load and throughput. Management issues include deciding whether imaging services are centralized with a corporate librarian or if individual departments will have their own scanners and control their own work flows.

Costs/Benefits
Imaging systems vary widely in cost. Systems are available to the home user or small business, given the low cost of writable CDs and associated hardware. Larger company applications can cost more than $100,000 but yield cost savings in many multiples of the

implementation cost. In areas in which real estate costs are high, using document imaging to replace large numbers of filing cabinets can eliminate the need to move to larger quarters and can significantly reduce the cost of archiving documents off-site and of long-term storage. Thousands of imaged documents can be stored on a small quantity of CDs as opposed to lots of boxes. Even document transportation costs can be greatly reduced.

Document imaging has reached some degree of maturity in the marketplace and many different vendors offer competing systems. Staying within industry standards for storage should help keep costs in line. Also, selecting a system that can use different hardware configurations will help reduce the cost associated with buying hardware from a single source.

Implementation Risks
Document imaging is a very high-impact application and as a result has risks that can be minimized through careful planning and execution. Involvement from user and technical departments early in the project's life cycle will help to minimize risks. Communications and training are essential, and lots of issues arise outside of the technical arena.

Implementation issues are significant in terms of the policies and procedures by which documents are imaged and archived. One way to minimize risk is to start with a small pilot project, try out the new procedures, the hardware and software, and settle everything down before going to wider distribution.

Planning is really key to successfully implementing imaging. Next, a working partnership with a capable vendor is essential. Involving the affected departments and getting their cooperation and feedback should have a big impact. Having the proper networking environment in place and dealing with the human factors is important. Document imaging succeeds best with hands-on project management and lots of cooperation.

Telephony

Telephony is the merging of telephone and computer-network technology. It offers the potential to add value to telephone usage by making databases available to outgoing and incoming telephone calls.

Description

The reality of business-grade telephone systems and PBXs is that telephone technology is starting to take on the characteristics of PC technology. That is, a supply of generic, interchangeable parts accompanied by some off-the-shelf software is starting to enable telephone systems to become commodity products. As telephone systems standardize, products will be differentiated by the add-on products and services that integrate various telephone-based services such as voice mail, voice response systems, and telephony.

Telephony applications enable the use of resources from the local area network working in an integrated fashion with the telephone system. Some examples of this application follow.

For marketing, your computer could show information relating to a caller on the incoming call prior to picking up the phone. For client support, as the phone rings, the computer display could show current issues relating to a client, enabling such responsive proactive support that the client thinks his or her account is your most important. Other telephony technology incorporates the capabilities of voice mail for supporting projects such as client satisfaction surveys or corporate opinion surveys.

Costs/Benefits

Telephony costs vary depending on the telephone system, local area network design and operating system, and the complexity and customization of the application. Two different types of software are fighting for standardization, one championed by Microsoft and the other by Novell. For now, the applications tend to have proprietary components in order to work with each PBX, and as a result the incremental cost requires an impact on 20 or more people to be cost effective.

For some applications, such as customer service, telephony saves time on the telephone and can dramatically reduce costs associated with the number of calls each customer service representative can handle in a day. For those applications, the savings far outweigh the costs.

Given the number of telephony components, the need for proprietary interfaces, and the newness of the software, it is impossible to quote costs in a generic sense. As the technology matures, the costs will diminish as will the number of proprietary components.

Implementation Risks

Risks associated with telephony implementations tend to be higher than with many other technologies. The technology is fairly early in its development cycle and tends to have more proprietary components than other more mature technologies. Working with an established vendor who can demonstrate working sites with similar applications helps to avoid being the pioneer for the vendor.

Communications within the company and training are crucial, since telephony represents a complete change in focus and direction. Understanding and buy-in from the corporate environment is crucial to the success of these leading-edge applications.

Multimedia

Full motion video and sound are beginning to make their way to the desktop as presentation vehicles, presentation aids, and training solutions. More business applications for multimedia will be appearing as the CD-ROM drive becomes a necessity on business computers. The multimedia computer that today is primarily a home computer for playing sophisticated games is expected to have a significant impact on business in the future.

Description

A multimedia-capable computer has the ability to play full motion video with stereo sound on a computer. Since multimedia requires huge amounts of disk storage, CD-ROM devices (and other optical disks) are one way of making multimedia available on a large scale. Multimedia is a high-impact presentation method, enabling you to make a personal presentation to many different people by storing your presentation on a CD.

Some uses for multimedia include interactive catalogs that incorporate product demos with music and voice-overs (like a television commercial), retirement plans that use interactive multimedia CDs to help plan members select investment options, commercial real estate that now can be viewed from the comfort of your office with video walkthroughs, and other uses too numerous to mention.

Costs/Benefits

The cost of producing a multimedia presentation suitable for production on a CD can approach the cost of a set of television commercials. Producing multimedia materials may be too costly for many. However, the cost of a multimedia-capable PC is now just a few hundred dollars more than a standard PC. It allows you to view multimedia CDs, produced by other companies, for many time-saving applications.

Multimedia computers will become a part of the standard business tool set, especially when personal video conferencing and telephony become more common. Larger companies already produce their own multimedia CDs; as with other technology, multimedia is becoming less costly and is more affordable for other companies.

Implementation Risks

There are few risks associated with producing a multimedia presentation when working with a professional service. Risks increase when you produce that presentation in-house; unless the in-house personnel have the equipment and expertise, then the risks should be the same as with a professional presentation.

There are no real risks of purchasing a multimedia-capable PC. These PCs are becoming commonplace and are a standard part of the business toolset.

ISDN

The digital telephone revolution is starting. One day in the not-so-distant future, noisy and slow analog telephone lines will be replaced by the crystal-clear digital capability of ISDN. The Integrated Services Digital Network (ISDN) is the first step in what will be a revolution in the telephone. Telephones will do much more than just carry voice; it is conceivable that the telephone could incorporate features of other appliances and have a more central role in people's lives.

Description

ISDN is fully digital telephone. It is to the analog telephone what CDs are to vinyl records. The analog telephone is not vastly different from the telephone invented by Alexander Graham Bell. ISDN uses the same two wires that analog telephones use, but splits them into two crystal-clear channels. This is called basic rate ISDN. The user gets two telephone numbers and can use the two lines separately or together. For separate use, ISDN can simultaneously carry voice and data. With combined use, the data rate can be doubled.

Primary rate ISDN provides 24 digital channels for any combination of voice and data transmissions. Like basic rate ISDN, channels can be combined for increased speed. Currently, there is much confusion in the market by the service providers of ISDN; not everyone who can receive analog telephone service can get ISDN. It requires a specific proximity to a digital-capable central office. Customer service and pricing is still iffy, but the rewards of scoring ISDN are really worth the effort.

Initial uses for ISDN include dedicated applications like telecommuting, remote office networking, Internet use, videoconferencing, and other data intensive applications requiring lots of bandwidth. Future uses for ISDN will include the standard telephone. Digital technology offers the ability to isolate interference and other uncontrollable phenomena affecting the quality of the signal. The standard use of a telephone line to simultaneously carry on a normal conversation while transmitting data in the unused bandwidth will become more commonplace. PBXs offer digital capability in a more proprietary format. The explosion of capability accompanied by the shrinking of costs will eventually force the issue.

Anyone who has used a standard modem has had the opportunity to wait 45 seconds or more for the modem to handshake and secure a connection. For short uses, such as a remote office burst E-mail on-demand application, ISDN can dial, connect, transmit, confirm, and disconnect in less time. An on-demand application initiates a connection based on a condition, such as a piece of E-mail being ready to send. It initiates its connection, performs its duties and disconnects automatically. ISDN provides an inexpensive way to make this method of communication fast and reliable.

Costs/Benefits
ISDN provides low cost, high speed, high reliability voice and data capabilities. It requires an ISDN capable modem, currently around twice the price of a 28.8K modem. Over time the price will drop and I expect ISDN to eventually replace current telephone service everywhere. Until then, expect some inconvenience in ordering, inconsistent pricing, and less than admirable customer service, unless you are one of the lucky customers where the service provider has gotten its act together.

The direct cost of basic-rate ISDN varies from around two to three times the standard analog telephone rate plus, in some cases, a usage charge by time or data volume. Since the line is totally digital, the phone company has the ability to meter it and charge by use, as opposed to time charges by analog phones.

Quality, speed, and convenience make ISDN a must for serious telecommuting, Internet use, or other data-transmission applications. It is cost effective and the technology is mature and reliable.

Implementation Risks

Most of the implementation risks associated with ISDN are associated with the difficulty of obtaining and setting up service. If you know someone who has successfully installed ISDN, you have a much better shot. Hopefully, demand for ISDN and experience by the service providers will simplify ISDN ordering and installation.

Once the line is successfully installed, the station equipment needs to be configured and tested. Recent literature suggests that this process is not always completely smooth. Given enough time, patience and, if necessary, assistance, ISDN can offer major benefits. Once the installation is complete, ISDN offers very minimal risks.

⑥ TELECOMMUNICATIONS AND COMPETITIVE ADVANTAGE

Michael Frank
Managing Director of Information Systems
ESI Securities Company

> Competition . . . the effort of two or more parties acting independently to secure the business of a third party by offering the most favorable terms.
>
> —*Merriam Webster's Collegiate Dictionary*

> The clock, and not the steam engine, is the key machine of the Industrial Age.
>
> —Lewis Mumford

A brokerage client who buys a few shares of stock is rarely aware of the mechanics that underlie the transaction. The introducing broker, executing broker, floor brokers, specialist, contrabrokers, clearinghouses, and banks that may get involved in execution and settlement are more or less unseen by the client. "Why are my fees so high?" is a natural question to ask of financial service providers. Explaining the mechanics is one answer, but finding ways to process more efficiently, thereby lowering transaction fees is a better response.

Not long ago, mainframe systems, isolated from the world, could provide efficiency by processing vast quantities of internal data. But the days of glass house computing are behind us. Today, information can be quickly and instantly shared among computer systems serving clients, correspondents, business partners, and service providers. This integration of transaction processing capabilities is made possible by telecommunications. Someday, historians may recognize telecommunications as the key technology of the computer age. In this chapter, we examine the use of communications technology to boost efficiency and to open new markets.

TELECOMMUNICATIONS AND THE STRATEGIC PLAN

Because of not daring to be ahead of the world, one becomes leader of the world.

—Lao Tzu

Quantity has a quality all its own.

—Josef Stalin

Technological solutions have a landscape-altering effect on a business. Because of increased efficiency, transaction costs are typically reduced. More than likely, customer demand or competitive pressure will force the savings to be passed on to the client. Thus, firms that embrace technology often find that a low volume/high price business is quickly transformed into a high volume/low price business. Inevitably, large scale introduction of new technologies has an impact on organizational structure, financial performance, and client relationships. It is therefore imperative that change be managed by the boardroom and not the back room.

The first step in devising an automation plan is to analyze customer needs. If you have a vocal client community, or a means of polling client opinion, you may already have specific automation requirements. However, knowing what the customers are asking for is not the same as knowing what they need. Very often, ways of improving efficiency are not immediately obvious to either the provider or the consumer. A joint study may identify procedures that are labor intensive, error prone, or expensive. These are the true targets for automation. You may also find that simply making your services more accessible provides an opportunity for revenue enhancement.

In the process of polling clients, it is key to identify their technical capabilities. It would be useless to build a sophisticated on-line system if your clients cannot take advantage of it. For example, if your technical solution requires a TCP/IP network, but your client only supports X.25, you may be making an expensive mistake. Unless your firm is a major market force, you need to meet your clients on their terms.

Businesses both produce and consume. It is as important to examine relationships with product and service providers as it is to talk with clients; a dollar of cost savings or a dollar of revenue is still a dollar on the bottom line. Every exchange of information with a supplier or service provider is fertile ground for automation.

One other area needs to be considered—internal efficiency. Lowering costs should be part of the overall strategy to increase competitiveness. At worst, lower costs will improve profitability. At best, they will allow the firm to remain competitive at lower price points and to weather bad times. Even technologically sophisticated firms often neglect to consider the inefficiencies of their internal operations. Study the paper flow in your back office or accounting area to identify areas for cost savings. Track the flow of a sample transaction from initial call to final payment. Figure out what a trading assistant does all day. A bit of honest introspection can reveal many routes to greater productivity.

The next step is to survey the competition. Understanding what competitors are up to will help identify competitive risk, as well as helping to size up opportunity. Information on competitors can be gleaned from trade magazines, consultants, clients, or personal contacts. The reader is urged to use only legal means to obtain competitive data.

At this point, specific opportunities should have been identified. Internal analysis of each opportunity can now begin. The analysis should include marketing, technical, financial, and human resources input. The process may require many iterations: A proposed technical solution may be too expensive to justify based on projected revenues, and may therefore need to be revisited. All participants in the process should reach a consensus on the impact of a proposed change.

At the end of the day, opportunities should be ranked according to cost, market risk/opportunity, and organizational impact. It is then up to the decision makers to select a course of action. See Exhibit 14-1.

E X H I B I T 14–1

Technology Decision Matrix

Business Aspects	What are clients asking for?
	What do they really need?
	What are clients technically capable of?
	How can vendors be more efficient?
	What are our internal processes? Are our internal processes efficient?
Competitive Aspects	Who are our competitors?
	What are our competitors doing?
	What are their capabilities?
Risk	Can someone else fill our clients' needs?
	Can we succeed technologically?
	Can we offer new services profitably?
Marketing Aspects	What pricing is acceptable?
	How much revenue is at risk?
	Are there new marketing opportunities?
	How much volume/revenue can be gained?
Technical Aspects	What is our current technical capability?
	What are the potential applications?
Financial Aspects	What are our costs?
	How much can we invest?
	What is the effect of altered pricing?
Organizational Aspects	Is staffing adequate?
	What training is needed?
	Are changes to the organization chart required?
	What are the human resource costs?
	What is the impact on corporate culture?

FROM THE BOARDROOM TO THE
BACK ROOM—IMPLEMENTATION ISSUES

Your true choice.

—AT&T advertisement

Don't fight forces—use them.

—R. Buckminster Fuller

In the process of strategic planning, specific business objectives are defined. Objectives should be owned by the line manager who is accountable for their success, both technically and financially. This manager will be responsible for developing a set of functional requirements that define the operation of the system from a user's perspective.

Functional requirements should then be reviewed by the technical staff to develop time and cost of implementation. This process may be iterative: Functionality will be added or removed based on the budget, time, and risk.

Organizations that are new to technical development generally have a very rough time with the scheduling and budgeting process. A combination of inexperience, optimism, and wishful thinking can result in a project that is over-budget and far behind schedule. It is a good idea to regard initial estimates skeptically, as technology projects are notoriously prone to cost overruns. For this reason, it is important to have a quality time-tracking and cost-control system in place at the outset of a project.

One of the key factors to successful implementation is the ability to manage the telephone companies you deal with. Not too long ago, most telecom services were provided by AT&T. Today, there is a choice of vendors for almost every service. That places more responsibility on the customer, but also provides the opportunity for competitive pricing. These are some of the things you need to know:

- Most vendors offer similar services. Although there are subtle differences in pricing, service quality, and product offering, there are no longer monopolies in the communications business. Comparison shopping is obligatory.
- Prices can be negotiated. Telecom pricing used to be one of the most regulated areas of the economy. It is now one of

the most competitive. If you are buying services in even modest quantity, it is generally possible to get a deal or a term discount.

- Delivery time is unpredictable. Thirty days is typical for most line installations. If you require accelerated delivery, expect quality to suffer.

- Don't expect your phone company to be especially sensitive to your needs. Your provider probably has an overall standard of 99.9 percent availability. However, if the .1 percent happens to be your line, you are out of service 100 percent of the time. It's all a matter of perspective.

- Because many vendors must cooperate to provide even simple services, problem resolution can be a frustrating process. Denial and finger-pointing are to be expected.

- Vendors will charge you if you dispatch them to repair a problem, and they determine that they are not at fault. "No trouble found" calls will be the largest component of your repair costs.

- Phone companies generally don't provide inside wiring, and where they do the quality is often poor. You should arrange for your own electricians for this piece of the job.

- You may lose money, your job, or your whole business as the result of a line failure, but the vendor cannot be made to reimburse you for more than the line charges.

- Telecom personnel tend to move around rapidly, due to the growth of the industry. Your relationship with the company providing the service should extend beyond the individual sales rep.

Line installation is usually only a small piece of the overall project plan, although it can be the slowest part of the process. Typically, there is software development and hardware installation that must be completed as well. This work can go on while waiting for the line to be installed by the use of dial-up modems. Remember the equation TIME = MONEY^N, where N is the number of tasks in the queue. The goal of good project management is to keep all resources as fully occupied as possible.

Technical management must keep the responsible line manager informed of progress, delays, and changes to the schedule. It is the responsibility of the line manager to ensure that this information is communicated among all interested parties. It is also the line manager's responsibility to ensure that an acceptance testing procedure is in place once the project is completed.

FROM THE BOARDROOM TO THE BACK ROOM—MANAGEMENT ISSUES

Quality requires minute attention to detail . . . personal involvement is essential.

—David Packard

If I dialed a wrong number, how come you answered the phone?
—from a James Thurber cartoon

Once a telecommunications system is in production, further issues need to be addressed. These include security, network management, cost control, and charge back.

Providers of financial services must be especially concerned about security. There is an element of trust between a customer and a financial institution which, once breached, cannot be repaired. In addition, it is easier to move large quantities of money and securities electronically than physically.

Here are a few general rules of thumb for providing electronic security:

- Something they know, something they have. To gain access to a secure system, a client should have unique knowledge of some bit of information and physical access to something that is available only to legitimate users. For example, it is possible for a network to be secured with encryption devices. Only terminals with a correctly configured encryption device can gain access. This is the something they have. A client logging onto such a terminal may be required to enter a unique password (something they know).
- There are intruders out there who are smarter than you are, and they want access to your system. Security is not a good field for overconfident people.

- There are many consultants who can help you with security issues, for a price. There are intruders out there who are smarter than your consultants.
- Electronic attacks come from unexpected directions. Do you erase your expired back-up tapes? Shred security-related information prior to disposal?
- The most damaging security breaches are internal. Your own personnel know what's vulnerable and what isn't. They have legitimate access to your systems and know how your internal procedures work. Are they bonded? Are your internal audit controls adequate?

It is also important to staff the network management function adequately. When an electronic link fails, it can be difficult or impossible to continue working manually. For this reason, the network must be monitored continuously. In the event of a fault, there must be adequate means to provide rapid restoral of service.

Typically, a network operations center or help-desk monitors circuits, modems, and routers electronically. The vendor of your telecommunications equipment should be able to provide tools for this purpose. In the event a circuit fails, the network operator should be able to restore service using dial backup capabilities or alternative services. Service contracts should be in place with all major vendors to provide repair and restoral for the various network components.

At the end of every month, despite your fondest wishes, you will be getting bills from equipment vendors, telephone companies, and consultants. You will need some controls for tracking costs. Internally, you want to be able to attribute costs to the projects and departments that incur them. This will allow measuring the effectiveness and profitability of your electronic initiatives. Externally, you may need to generate billing to clients for services rendered.

It is necessary to carefully monitor telephone company billing. Telephone billing is confusing and obscure. Each piece of a circuit may be billed individually, service can be billed late, repair charges can be difficult to track, and administrative charges can be misapplied. In addition, tariffs may be applied incorrectly or the bill can be plain wrong. As your operation grows, it will become necessary to apply resources to the task of keeping your vendors honest and accurate. There are auditors and consultants who can do this on your behalf, but they frequently work on a contingency basis, keeping a large percentage of the errors they find and correct.

THE INTERNET

Every separation is a link.

—Simone Weil

Reforms are less to be dreaded than revolutions, for they cause less reaction.

—Mr. Justice Darling

The public Internet has been around for many years, but has only recently received major media attention. In concept, it is a set of interconnected TCP/IP networks, all offering a common set of services. These networks may be operated by anyone with the resources, and entering the Internet at any point enables a participant to access any part of the net.

The design of the Internet is very open, in part because it was originally conceived to support academic research. A message sent through the net can traverse any available path, and link any sender with any receiver. Because the total number of participants in the Internet is in the millions, it is easy to see why there is so much interest in using it to market electronic services.

Of the facilities available on Internet, World Wide Web has received the most publicity. The Web is a teletext facility which allows exchange of information in graphical format. It is well suited to consumer marketing and information exchange.

Internet security has been a topic that has drawn much attention. Using such a public, open forum for transacting business is clearly somewhat perilous. There are many holes in the security mechanisms, and millions of potential hackers to exploit them. Some of these holes can be plugged using a security fire-wall. This is a system which strictly limits traffic to permissioned users and allowable transactions. Yet even the best-designed fire wall is breachable. To provide protection in transaction-processing situations, data encryption is mandatory.

An alternative, or supplemental technique for providing data security is the use of a portable authentication device. A portable authenticator resembles a credit-card-size calculator. It will produce a new password every few minutes, which will be displayed in a liquid crystal window. This can be keyed into the application, and functions as a password or encryption key. The resulting message can be decoded only by a synchronized server.

No matter what security technique is employed, protecting Internet security must be considered an ongoing process, rather than a cookbook solution. The number of hackers grows every year, and the cleverness of their attacks is limitless. Security measures implemented today will be antiquated tomorrow.

Message traversal time is another concern in transaction-processing applications. Because the topology of the Internet is constantly changing, it is impossible to predict the time it will take a message to cross the net. In fact, messages can be lost or connections broken unexpectedly. This characteristic tends to limit the usefulness of Internet for processing institutional applications.

Internet has recently received interest from the financial community. Several applications have begun to appear:

- E-mail. As a technique to communicate between branch offices, or between clients and customer service personnel.
- Advertising. The Web offers an easy and colorful vehicle for advertising.
- Distribution. Distribution of reports and research is a safe use for Web technology.
- Transaction processing. Internet is a cheap way to provide on-line access to a wide audience. However, there are two drawbacks: security concerns and indeterminate network performance.

It is not necessary to operate your own Internet site. In recent years, a whole industry has opened up to provide Internet access. An access provider can provide facilities to house your Web site, provide access to public E-mail, and implement security fire-wall protection.

SOME TECHNICAL BACKGROUND

Standards

We have a standard for everything.

-Leo Tolstoy

Imagine landing on a distant planet. You don't know the language. You don't even know if the inhabitants use sound to communicate. You need to understand the language and the transmission medium to share your thoughts. Only when both parties follow the same rules can they communicate.

A standard is a written specification that establishes the technical characteristics of a communications facility. Standards have been established for everything from the wires in the wall to data encryption techniques. By following an established set of standards, two parties can communicate.

Standards often begin as the proprietary design of a telecommunications company or equipment manufacturer. If the design becomes popular, the user community will often call for standardization to reduce costs and technological risk. The manufacturer may support the standardization process as a means of capitalizing on a technological head start, or may resist standardization in an attempt to retain marketplace control. Standards may also be initiated by government bodies or user organizations to promote interoperability.

The process of establishing a standard involves users, vendors, and regulators of telecommunications facilities. You may be familiar with the various standards organizations: Consultative Committee for International Telephone and Telegraph (CCITT), International Organization for Standardization (ISO), Electronics Industry Association (EIA), American National Standards Institute (ANSI), and The Institute of Electrical and Electronics Engineers (IEEE). These agencies and organizations provide the forum for discussing and establishing new standards. Needless to say, it is a complex political process. Although the standardization process can be time consuming, the resulting set of technical specifications provides the common ground on which all modern telecommunication is based.

OSI: The Mother of All Standards

OSI (Open Systems Interconnect) is a sweeping set of standards that defines a set of protocols. But even more important than the protocols it defines, OSI establishes a scheme by which all protocols can be classified and discussed. Refer to Exhibit 14–2 for a brief description of the seven layers of the OSI model.

EXHIBIT 14–2

Seven Layers of the OSI Model

7. Application	Defines high level access into communications systems. Examples: RPC, TELNET.
6. Presentation	Rules for data transformation and formatting. Examples: DES, Sun XDR.
5. Session	Rules for establishing and terminating a communications session.
4. Transport	Guarantees end-to-end reliable delivery of information. Examples: TCP.
3. Network	Defines how a logical connection is established, including addressing, routing, and flow control. Examples: X.25, IP.
2. Data link	Defines how a device gains access to the channel, including framing and error control. Examples: HDLC, SDLC, CSMA/CD.
1. Physical	Defines physical and electrical interconnections. Examples: RS 232, V.35, 10BaseT, Coax, T1.

A Sampling of Standards and Where to Apply Them

> And now I will explain why one man's meat is another's poison.
> —Lucretius

It is beyond this brief discussion to provide a comprehensive analysis of telecommunications standards. Exhibit 14–3 summarizes some of the key technologies and where they may be employed.

EXHIBIT 14–3

A Sampling of Standards

10BaseT	Standard for Ethernet connections using twisted pair cabling.
212, 208	Older standards for modems, rarely used these days.
ATM	Like Frame Relay, a packet-oriented technique for passing data.

EXHIBIT 14–3 (continued)

	By limiting error detection and fixing packet length, extremely high transmission speeds are possible.
Bridge	Device for allowing data traffic to travel over multiple networks. Bridges provide limited traffic management based on source and destination address. Bridges operate with low-level protocols, such as Ethernet.
CSMA/CD	Carrier Sense Multiple Access with Collision Detection is a technique for negotiating usage of a shared channel. In a CSMA/CD environment, a device wishing to transmit proceeds as follows:

1. The device listens to the channel.
2. If there is no data traffic, it transmits, or else it waits and repeats step 1.
3. As data are being transmitted, the device continues to listen to the channel. If another device is simultaneously transmitting, it will detect the collision, and go back to step 1.

CSU/DSU	Device for communicating data on a digital line.
DS0	A telecommunications line capable of transmitting data at 56kb per second.
Ethernet	A protocol for transmitting data on a shared channel. Typically, the channel will be coaxial or twisted pair cabling, although both radio and optical variations are available. The underlying principle of Ethernet is CSMA/CD (qv).
Frame Relay	Packet-oriented technique for passing data with minimal error correction. This allows cheap, high-speed data transmission. Although most frequently associated with TCP/IP applications, Frame Relay can be used for almost any type of traffic, including digitized voice.
Internet	Public data communications facility built on the networking capabilities of its participants.
LU 2	SNA protocol for host-to-terminal communications. LU 2 is most commonly associated with IBM 3270 terminal devices. Occasionally, LU 2 is used for computer-to-computer applications, although implementation can be clumsy in comparison to LU 6.2.
LU 6.2	SNA protocol for peer-to-peer communications. LU 6.2 is most commonly used for serial communications between a host computer (usually a mainframe) and a remote client computer.
Modem	Device for communicating data on an analog line.
Multiplexor	A device which can split a telecommunications circuit into multiple channels. Multiplexors can be broadly classified as time division or statistical. Time division multiplexors provide equal bandwidth to all channels by providing access to each channel

EXHIBIT 14–3 (concluded)

	for a fixed interval with a round-robin technique. Statistical multiplexors divide the line according to the activity on each channel.
Router	Device for allowing data traffic to travel over multiple networks. Routers provide the ability to control traffic according to source and destination address. Routers operate with relatively high-level protocols, such as TCP/IP or Novell IPX.
RS232	Standard for the electrical connection between a device and a short-haul communications line. Although the standard is most often associated with the familiar 25-pin connector (DB25), RS232 can be implemented with 9-pin connectors (DB9) or modular connectors (RJ45). RS232 is most commonly applied when baud rate is 19.2kb or less.
SNA	Suite of telecommunications protocols originally developed by IBM. The SNA protocols typically break out into Logical Units (LU) and Physical Units (PU). LUs roughly correspond to the higher levels of the OSI stack, while PU's correspond to the lower levels.
Switched Ethernet	An Ethernet variation in which an intelligent hub provides a virtual private Ethernet between two communicating workstations. In true peer-to-peer networks, large gains in performance and throughput are possible.
T1	A telecommunications line capable of transmitting data at 1.44mb per second. A T1 line often multiplexed to provide up to 24 DS0 circuits.
TCP/IP	Protocol for providing assured delivery over a common channel. TCP/IP is most commonly used on local area networks or the Internet.
Token Ring	A technique for negotiating usage on a shared channel. With token ring, a special message (token) is circulated among all the devices sharing the channel. If a device wishes to transmit, it must wait until it receives the token.
v.32, v.42, v.32bis, v.42bis	Standards for modems. Standards cover speed, modulation, error correction, and data compression techniques. Can apply to either synchronous or asynchronous devices.
v.35	Standard for the electrical connection between a device and a short-haul communications line. v.35 is usually employed where speeds greater than 19.2kb are needed.
X.25	Packet switched protocol. X.25 defines a technique that allows a message to be divided into fixed-size packets for network transmission. The X.25 packet will contain both data and routing information, allowing information to be transmitted over a switched network.

ⓖ OBJECT TECHNOLOGY
IN FINANCE

Ralph Frankel
Principal
CSC Consulting

Perhaps the most important new technology of the '90s that is here to stay is object technology. As with other technologies, it comes as no surprise that Wall Street and the financial community are at the very forefront of object technology. Investment firms were the first companies to experiment with this promising technology and the first to actually build production systems that utilize it. In this chapter we introduce the technology and discuss its advantages, technical and otherwise.

As most readers already know, object technology differs from structured programming in that an object combines process (the functions or methods) with data (instance variables). While some companies have reported tremendous successes using object-oriented (OO) technology, other companies have reported no return on investment after significant investments over two or three years. This chapter addresses many of the pitfalls and serves as a guide for the chief information officer (CIO) or manager of application development in avoiding similar problems in the migration to this technology.

A BRIEF INTRODUCTION TO OBJECT-ORIENTED TECHNOLOGY—KEY CONCEPTS

The most important concept is that of a *class*. A class has both data (attributes) and operations (methods). It is this marriage of operations to data that provides an object with much of its unique behavior. Typically, each operation operates on its own data and also provides other types of business operations (calculations, event generation, notification to other objects) that provide greater value. A class's data are referred to in different terms depending on the language: C++ refers to the class's data as *member variables*. Smalltalk and Objective C refer to them as *instance variables*. Similarly, C++ refers to the class's operations as *member functions*, whereas Smalltalk and Objective C refer to them as *methods*. For consistency, we will adopt the Smalltalk naming convention, but readers should be aware that these terms are interchangeable.

Class versus Object

The literature sometimes uses classes and objects interchangeably, but it is generally understood that an object is an *instance* of a class. The class provides for the general template or description of what each object that is a member of a class will be. Until the object has been created, the system has not allocated any memory for the class's instance variables. Each object will have specific sets of values assigned to its instance variables. Two distinct objects of the same class will typically have different sets of values for those same instance variables. For example, the *car* class may have the following objects: Ford, Chevrolet, and Cadillac. The class serves as a template that defines the attributes and methods that each of its instances will possess. The *car* class's instance variables may be color, serial number, model, and engine type. Each object of this class will have different values for each of these instance variables.

The three major features of object technology are inheritance, encapsulation, and polymorphism.

Inheritance

Inheritance provides for the ability of one class to inherit the attributes and methods of another class or group of classes. The class that is inheriting is called a *subclass*. The class that provides the inherited instance variables and methods is the *superclass*. Through the use of inheritance a subclass has access to all of its superclass's instance variables and methods. A subclass must satisfy the *is-a* association—this means that the subclass is a type of superclass.

Usually the subclass is similar to its superclass in many ways, but it adds some functionality or enhancements that is not provided by the superclass. Other times, it will not add new functionality, but change existing functionality. The power of inheritance allows for reuse of design and code. New functionality can be added by subclassing an existing class, and adding a single method or two, or perhaps modifying an existing method. The rest of the behavior provided by the superclass remains in tact without requiring any modifications. Thus the subclass is able to leverage the behavior already created in the existing superclass.

As an example, consider the *employee* class that maintains all the data of employees within a company. The *employee* class will maintain basic employee information: name, address, Social Security number, salary, years with the company, and so forth. We may want to create two subclasses: *manager* and *worker*. Both subclasses satisfy the is-a association—they are both types of *employee*. The *manager* class will maintain information that is unique to managers: the group of people they manage, the manager's bonus plan, and so on. This information provides an extension of behavior that is not provided by the *employee* class. The *worker* class may have information that pertains only to workers—the name of the worker's boss, or the worker's skill set. The inheritance mechanism provides the utility that we do not have to recreate any salary and address processing for workers or managers. If we want to query a *manager* object what its salary is, it will use the superclass's method that already provides us with this functionality.

Sometimes a class might satisfy an is-a relationship with more than one class. In this case, a subclass can inherit the instance variables and methods of several superclasses. This is known as *multiple inheritance*. Some languages (notably C++) support multiple inheritance whereas other languages (Smalltalk, Objective C) do not. Consider a situation which is commonly used by some of the object database management systems (ODBMS) vendors. Let us assume that we want our *manager* class to be persistent (i.e., we will store all manager information in a database). Assume the existence of a *persistence* class that provides us with database connectivity. It will provide behavior such as: connect( ), fetch( ), or save( ). If we want our *manager* class to be persistent, we will subclass the *employee* class as well as the *persistence* class.

Encapsulation

Encapsulation is the mechanism that provides for hiding of data and implementation. An object provides its interface to the outside world—it is through this interface that the outside world can act on the object's data. Only the object can change its own data—other objects may have read-access to an object's data (if the object provides access methods that will return this information), but it cannot alter the object's data. The data are encapsulated within the object. C++ provides for three types of data hiding: *private, protected*, and *public*. Private data are the default—only the object has access to the data. Protected data means that subclasses also have access to the superclass's data. Public data are data that all objects have access to—this is another way of saying that the data are not encapsulated. This should be used sparingly, if at all. In Exhibit 15–1 we illustrate encapsulation in greater detail.

In the same way that an object's data are hidden, so too is its implementation. The manner in which an object performs its operations is hidden from other objects. The object can be considered as a stand-alone black box that just works. For example, the outside world need not know if an object maintains a list as a linked list or as an array. The object will provide its interface (or its signature) to the outside world which provides the specification of how other objects are to interact with this object. This interface provides all the methods, arguments, and return values. However, the implementation specifics are completely encapsulated within the object. The advantages of encapsulation are:

• **Improved maintenance**   The side effects and bugs that ripple throughout a system that frequently occur in non-object-oriented program (OOP) systems do not exist in an OO environment. If an object's instance variable has become corrupt, we need only examine the set of methods provided by that object that operates on the instance variable. Since the instance variable is hidden from the outside world, the only possible manner in which the instance variable changed was via one of its methods. Similarly, OO systems are easier to enhance because if the need arises to change a method's current implementation to a different algorithm, no adverse effects occur on the rest of the system. The method may be rewritten, but the object's interface and the manner in which it is acted on by other objects in the system do not change.

E X H I B I T 15–1

Demonstration of Object's Encapsulation

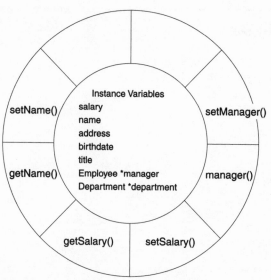

The object's data are hidden from the outside world—the only access to the object's data is through its interface—its methods. To change the employee's salary, one must invoke the setSalary() method on the *employee* object.

- **Reuse**   Since an object is a black box that provides functionality, it can be used as a separate component in any application. As long as the object conforms to its protocol, we should theoretically be able to successfully embed it in any application.

Polymorphism

Polymorphism refers to the ability of different classes in the system that have operations that are similar in intent, but implemented differently, to possess the same method name. For example, consider two separate classes, *queue* and *stack*. They both allow for objects to be inserted in them (a push), and to be removed from them (a pop). Thus they both provide two methods: push() and pop(). However, although the signatures are identical, their implementation is significantly different. The *queue* class will pop objects from the front of the list (the FIFO paradigm) whereas the *stack* class will pop objects from the end of the list (the LIFO paradigm).

E X H I B I T   15–2

Sample code snippet in C

```
switch(structure_type)
{
case QUEUE:
      queue_pop();
      break;

case STACK:
      stack_pop();
      break;

default:
      break;
}
```

In a non-OO programming language we would have to declare
two separate methods: stack_pop() and queue_pop(). We would
also have to insert some if-else or case statements in the code to
determine which function must be called. Exhibit 15–2 indicates
what this code snippet would be like in C.

Furthermore, utilizing a structured programming language,
as we introduce new data structures in our system that will have a
pop() function, we will have to not only create a new function, but
also modify every section of source code that calls these functions
and alter the case statements. The result means a bigger software
system that is more difficult and costlier to maintain in that
changes must be made throughout the system and the enhancements are more prone to software bugs.

Let us consider an investment example. Consider a *portfolio*
class composed of different fixed-income instruments. There are
Treasury bonds, municipal bonds, notes, and mortgage-backed
securities. Our system must calculate the yield of the entire portfolio. Through the use of polymorphism, this code becomes a piece of
cake. Each security defines its own yield() method. A municipal
bond knows what its yield is, and a T-bill knows how to calculate

its yield. The *portfolio* object will ask each security in its portfolio to calculate its own yield. The portfolio object does not have to know what type of security is being asked to return its yield. The only requirement is that each security adhere to this protocol: It must have a defined method named yield( ).

Object-Based versus Object-Oriented

One of the critical distinctions in the understanding of OO is the difference between an object-based system and an object-oriented system. Many vendors that claim to be object-oriented are in fact only object-based, which may or may not satisfy an organization's information technology (IT) requirements. An object-based system provides for encapsulation—it is a black box that just works. It has an interface and it can be embedded within another program. The best example of this is Visual Basic Controls (VBXs and OCXs). The behavior and internal algorithms are hidden from the rest of the system, as are its internal attributes. However, there is no provision for either inheritance or polymorphism. If a component's existing functionality provides for 80 percent of one's needs, but one must extend some of its functionality without the ability to subclass and extend the class's methods through overriding and extensions, this becomes a difficult task indeed.

Messaging

Another critical concept of OO is messaging. An OO system is built as a group of objects that message each other. Each object can be thought of as a separate component of software (the black box) that is invoked by sending it messages which are the object's interface. When object A messages object B, it is simply invoking one of object B's methods. The object that invokes the message is referred to as the sender. The object that receives the message is the receiver. Typically, the receiver or one of its superclasses will provide the implementation for the invocation. If the receiver provides an implementation for the method it has been asked to execute, it will execute its own method. Otherwise, the superclass will be asked to provide the implementation. The request to service this message will move up the class hierarchy until an object that responds to this message is found.

The notion of separate objects, each one being a working component capable of sending and receiving messages, allows for the ability of objects to message each other either from within the same application (in the same address space) or outside the application (a different address space, perhaps running on a different host). If object B is running on a different machine, it is referred to as a *remote object*. Object A can still invoke object B's methods without knowing where object B resides. This is performed by the use of object request brokers (ORBs). An ORB maintains the directory services and mapping of methods from objects running on two different machines. Therefore, although it appears that object A is messaging object B directly, in reality what is taking place is indirect messaging—the ORB is acting as the intermediary between the sender and the receiver. This is performed seamlessly and transparently. The Object Management Group (OMG) has defined a standard for distributed object communication known as common object request broker architecture (CORBA). CORBA 2.0 is emerging as an industry standard that has been adopted by most of the OO industry, with Microsoft, to no one's surprise, being the lone holdout. Microsoft has a competing paradigm for distributed computing known as common object model (COM). This framework is built on top of Microsoft's object linking and embedding (OLE) technology which the firm has aggressively pushed as the desktop standard for interapplication communication.

Often, the receiver object is not known at compile time—it is only determined at run time. Smalltalk and Objective C provide for dynamic binding, so that the method being called and the object receiving the message are bound at run time. C++ is statically bound—it must be determined at compile time which object is the receiver. There are provisions through the use of virtual methods to circumvent this restriction, but a discussion of how this works is beyond the scope of this chapter. Suffice it to say that Smalltalk and others like OOPs provide far greater elegance and ease-of-use in support of this important feature.[1]

---

1. For a detailed description of message dispatching in C++ and Smalltalk, see G. *Pooch,*
   Object-Oriented Design with Applications (Redwood City: Benjamin/Cummings, 1991),
   pp. 118–21.

EXHIBIT 15-3

Security Firm Hierarchy Using Object Modeling Technique (OMT)

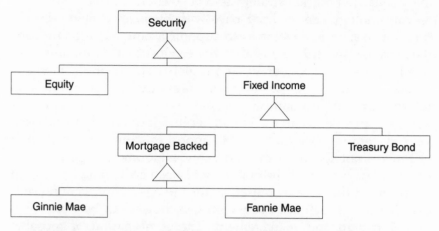

A simplified version of the class hierarchy for a security firm using OMT notation.
Each rectangle represents the name of a class. The triangle denotes a subclass,
where the classes beneath the triangle are subclasses of the class above it.

In the investment industry, we are beginning to see rich sets of class hierarchies. In Exhibit 15–3, we depict an extremely simplified version of a security hierarchy for fixed-income instruments.

THE BUSINESS CASE

Why is the OO revolution taking place? Now that we have introduced some of the basic concepts of OO technology we can discuss some of the benefits that OO will bring to an IT organization. The critical objectives of an IT organization usually are to improve time to market, improve quality, and reduce software development costs.

Time to Market

Reports have shown that corporate America now has a five-year backlog of mission critical applications. Despite an abundance of popular development tools that have improved programmer productivity, there seems to be no improvement in the time it takes to develop large and complex software systems. In fact, the percentage of failures of large projects is alarmingly high. Furthermore, we have seen a new trend that has shaped businesses in the '80s and '90s—businesses are becoming increasingly complex and seemingly shift their market strategy and business focus overnight. Current technology cannot keep pace with business change—by the time the system is developed to support a new business process, the market opportunity has already been lost to a competitor. Economic forces such as deregulation, global competition, mergers, and acquisitions are putting new pressures on companies to improve their IT dramatically. We have seen cases in which a company was unable to enter a market because it did not have the software system in place that would support this initiative. Although OO might not speed up the software development process in the first few projects, once the objects have been created and placed in a repository, they can be reused again and again. Software reuse is still difficult to achieve even with OO, but it can be done with proper design and management. The combination of reusable objects and the reduced lines of code in a well-designed OO system will have, can shave months (and years for large-scale projects) off development schedules.

Quality

The larger the project and the more lines of code in the system, the more difficult it is to maintain and to debug. Using OO, this is greatly simplified. Through the use of polymorphism and inheritance, OO systems have far fewer lines of code than a traditional system, thereby reducing development time and the total number of defects (bugs) in the system. Furthermore, debugging and enhancements are greatly simplified because of encapsulation. It is far simpler to isolate the method that changed the data to the incorrect value or to isolate the method(s) that need to be modified to create the enhancements. Often, the enhancement might entail no changes to the existing classes, but rather the creation of a new class that subclasses an existing class and provides the new functionality through the creation of new methods or through overriding its superclass's method. Studies have also shown the economic value of catching bugs at the earliest possible time. Once the software has been released, the cost of isolating the bug, fixing it, sending out patches or reconfiguring the software for all users, runs into the thousands of dollars. It is clearly in a company's best interest to catch bugs in the development phase. Using OO, this becomes easier, because the initial unit test is on the object itself, and it is a relatively simple task to determine that it functions as a true reusable software component.

Cost Reduction

When building large software systems, we should focus not only on the cost of development but also on the cost of maintenance and the software life cycle; that is, how long will the software system stay in production before it becomes totally obsolete. Software maintenance typically eats up between 80 to 90 percent of all software development costs. Furthermore, as business becomes more complex, and significant change is introduced at ever-increasing speeds, we are seeing software systems that become obsolete within the first year of the life cycle. This is a worrisome observation considering that there are legacy systems churning away into their third decade. Industry analysts have noticed that major systems usually require reengineering every 10 to 15 years. It comes as no surprise therefore, that any technology that reduces maintenance costs and provides for flexibility and scaleability that will increase the software's longevity is a tremendous boon for the corporation. With IT budgets of major corporations running into hundreds of millions of dollars, proper use of object technology can save a company millions of dollars on an annual basis.

OBJECT-ORIENTED ANALYSIS AND DESIGN

The key to good OO development starts with analysis and design (OO A&D). It is through object modeling that an accurate model of the company's business processes can be described. One of the advantages of OO technology that is frequently mentioned is its ability to model the real world. Since an object contains both data and process, the object's behavior is closely patterned after the company's business. An *invoice* class models the behavior of invoicing. An *order* class will model the company's business process for accepting and creating customer orders. The *portfolio* class will model the portfolio manager's portfolio. Each of these classes provides for the real-world behavior and functionality of its business process that it is modeled after. Communication between the business community and the object modeler is improved because users understand what the object does. They can see the object in terms of their own business processes.

Let us consider our *portfolio* class in more detail. What operations do portfolio managers perform on their portfolios? They undoubtedly perform the following operations:

1. Add/delete securities to the portfolio.
2. Purchase/sell shares of a security in the portfolio.
3. Add/delete customers to the portfolio.

In addition to those operations, portfolio managers also will want to extract useful information from their portfolios.

1. The portfolio's current value.
2. The value of particular securities within the portfolio by security and industry.
3. The portfolio's current risk.
4. A customer's value in the portfolio.
5. The current number of shares and the share value of the portfolio.

It is the OO analyst's job to convert the business processes into an *object model*. At a bare minimum (see the following section), the object model will contain the following:

• A description of all objects in the system.
• A description of each object's instance variables and methods.
• The associations of one object with another, with particular emphasis on a class hierarchy (superclass and subclass associations).

There is no consensus on when analysis ends and design begins. Jacobson and Rumbaugh both suggest that analysis reflects the business model without any hardware/software constraints.[2] The design model must map the object model into an implementation—it must take into consideration the programming language, the operating system, the hardware, the database, specific

2. I. Jacobson, *Object-Oriented Software Engineering*, (Reading, MA: Addison-Wesley, 1992) and J. Rumbaugh, et al., *Object-Oriented Modeling and Design*, (Englewood Cliffs, NJ: Prentice Hall, 1991).

algorithms, and all other issues (external interfaces, throughput, etc.) that would effect the implementation.

The Importance of Analysis and Design

Although analysis and design is a critical success factor in any system, the benefits of OO will not be realized unless management recognizes that OO A&D is a top priority in any OO project. Without the investment in A&D, systems will be implemented without yielding the reusable objects that serve as the *raison d'être* of object technology. Management should be aware that training in an OOP does not automatically entail knowledge of object modeling and OO A&D. In fact, we've often observed that some very good programmers make the worst OO designers. Adoption of OO technology requires a complete paradigm shift and new form of software development. The key to its success starts with a proper foundation in OO A&D.

The Object-Oriented Methodologies

Five or six methodologies are currently fairly widespread. To discuss each one would itself require a complete textbook, so we can only introduce the main ones here. The methodologies follow two different approaches, evolutionary and revolutionary. The evolutionary approach is intended to bridge the gap with conventional structured analysis so that analysts who have worked with E/R models data flow diagrams (DFD) and process models will pick up the OO models relatively easily. The revolutionary approach is a different way of presenting the models—it is not intended to evolve from structured analysis.

The leading methodology in the first camp is Rumbaugh's object modeling technique (OMT).[3] In the second camp, the leading methodology is Ivar Jacobson's use-case methodology.[4] Although Jacobson has provided for a complete project-life-cycle methodology, use cases have enjoyed strong support at the early phases of the software life cycle, particularly in the requirements phase, represented in the requirements model.

---

3. Rumbaugh, *Object-Oriented Modeling*.
4. I. Jacobson, *Object-Oriented Software Engineering*, 1992.

Object Modeling Technique Highlighted

The three major models that describe the entire system are the object model, the dynamic model, and the functional model.

The *object model* describes the static state of the system. From the object model, one can determine the class hierarchy, the instance variables of each class, and its methods. The associations of one class to another is also depicted. Associations provide the same type of class relationships as do entity relationships (E/R). The *employee* class is associated to the *company* class with a *works-for* relationship. Cardinality is provided, in a similar fashion as E/R diagrams. The model indicates if an association is one-to-many, many-to-many, optional, zero-or-more, or at least five. However, two specialized types of associations are not seen in the E/R. These are:

- The *is-a* **association**—The is-a association captures the relationship of a subclass with its superclass.

- The *part-of* **association.** Often a complex object, in addition to containing instance variables of simple data, also contains other objects. For example, the *car* class might have an *engine* class as one of its aggregates. This should not be confused with a superclass/subclass association. The *car* class is not the superclass of engine; however, the *engine* class is a *part-of* "car." Each instance of *car* will also have an instance of *engine*.

The static object model does not indicate how the system actually works. The dynamic model describes the collaboration of different objects in responding to an event. Included with the dynamic model are event traces and state transition diagrams. The event traces show the messaging from one object to another. They describe the flow of control in the system and indicate which object is receiving a message and which object is sending a message. State transition diagrams show the inner workings of a single object and what events must occur (what methods must be invoked) that will cause a transition of this object from one state to another. Event traces do not describe state transitions and state transitions do not describe the object's interactions with other objects, so both sets of diagrams are needed to provide the complete picture. It is not necessary to create an event trace or a state transition diagram for each object or event in the system. The model should capture the most important events. The simple events are often so trivial that they need not be captured as a separate diagram.

The functional model is the least important of the three, and is often ignored entirely; however, it is still useful in certain situations. The functional model captures the data flow in the system, showing the flow of data from one object to another. It very closely resembles traditional data-flow diagrams.

Use Cases

Use cases have become quite popular over the past few years. Whereas the object model describes the developer's view of the system, the use case describes the user's view of the system. As such, the use case is arguably the best approach to gathering requirements and defining the system's functionality. The use case provides a detailed description of the user's interaction with the system and traces this interaction through a complete thread or business process. In Jacobson parlance, the user is often referred to as the *actor*, describing the role that he is currently playing in interacting with the system. As Jacobson suggests, use cases provide the following benefits:

- Defining functional requirements.
- Deriving objects.
- Allocating functionality to objects.
- Designing the user interface.
- Integration testing.
- Defining test cases.[5]

Of particular benefit is the ease with which object definitions and functionality is identified through use cases. Unfortunately, this benefit has not been given enough attention by the other OO methodologists. With some exceptions, the other methodologies do not provide a meaningful way to capture the objects—they merely provide a notation to represent the model once it has been identified. The key to successful OO modeling is largely determined by

---

5. Jacobson, "A Growing Consensus on Use Cases," *Journal of Object-Oriented Programming,* March 1995.

the modeler's ability to determine what is an object in the first place and what operations the object must provide. Use cases provide a huge benefit to facilitate this effort.

In addition, use cases also provide for the interaction of several objects in satisfying a particular function. The design of object frameworks is of critical importance in building large and complex reusable objects. Objects that interact with each other frequently are tightly coupled; objects that interact with each other sparingly are loosely coupled. The more object associations one creates via tight coupling, the more one creates an object framework that is harder to learn and reuse. On the other hand, when objects that must work together are not grouped into a framework, each object as a stand-alone entity is virtually unusable.

KEY SUCCESS FACTORS

Management Support

Introduction of a new technology will always be met with resistance in certain camps. There is always a group of skeptics who have seen previous transitions to new technology fail, and they question why this technology will be any different. Another group feels constantly threatened by new technology and resists any attempt at change because of fear of the unknown and/or a threat to job security. If this technology is to take root and firmly establish itself as a standard in the organization, it is key that management buys into it and supports it to the hilt. Management must also obtain the buy-in of the naysayers and the skeptics.

The Paradigm Shift

Management support must go far beyond a few short speeches or hastily written memorandums. Management must be prepared to manage the paradigm shift to object technology. Object-oriented technology represents a radically new approach to software development. It represents a different manner of thinking, a different way of capturing requirements, a different approach to analysis and design, a different style of project management, and a different approach to programming. To migrate an organization from old to new is always a difficult and arduous task that takes planning, time, investment, and significant effort. New teams of OO analysts and OO programmers must be formed. Significant training must take place on an on-going basis. All this must be done while keeping the naysayers at bay. Even after the organization has been reorganized, it must be realized that the first few projects will be a learning experience for most of the staff. The return on investment (ROI) that one may be expecting will almost certainly not happen in the first year and perhaps not even in the second year. The better one understands the pitfalls and extends the horizon for deriving cost benefits, the more successful one will be in the long term.

Project Staffing

As with any other experiment with new technology, one of the keys to success is the identification of key personnel who will lead the foray into uncharted territories. Too often, immediately after training has been completed (the new term, *just-in-time training*, has become quite popular the past two years), the project team is thrown headfirst into the new project. This could be quite effective if there are several experienced people in the mix. A migration to OO technology without some experienced people on board is a sure sign of trouble. The reliance on an experienced outside integrator or consultant to provide assistance in the first project or two is highly advisable, providing that he or she not only provides, the benefits of expertise and experience, but can also impart some knowledge to the newly trained staff.

Remember that the staffing plan must provide coverage for each area of object-oriented technology . One must ensure that qualified OO analysts who have knowledge and experience with at least one type of OO methodology are on board. It is not imperative that the experience be with the same methodology that has already been selected as the organization's standard.

The Project Scope

After the staff is in place and ready to go, the team is ready to start its pilot project. If this is the corporation's first experience with object-oriented technology , this decision will be critical. Too often, the most important and ambitious project is selected as the pilot. The larger the project, both in staff and complexity, the greater the chances of failure. This is true with any technology; it rings even truer with a new technology and approach such as OO. The project should be visible, but it should not be the current most mission-critical project in the organization. We recommend that the project's scope and staffing be limited to a manageable size. A 5-person project over a period of four to six months will probably result in success; a 20-person team over a year will probably fail. The key is to start small and grow slowly.

Project Management for Object-Oriented Technology

Object-oriented technology cannot succeed without proper project management. It is critical to have a project manager who is familiar with OO concepts and understands the OO project life cycle and how it differs from traditional approaches. With a proper understanding of OO, it is actually easier to build software; programmers can be assigned a complete object to implement, and the object and object framework becomes the metric for measuring progress. The key rules are

- Plan for iterative design and implementation.
- Ensure that there is an object model in place before implementation begins.
- Ensure that the object model is updated as new objects are "discovered" during the implementation phase.
- Assign tasks based on objects.
- Ensure that there is a software librarian responsible for reusable objects.
- Ensure that programmers are not reinventing the wheel but are trying to reuse other people's objects.
- Have the OO gurus work on the OO tools and frameworks that the less-experienced programmers will use. This will greatly increase the latter group's productivity despite their limited knowledge of OO tools or concepts.

Organizational Issues

Dealing with Mainframe Holdovers

One of the difficult organizational issues that confronts managers who have made the plunge to OO is the determination of qualified holdovers. IT executives have observed that only 30 to 50 percent of mainframe programmers can make the cut to OO. One of the reasons that Smalltalk has enjoyed recent popularity is due to the relative ease with which COBOL programmers can be trained in Smalltalk. It is far easier for a mainframe programmer to learn Smalltalk than C++, the latter presenting a formidable learning curve.

Dealing with the OO Purists
On the other side of the coin are the OO purists. This group, in fact, loves OO so much that they forget their main responsibility is to create mission critical software at increased speed and quality. One of the main reasons that some organizations have not witnessed any benefits from OO is due to poor management of this group. Typically, the purist has little interest in the business domain, does not understand the company's business, and wants to spend the whole time creating the greatest OO framework that will, in all likelihood, be used by no one else. Despite the purist's knowledge of OO, such a contribution to a project will not be significant and could even be detrimental. We have seen too many projects where six months are spent building application frameworks on top of high-end developer tools before a line of application code is written. While tools and frameworks can be valuable, they must be chosen wisely. Successful managers should recognize the purists' agenda may be different than their own—the purists are probably not committed to their companies or projects but to the technology itself.

Creating an OO Culture
The most difficult task managers face is the creation of a new corporate culture. For OO to succeed, the entire process for software development must change. There will undoubtedly be resistance and some of it will come from the OO programmers themselves. Programmers traditionally resist resorting to formalism in their programming efforts—they believe that it is an imposition on their creativity. In many organizations, programmers start coding as soon as the requirements are complete. In an OO environment, this must change. In addition to the other benefits provided by rigorous analysis and design, software reuse can only come about through a published description of all objects in the system that all programmers have access to.

PREPARING FOR REUSE

When you are one or two years into your paradigm shift, you will have successfully transitioned a large percentage of your organization to OO development. All your key OO personnel will be in place, from your programmers through your project management staff. Yet, you may not notice any significant software reuse from your structured programming days when you had reusable software libraries. Where did you go wrong?

At the outset, recognize that achieving software reuse is less a technical issue than an organizational and cultural issue. Assuming that objects have been implemented that are reusable, what must be done to maximize reuse? The main issues are twofold; information and organization. From an information perspective, developers must be aware of what is in the object repository. Object browsers and text-search engines should be part of the development environment—these tools provide developers with information concerning the objects suitable for reuse—either to be used in whole or to serve as a basis for subclassing where the developer's role will be to add the needed behavior to a new subclass. Occasionally, developers recognize that the current classes are not robust enough for their purposes so they might make changes directly to those classes without subclassing.

The second key element that must be in place to maximize reuse is a culture of reuse. Organizations must be converted into this culture so that programmers are creating reusable software, not only for themselves, but for their entire organizations. In this culture of reuse, developers are encouraged to first select an existing class to work from, rather than reinvent the wheel and create their own class from scratch. Part of the programmers' annual review and reward structure must look at their contribution to the reusability culture—how often were their objects checked out of the repository and reused by other developers; how often did they choose an existing class rather than create their own. Senior architects must take responsibility for the object repository and determine which objects are candidates for reuse on a given project. It is always difficult to shift old ways of working, but software development as an engineering discipline has not advanced the way it could or should. Management must create a culture where more attention is paid to the process of building software.

PLANNING TOWARD A SOFTWARE DEVELOPMENT PROCESS

Most of the methodologists have emphasized OO as a complete project life cycle. Jacobson refers to his methodology as object-oriented software engineering (OOSE).[6] This is an essential concept— OO is not only a technology, it is an entire methodology for developing complex software. The Software Engineering Institute has described a metric for evaluating the software development proficiency level that an organization has reached. This is referred to as the capability maturity model (CMM). At the lowest level, level one, there is no process for developing software. Each developer works independently and there is no set approach of any kind. At the highest level, level five, there is a rigorous approach to software development that is published, adhered to by all developers, managed accordingly, and optimized. The optimization process requires a regular self-examination of the organization's implementation of its methodology to ensure that it is on target and to make corrective shifts in direction to constantly improve the process. The CMM does not require OO to be the methodology in place; however, a shift to OO as an all-embracing method for software development should immediately place an organization at level 3. An understanding of the process is therefore essential to yield the greatest benefits of object technology.

The Object-Oriented Project Life Cycle

The traditional life cycle follows these basic steps: requirements, functional specifications, analysis, design, implementation, testing, and rollout.

Traditional methodologies require that these activities be done following a waterfall approach—one cannot advance to the next stage until the previous phase has been fully completed. The OO approach (regardless of the methodology one selects) follows an iterative approach—each phase is revisited several times before it is completed. More powerful development tools and RAD tools have made this approach quite popular even for more traditional client/server projects.

---

6. Jacobson, *Object-Oriented Software.*

E X H I B I T 15–4

The Spiral Project Life Cycle

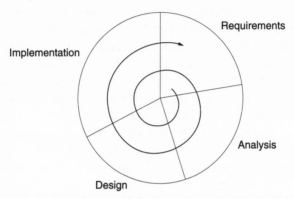

The figure above depicts several iterations of requirements, analysis, design, and implementation.

Exhibit 15–4 depicts the OO approach. Note that during the entire project life cycle, requirements, analysis, design, and implementation are all done iteratively. It is common to cycle through these different phases several times until the project is complete.

The end result is a project that is completed in a much shorter time span than when using the waterfall approach. The benefits are significant:

- A shorter development life cycle.
- Requirements can be validated and confirmed (through the use of prototyping) with users at a much earlier stage in the project.
- Integration of new requirements is easier to achieve.
- Some of the harder requirements or design areas that take longer to pin down need not be a bottleneck—the rest of the project can continue. The remaining requirements will be integrated in the next iteration.

Large projects have traditionally suffered from obsolescence by the time the system is rolled out. Often so many requirements are changed or added that the newly created system is unusable. In these situations, the iterative approach is an absolute necessity. The system must have the capability to integrate new requirements at any point in the project life cycle.

Object-Oriented Architecture

Companies have long ignored the importance of a proper architectural framework in building large systems. Performance engineering is critical in determining what design compromises will be required (flexibility versus performance) and what other design concepts should be added. Unfortunately, for some inexplicable reason, too many OO projects were developed with a lack of architecture and system design. In addition to traditional design and architecture issues, there are new ones that are unique to OO systems. Issues that must always be taken into consideration:

- Mapping of relational data to and from object instances (referred to as the *impedance mismatch*).
- The number of object instances that will be in memory.
- The system's performance requirements.
  - The system's response time.
  - The system's throughput.
  - Scaleability requirements—how many users must the system support, how many transactions, how many database queries.
- Concurrent database updates.
- The complexity of object interactions (to implement a method, how many objects must message each other to complete the task).
- The depth of the class hierarchy.
- Cacheing requirements.
- Object messaging.
- Use of distributed objects.
- Two-tier versus three-tier architectures, replication of services.
- Integration of OO with non-OO systems or subsystems.

Always remember that the object model represents the state of the system in a pure form. Once hardware, software, and RDBMS decisions are made, the pure object model must be converted into a design model that must deal with the real world of bits and bytes. Compromises must be made; often a pure object model represents a class hierarchy that is too deep. Typically, a hierarchy that goes beyond four or five levels is already too deep. The deeper the class hierarchy, the more baggage it contains; when it becomes too large it also becomes less reusable, as it is more difficult for developers to understand and maintain. In addition, the deeper the hierarchy, the worse the system will perform.

Relational data does not map readily into objects. This is particularly true when one object contains other objects—to read a complex object from a relational database requires a sophisticated SQL query that requires a multitable join. Poor design of reading relational data and mapping it into objects will result in unacceptable performance and has resulted in the failure of more than one OO system.

Object-Oriented Testing

An optimal process for OO software development cannot be fully realized unless the organization has developed a different process for OO testing. OO systems are tested in a different manner than traditional software; once understood, this testing becomes simpler and more productive.

The key difference is the unit test. In OO, unit testing represents testing the object itself. Functionally, if an object performs in accordance with its signature (it properly implements all of its methods), than it has been unit tested. In addition, part of the object's unit test must consider the place this object occupies in the class hierarchy. Does the object override superclass methods properly, if required to do so? Since an object inherits all the methods of all its superclasses, testing on the object must involve testing of methods provided by the superclasses as well.

If requirements were created via use-case analysis, the use case can be used as a basis for system testing. For each case in the system, several test scripts should be constructed that will determine if the system properly implements the use case.

RISK FACTORS

At this point, you should have a strong idea of what is entailed in delivering a successful OO project. Whereas the sections before described what must be in place for object technology to succeed, it is also important to be aware of some of the mistakes that are common in the industry and have led to near disasters in attempts to embrace OO. Many of the points raised here are mostly common sense; unfortunately, common sense is all too rare a commodity.

Lack of Analysis and Design

The real payback of OO requires a significant investment in OO A&D. Although all complex systems, OO or otherwise, must require significant analysis, it is all the more critical with OO. It is not unusual for the A&D (analysis and design) phase of an OO project to take longer than its non-OO counterpart. This is particularly true during the first few OO projects that the organization has initiated, until a repository of reusable objects has been established. The common approach used by many firms is to plunge straight into OO with OOP. However highly skilled C++ or Smalltalk programmers are as developers, they do not necessarily have any skill in OO analysis and design; on the contrary they often have no concept whatsoever of how to design an OO system. There is a critical need to ensure that a senior OO modeler can create the object model and can map the model into the OO programming language or environment.

Lack of System Design and Architecture

Even a well-conceived object model can still result in a system that fails to perform adequately. There must be a strict adherence to the system's performance requirements. For some reason, many OO modelers are capable of creating the object model but do not have the software engineering skills to take the object model into design. Careful consideration must be given to the topics discussed in the earlier section.

Lack of Software Development Process

An OO approach to software development is a disciplined approach. There must be a documented methodology that is strictly adhered to. Failure to do so will result in code that may work, but will not properly represent the object model. Chances of reuse become slim to none without the development process firmly in place.

Building a Design and Architecture around a Tool

In the never-ending search to find the silver bullet, IT departments are always looking for the tool that will ease the pain of software development. The tool always seems to be selected before the performance and system requirements (throughput, data volumes, real-time messaging, network traffic) have been identified. It is absolutely folly to retrofit the tool to the architecture. Time and again projects have failed because either the tool selection was poor, or the attempted implementation with the tool was poor. Remember, the silver bullet does not exist. Some tools may yield more productivity than others, but ultimately it takes a lot of hard work and strong management to develop successful systems.

Know Thy Vendor

As much as we think that we know how to deal with our vendors, it is amazing how often IT organizations make selections based on the marketing literature or the recommendations of their programmers without doing a proper evaluation of the vendor's product. Especially when selecting an OO tool that will be used to create an enterprise system, one must ensure that the tool can support the scaleability that the system will require. Do not take the vendor's word—make sure that the product is properly evaluated for its performance, scaleability, architecture, flexibility, and robustness.

Parting Words

With proper management commitment, tight control of the project's scope, and key experienced staff on board, successful delivery is achievable. Remember that proper management and organization will be every bit as critical as pure technical capabilities. The journey may at times seem to be more trouble than it was worth, but ultimately, once the organization has assimilated OO as a core competency, it will be a journey that will never end.

REFERENCES

Booch, G. *Object-Oriented Design with Applications*. Redwood City, CA: Benjamin/Cummings, 1991.

Graham, I. *Migrating to Object Technology*. Reading, MA: Addison-Wesley, 1995.

Jacobson, I. "A Growing Consensus on Use Cases." *Journal of Object-Oriented Programming*, March 1995.

Jacobson, I. *Object-Oriented Software Engineering*. Reading, MA: Addison-Wesley, 1992.

Rumbaugh, J.; M. Blaha; W. Premerlani; F. Eddy; W. Lorensen. *Object-Oriented Modeling and Design*. Englewood Cliffs, NJ: Prentice Hall, 1991.

Wirfs-Brock, R.; B. Wilkerson; L. Wiener. *Designing Object-Oriented Software*. Englewood Cliffs, NJ: Prentice Hall, 1990.

16

⑥ FINANCIAL COMPUTATIONAL INTELLIGENCE*

Dean S. Barr
Chief Investment Officer
Advanced Investment Technology

Financial time series forecasting is perhaps the most complex and thus difficult of all times series prediction disciplines. Financial data are notoriously noisy and highly dimensional (many degrees of freedom). Extreme events are common, which produces nonuniform return distributions. Indicators or factors driving financial time series may be correlated or spurious. Often the underlying structure of the time series is unknown at worst and a moving target at best. While one might easily dismiss financial prediction as too difficult or results as statistically insignificant, it is not impossible. Moreover, recent advances in computational processing speeds, coupled with powerful new explanatory tools, have the potential to revolutionize the whole field of financial time-series prediction. Indeed, this relatively new development has launched a new discipline termed *financial computational intelligence*. At the core of this methodology is the dependence on building models from data observations unlike established and traditional modeling, which is based on a theory.

*Acknowledgments: I would like to thank my colleagues Dr. Ganesh Mani, Dr. Sam Mahfoud, and Doug Case, for their helpful advice. I would also like to thank Kathy Hanson for her editorial comments and her gentle nudging to prod completion of this work.

Every active portfolio manager implicitly engages in financial time-series forecasting. Typical questions commonly asked when making investment decisions include: What should the excess-return expectation be? What kind of factors drive the returns? Will the same factors that worked historically work in the future? Put in a financial computational intelligence context, the same questions asked are: Is the time series random or predictable? What kind of system produced the time series? Are factor sensitivities stationary or do they migrate with time? In essence, financial computational intelligence attempts to quantify answers to complex investment questions.

THE TOOLS FOR FINANCIAL TIME-SERIES FORECASTING

The tools necessary to address questions of this sort include fast computer-processing capability and clever/smart algorithms. These tools are inexorably linked in tackling complex financial forecasting problems. However, the critical issue is not computational power for brute force sake, it is designing clever algorithms.

The reason for this is that one can never have enough computational power to solve, with certainty, most complex problems. In financial forecasting, even trivial problems can be unwieldy. For instance, given just two financial variables, where both can take a value from 1 to 10, the number of possible ordered paired outcomes is 10^2 or 100. Suppose one wishes to design a buy/sell strategy based on the values of these two variables. Such a strategy would specify, for each of the 100 possible pairs of variables, whether a buy, or sell decision is warranted. The number of possible buy/sell strategies that a computer could learn is 2^{100}, which is greater than 10^{30}. That's more strategies than a million of the world's fastest computers (even running at a trillion evaluations per second) could evaluate in a lifetime. To make matters worse, the number of possibilities increases greater than exponentially as the number of variables grows beyond two. One might easily be awestruck by the exponential increase in computer power versus price over the past three decades. However, this increase is no match for the above-mentioned explosion in problem complexity.

EXHIBIT 16-1

Accuracy in Relation to Speed of Humans and Machines

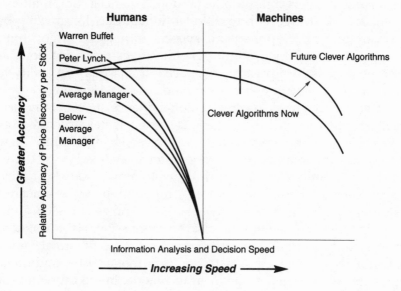

The amount of available financial information (not to mention the number and complexity of financial instruments) is enormous. Compounding the problem is that ever-increasing amounts of information are available to all market participants at the same time. The need to assimilate and process financial information efficiently, quickly, and accurately is paramount. Invariably, financial forecasting success is a function of possessing a qualitatively better processor (brain) or processing the same information quicker, thus enabling one to view more opportunities to succeed.

Exhibit 16-1 depicts the trade-off between information analysis and decision speed and relative accuracy of price discovery per opportunity. Simply stated, this graph attempts to demonstrate that given ample time to make an investment decision, one is more accurate than if required to make the same decision in less time with more information. Every investor creates a personal accuracy curve. Obviously, some investors possess more accurate processors than others, thus creating qualitatively differentiated curves. However, at a particular point where an investor is required to make an investment decision with increasing amounts of information and with little time to analyze, all investors reach a point of cognitive dissonance and decisions become random. Financial computational intelligence contrasts with traditional human decision making by incorporating faster processing speeds with clever algorithms. While these algorithms might generate investment decisions as accurate as those of investors, the speed of analysis and ability to view and assimilate more information provides a clear edge.

Clever algorithms in computational finance are generally classified as nonparametric techniques. These tools infer structure from observable facts and are thus data-driven search algorithms. These techniques are commonly called nonlinear estimation methods. Specifically, nonlinear tools include well-known statistical techniques such as kernel regression, projection pursuit, k-nearest neighbor algorithms, neural networks (NN), and genetic algorithms (GA). They are mathematical tools, as is regression. However, nonlinear algorithms fit curves, and linear techniques fit straight lines. In Exhibit 16–2, a series of data points is modeled by traditional regression analysis and a nonlinear technique. In theory, nonlinear proponents hope to better represent the underlying structure of the time series than do linear techniques. Why is this important?

NONLINEAR COMPLEX SYSTEMS

Much has been written about efficient markets. It bears noting that the early theories providing the foundation of efficient market theory are systematically under attack. What is clear from a financial time-series perspective is that financial markets are complex systems and almost all complex systems are nonlinear. A recent study by Zhuanxin Ding of the University of California, San Diego, examined the correlation of past and future returns on the S&P 500 between 1928 and 1991 and found that when all the returns are made positive, the correlation of past and future returns is statistically greater than if the signs of the returns are left unchanged. Professor David A. Hsieh at the Fuqua School of Business, Duke University, also concluded that price changes of asset returns are not autocorrelated, but the absolute values of changes are strongly autocorrelated.[1] Nonlinear processes can generate this type of behavior; linear processes cannot!

E X H I B I T 16–2

Illustration of Nonlinearity

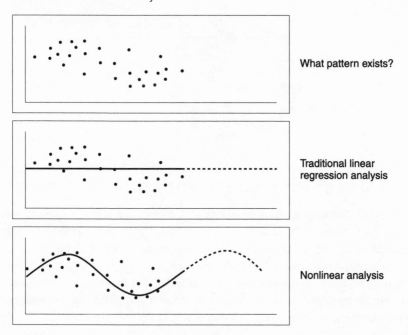

What pattern exists?

Traditional linear
regression analysis

Nonlinear analysis

Exhibit 16–3 demonstrates another very important aspect of nonlinear techniques in financial market analysis. Nonlinear models represent a considerably larger set of possible model relationships than do linear models. To a large extent, most linear relationships have been exploited by active managers using traditional techniques. The linear techniques are well known and often used. The next frontier of exploration and the most fruitful is nonlinear relationship discovery. It has the benefit of newness, as recent advances in computing power allow for experimentation and discovery. Further, it provides the promise of oversized returns because of the relatively high barriers to entry and the lack of participants actively pursuing these techniques.

---

1. D.A. Hsieh, "Nonlinear Dynamics in Financial Markets: Evidence and Implications," *Financial Analysts Journal*, July–August 1995, pp. 55–62.

Relationship Models: Linear versus Nonlinear

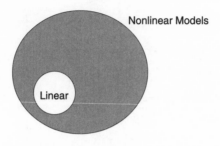

NEURAL NETWORKS AND GENETIC ALGORITHMS

Classical computational intelligence algorithms most commonly used in financial time-series forecasting include neural networks and genetic algorithms. Both techniques learn from data but their search methods differ. Neural networks are mathematical connectionist models. They attempt to emulate brain-style computation by processing patterns of data that evolve over time in an attempt to emulate a relationship between the data (factors) in the model and the output (future return). Investors do this when they attempt to distill meaning from the relationship between interest rates, gold and grain prices, and so on.

In Exhibit 16–4, a neural network examines each point in the time series and stores the juxtaposition of each factor in relation to the other while referencing the output; in this case, the return of the time series. These learned patterns are stored as weights. As in regression, the model attempts to minimize the error between the input derived solution and the actual output solution. However, neural networks are inherently adaptable models. Regression models must be adapted. A training algorithm changes the weights of each of the factors in a feed-forward process of trial and error. A connectionist representation of a neural network is provided in Exhibit 16–5. It contains an input layer (factors), a hidden layer, and an output. Nonlinearity is introduced in the hidden layer as each of the inputs mathematically interrelate before being processed and compared with the output. Removal of the hidden layer creates a regression model.

EXHIBIT 16-4

Data Pattern Phase Plane

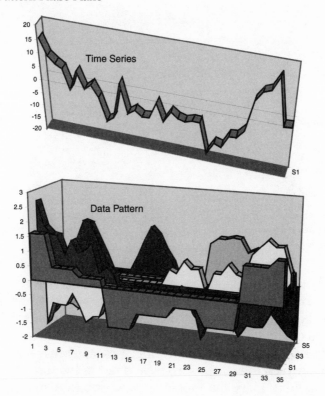

Neural networks are very powerful pattern recognition tools. Significantly, neural networks learn the most significant patterns first. However, their powerful learning algorithm also enables them to learn both significant patterns and spurious correlations. Great care and experience must be used in building neural network models as it is practically impossible to examine the weight matrices once constructed. The matrices are complex as even a five factor model would create a complex mathematical function that would be difficult to examine. Detractors commonly call neural networks *black boxes* because of this characteristic. Genetic algorithms (GAs) also learn patterns from data but encode patterns as rules. Genetic algorithms derive their power from crossover and from simultaneous testing of many components. Crossover, in combination with

EXHIBIT 16–5

Sample Neural Net

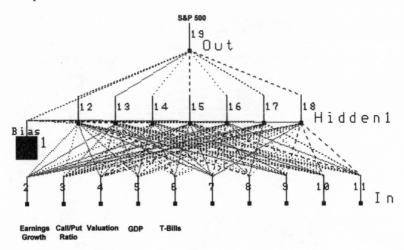

survival of the fittest, allows the best components of differing solutions to combine to form even better solutions. Although the GA visits a fixed number of solutions each generation, it effectively samples a much greater number of components, leading to a highly effective search. It is essentially these components—the genetic material—which the GA processes, and not individual solutions.

In Exhibit 16–6, the crossover and subsequent mutation is illustrated. In a financial application, a GA may discover that one variable or component, such as price/earnings ratio, is a better indicator of future return than another variable, such as earnings momentum. In this case, the GA would place more emphasis on the price/earnings variable and less on earnings momentum. One advantage that GAs offer over NNs is the GAs ability to learn user-comprehensible rules, along with the reasoning underlying each rule. As an example, a GA might generate the following rule:

If Earnings Momentum >10% & Volatility >7% &. . .
Then Future Return Forecast = Up

This reality-check feature provides comfort to detractors of black boxes. Do these nonlinear techniques work?

Increasingly, money management firms are actively researching and in some cases as in our firm, Advanced Investment Technology,

EXHIBIT 16–6

One Generation of a Genetic Algorithm

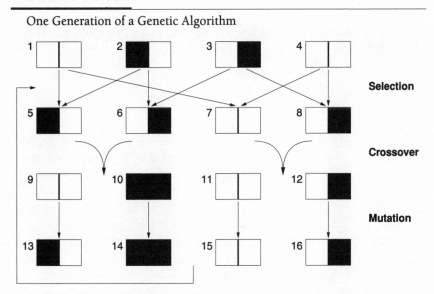

Inc., are managing significant investor capital with a good deal of success using nonlinear techniques. The academic community is also actively researching nonlinear techniques in their application to financial asset pricing with some interesting results. The Santa Fe Institute sponsored a time-series-forecast competition and found that many of the best submissions were neural networks.[2] Perhaps more significant, a recent paper by Hutchinson, Lo, and Paggio of MIT's Sloan School of Management, stated that "network pricing formulas may be more accurate and computationally more efficient alternatives when the underlying asset's price dynamics are unknown."[3] Findings like these combined with growing success by practitioners will undoubtedly move financial computational intelligence into the mainstream. In fact, one could argue rather convinc-

2. N.A. Gershenfeld and A.S. Weigend, "The Future of Time Series: Learning and Understanding," *Time Series Prediction: Forecasting the Future and Understanding the Past*, The Santa Fe Institute, 1993, pp. 1–7.

3. J.M. Hutchinson, A.W. Lo, T. Paggio, "A Nonparametric Approach to Pricing and Hedging Derivative Securities via Learning Networks," *IFSRC No. 277–94, International Financial Services Research Center*, Discussion Paper (Cambridge: Sloan School of Management, Massachusetts Institute of Technology, 1994) pp. 1–49.

ingly that these new approaches represent the natural evolution of quantitative money management.

In summary, the world is not flat and asset prices do not move in straight lines. For this reason, financial computational intelligence is here to stay.

REFERENCES

Barr, D., and Mani, G. *Neural Networks in Investment Management: Multiple Uses. Proceedings of the Second International Conference on AI Applications on Wall Street.* Gaithersburg, MD: Software Engineering Press, 1993.

Gershenfeld, N.A., and Weigend, A.S. "The Future of Time Series: Learning and Understanding." *Time Series Prediction: Forecasting the Future and Understanding the Past.* The Santa Fe Institute, 1993.

Hsieh, D.A. "Nonlinear Dynamics in Financial Markets: Evidence and Implications." *Financial Analysts Journal,* July–August 1995.

Hutchinson, J.M.; Lo, A.W.; and Paggio, T. "A Nonparametric Approach to Pricing and Hedging Derivative Securities via Learning Networks." *IFSRC No. 277-94, International Financial Services Research Center, Discussion Paper.* Sloan School of Management, Massachusetts Institute of Technology, 1994.

Mahfoud, S., and Mani, G. "Genetic Algorithms for Predicting Individual Stock Performance." *Proceedings of the Third International Conference on Artificial Intelligence Applications on Wall Street.* Gaithersburg, MD: Software Engineering Press, 1995.

Packard, N.H. "A Genetic Learning Algorithm for the Analysis of Complex Data." *Complex Systems,* 4, no. 5 (1990).

17

⑥ DATA/COMPUTER SECURITY

Don Berliner
*Senior Vice President, Management
Information Systems and Analysis
Kenmar*

Nothing in this chapter is burglar-proof or even foolproof. What we suggest are some fairly simple and practical measures that can make it more difficult to lose data due to accident or maliciousness. You still have to decide what suggestions make the most sense in your situation. (Note that my emphasis is on PCs and Novell networks. Thus, the examples used are specific to those environments although the thrust of the content is relevant to any environment.)

HARDWARE: PHYSICAL SECURITY
DON'T LET 'EM TOUCH IT!

When it comes to the security of an individual workstation, you are probably concerned about several different things. First, you don't want that workstation (or any piece of it) walking out the door with an employee, competitor, or stranger. Second, you would prefer not to see it harmed in any way. To prevent theft or damage, you can simply lock up the thing. If your office door has a lock, lock it. If not, you can buy cable and lock combinations that tie the computer to the desk. That way, a really ambitious thief will be forced to take the entire desk unit along with the computer. Why don't most people do that? It is a simple but ugly-looking solution.

What you can do fairly easily is lock the computer, using the key lock located on most computers available today. Why don't most people use those? Laziness, I suppose. Or, perhaps fear of keeping yet another key in a safe place or on an already crowded key ring. This CPU lock is not a real ironclad defense, of course. But, at least it is an easy way to stop the casual thief.

Another simple step that few people take advantage of is the start-up password. Many computers today have the option to require a password after the machine is turned on but before any real action takes place. Why not do this? Other than the inconvenience of remembering yet another password in your life's collection, this is a simple way of keeping others out of your PC. Of course, some office environments where machines are shared would necessitate sharing passwords. And, there is always the little office rascal who one day decides to change it and not tell the others.

One legitimate problem with start-up passwords is in office settings in which machines are rebooted automatically and are left unattended. If the machine is used for remote access, for example, it most likely requires some software to be loaded automatically on start-up. With a start-up password, the machine would sit unattended at the prompt for a start-up password and never get to the point of loading the software allowing the remote access.

How about the floppy drives? Most computers have them and you may want to restrict their usage. Maybe you don't want employees routinely taking home your entire customer file on a single 3½-inch disk slipped into a shirt pocket. Sure, they could still walk off with a printed list. But, a 150-page printout is still not as tempting as one single floppy disk. Readily available freeware and shareware programs can completely turn off the floppy disk drives, both in the stand-alone PC and in network settings. In one case, all you need do is run a short program (from some start-up file) so that users aren't even aware of it. Even on the off chance that they see its name when it runs, they are highly unlikely to know how to reverse its effects.

Surely you could disable the floppy drives mechanically, inside the PC case. The only problem with this is that, should you need to do something requiring floppy disk access, you would have to take the time to reverse the process. A software solution is a lot easier to reverse.

When in the start-up process should you execute this protection? Usually you want to turn this on as early in the process as you can. That way, by the time the user has rubbed her eyes or sipped his coffee waiting for the computer to boot up, the deed is done and you are protected. Many network administrators prefer to wait until the user logs into the network to execute any protection from the fileserver. The only drawback to this is that it won't be effective if a very savvy user manages to interrupt the bootup process before it proceeds to log in.

If you decide not to worry about the floppy drive, the hard disk drive will only add to the problem. Why should you care about the hard disk, which generally cannot be stuffed into a shirt pocket and spirited away? It is not too much of a stretch to imagine an evildoer copying crucial files to the hard disk while attached to the network, and then copying the files to a floppy disk when it isn't deactivated.

Generally speaking, you cannot restrict access to the hard disk because at the very least it is normally the boot device from which the PC starts up. Unless, of course, you bring in a diskless workstation which naturally eliminates the issue. A diskless workstation is then set up to boot from the network itself. These haven't exactly infiltrated the networking world because, I suspect, it is still more convenient for the network manager to deal with and troubleshoot normal hard-disk-booting computers. (For more solutions to the hard-disk question, please see the next section.)

Okay, so it is the rare MIS manager who insists that all workstations be locked up both in a physical and a logical or software sense. But, when it comes to network file-servers, you are taking much more of a risk by not doing so.

First and foremost, and very simply put, keep your file servers in a secure physical environment. Treat them as royalty: Don't let them mingle with the riffraff (translation: common workstations). Disgruntled or misguided individuals could cause quite a bit of damage if they gained access to a file server. I know file servers are the central linchpins of your network but at least place them in a corner of the amphitheater, not center stage. You want them out of the spotlight. Even better is a separate room; better still is a *locked* separate room. Just make sure that somebody (like a network administrator and his or her associates) still has access.

SOFTWARE: INTELLECTUAL SECURITY
DON'T LET 'EM TOUCH IT

The next consideration after physical security is logical or software security measures. What can you do to protect malicious or innocent damage to a workstation's hard disk, for example? One simple course of action is to make the workstation's key start-up files read-only. (Of course you have to remember when making any changes to those files to remove that attribute first.) The next, even better alternative, in the recent DOS-only past, might have been to run a program that makes the entire disk read-only. However, the advent of the Windows age has complicated the hard-disk-protection situation. Windows itself and many of the applications that run within it insist on writing temporary files to the hard disk. Thus, you cannot totally lock up the hard disk or make it read-only.

Available hard-disk security programs enable you to encrypt your hard disk so that even if the boot-up process is interrupted at the earliest possible point, the hard disk would read like alphabet soup. These programs do not enjoy widespread popularity mostly, I suspect, because PC administrators are extremely nervous about the robustness of such encryption. What happens if the secret decrypting passwords are lost or forgotten? Does that necessitate an entire redoing of numerous hard disks? It sounds like more headache than it is worth.

One solution I have heard suggested sounds silly at first, but could be a simple way of at least discouraging the wanton copying of files to the hard disk instead of the network. And it doesn't get in the way of Windows or applications needing to write temporary files to the hard disk. Just copy some nonsense files of sufficient size to the hard disk to eat up most of the disk, still leaving some room for those temporary files. Mark them hidden and read-only too. Then, a user will be effectively blocked from storing anything substantial on the hard disk. Of course this will only deter the beginner; anyone who knows how to find, unmark, and erase files can thwart this.

In a networked situation, after a workstation boots up, the user must somehow then be connected to the network. It is highly recommended that you set things up to automatically lead users to some type of log-in screen, preferably one from which they cannot

escape, interrupt, or drop out of. McAfee Associates' Saber Menuing system, for example, provides a log-in preprocessor program
that "splashes up" a bulletproof screen that allows only a log in.
The only other thing a user can do is totally reboot the computer.

Every user ID on the network should have its own password.
Obvious? We have seen networks on which the network supervisor—the individual with the ability to see, change, and delete anything on the entire network—did not have a password. In addition
to requiring passwords, require that they be at least four or five
characters long, that users change their passwords at least once a
month, and that they cannot use the same password over again for
a while. Then, if an interloper somehow discovers a user password
(or a user insists on using a very simple word, e.g., his first name),
at least there is some guarantee that the window of opportunity
won't stay open for too long.

Users have been known to complain about having to change
their password once a month. Can you imagine that today's knowledge worker, accustomed to working at a sophisticated computer
on a complex network, complains about the need to think of 12
unique five-letter words a year to remember?

And, yes, the supervisor ID needs a secure password as well.
It is also a good idea to have the network supervisor create a relatively "normal" user ID for her use as well. Many network experts
advise the supervisor to use the supervisor ID only when necessary
to do supervisor-like things. Otherwise, log in as the normal user.
This not only keeps the supervisor's ID more secure but it also
allows you to experience any problems on the network that you
might not if you restricted your log-ins to using the privileged
supervisor's ID. You might want to keep a fairly normal test-user
ID on hand, too, one that you could jigger with to test various
aspects of security you set up.

Novell networks give you the option of turning on intruder
detection and lockout features. Intruder detection simply locks out
a user who tries to log in and repeatedly types in the wrong password. You can set the number of attempts allowed as well as the
length of the lockout time-period, during which the user is literally
locked out of the network. After that time passes, the user can try
again. Obviously the intent is to guard against someone attempting
to guess another user's password. With enough time and enough

guesses, anyone could eventually ascertain someone's private password. Locking the ID after a few attempts can be a real discouragement.

You also have available to you the ability to allow users to log in only from certain workstations (station restrictions) and during certain times of day (time restrictions). Thus, if you need to make sure that marketing stays off of accounting's machines or that no one logs in after 11 PM Sunday night, you can do it. Time restrictions also can automatically log all users off the network at a particular time (say 2 AM), in case they forget to do so.

Within the network landscape, there are a lot of different ways you can set up users' file-space real estate. At a minimum, you will want a user-specific area (in which would be stored any user-specific configuration files as well as any truly private files a user may want to keep) and various shared areas (usually oriented around a user's membership in a group; e.g., *finance, MIS, sales*, etc.). The latter allows for the sharing of files among members of the group, one of the most useful attributes of a network.

A major responsibility of the network administrator is to set up a logically organized system of trustee rights; for example, who is allowed to access what files on the network and in what manner (read, write, create, delete, etc.). Of course, the easiest thing for the administrator to do is to simply give everyone total access to everything. I guess you could say that is certainly a logically *organized* way of handling the situation. And it is definitely easy to administer.

But it accomplishes nothing. The built-in network security system is an extremely useful tool that should be used to its fullest advantage not only when initially setting up a network but on an ongoing basis thereafter! In fact, this is one aspect of a network that an administrator most likely is in constant connection with during the lifetime of the network.

Trustee rights fall into at least two different categories—subdirectory and file-based. You will generally make most use of the first, and will only use the second on a rare occasion. Subdirectory trustee rights dictate who can have what kind of file access to every file in a particular subdirectory. Obviously, to make optimum use of subdirectory trustee rights, you need to have set up a logically organized subdirectory structure on your network (starting with the group- and user-oriented configuration mentioned above).

In conjunction with that, it is very useful to attempt to organize the rights structure as much as you can around the network groups rather than the users. Let's say you have a network of 250 users organized into 15 groups (certain users are very likely members of multiple groups). In simple numbers, it makes your job a lot easier to assign and manage the trustee rights at the group level rather than to deal with it at an individual user level.

Analogously, it is much easier to assign the group rights to *groups* of files, such as a subdirectory, at a time, rather than to individual files. The individual-file-right assignment is left for those situations that are quirky exceptions to the general rules of your network file structure.

The trustee-rights system is quite sophisticated in that you can assign one group read-only access to a subdirectory and another read-write-create-delete access. This accommodates the situation in which one user group (e.g., administration) needs the full range of access to maintain (input, edit/update, delete) records in a database whereas another group (marketing) only needs to view the data.

(Realistically, the choice of the phrase *needs to* is a weaselly way of saying that marketing really should be protected from inadvertently wiping out portions of the database! Furthermore, a properly set up file-security system would, in this example, get marketing off the hook in case some important records *did* get deleted, and would better help you pinpoint the cause.)

You do want to pay some attention to how subdirectory trustee-rights extend down the levels of the subdirectory tree. Huh? Well, in Novell's Netware V3.X, for example, the rights you assign at a subdirectory are, by default, inherited by that subdirectory's subdirectories. By way of example, let's say you set up an *APPS* (as in APPlicationS) directory to house all your application software that users need to access, and within that general category you also set up a *WORD* subdirectory (in which you have installed the word processor software), a *SHEET* subdirectory (for the spreadsheet software), *GRAPHICS*, and so on for each major application.

Now, let's also assume that you want to limit certain groups' access to certain applications. At the same time, though, to keep things nice and simple, you have assigned the EVERYONE group on the network read-only access to the APPS directory. By default then, *everyone* has access to *every* application subdirectory. Now, you could store the applications you wish to limit outside of the APPS subdirectory altogether. But this messes up your attempts at neat, logical file structure organization. A snazzier way to do this is to just explicitly assign the most limited set of trustee rights at the specific application level. In other words, assign "N" (No rights) rights for that group to the application; this overrides the inherited rights from the APP subdirectory and prevents those users from even seeing what files are in the application nor reading from, writing to, creating, or deleting the files themselves.

Depending on the file structure and trustee-rights structure, this can all get somewhat confusing to keep straight, especially when you need to quickly determine what rights a specific user has in a specific directory. This is compounded by the fact that, at least with Netware V3.1X, there is no built-in way to ascertain a user's or group's *effective* rights to any specific subdirectory. The effective rights are those rights that a user can actually exercise in a particular subdirectory, resulting from the interaction of explicit rights assigned to the current directory's parent directory and its subdirectories and how the particular subdirectory inherits those rights, among other things. This speaks to the necessity to buy additional third-party software that augments Netware's inherent rights-auditing functionality by displaying the true nature of effective rights.

Another security tool, in addition to the use of user-group trustee rights assigned to subdirectories is the concept of user or group *equivalence.* You do want to use this feature very selectively because it is fairly easy to overlook that you have made user *Mary* equivalent to the *supervisor* temporarily to handle security affairs during your vacation.

Every so often you ought to run a security "fire drill" to check for inadvertent leaks that you may have allowed to seep into the system. Novell has its *SECURITY* program that does a very mild overview of some of the obvious possible holes in your network security (e.g., more rights than are normally appropriate assigned to a user or group, a user not required to change passwords periodically, a user whose password is the same as her user ID, a user ID that has not logged in for a substantial length of time, anyone who has *supervisor* equivalence). As usual, there are third-party utilities available that go much deeper than Novell's own. Particularly fun are the password-checking programs that compare your users' passwords with thousands of the most obvious choices to determine how easy it would be to break into a user's ID.

Now that you've got the file-servers (and any other network components, e.g., hubs, routers, communications servers, network modems, backup tape drives, etc.) physically isolated as much as you can from casual observers, you can go a simple step further and install a passworded screen-saver on each server too. Novell provided its own simplistic one in Netware V3.X, in the *MONITOR* program (the infamous creeping snake that crawls across the screen). There are many others available, some adding functionality by using a graph of fileserver activity (CPU utilization, for example) as the image that pops across the screen. Some are actually part and parcel of other programs that provide extensive file-server statistics and include the locked screen-saver as an extra.

Don't Let 'em *See* It

There are two very diverse philosophies here: First, let the network security system totally regulate user access and thus let the users access the operating system directly (whether it be a DOS prompt or native Windows). Second, keep the users within a highly structured menuing system to tightly control the things they can do on the network, and even *how* they can do them.

The first option lessens the administrative workload in that you are essentially saying to the users "I'll manage the underlying security system, I'll tell you where applications are located, and you do whatever you need to do in running applications." The second option requires additional front-end and continuing network administration in that you have to maintain some sort of network menu-control system.

However, the major advantage inherent in the second option is that, if a user has a problem, the network administrator knows precisely the series of steps that the user followed in running a particular application, thus greatly easing the headache of troubleshooting. None of the usual questions (Did you change into the subdirectory before running the word processor? Did you add the option necessary to run this graphics program optimally on a network? and so on) are necessary to help lay the groundwork for solving the problem. You know what the steps were because *you* laid them out in the network menu to begin with.

The idea of keeping the users in a tightly controlled menuing system from the moment they enter networkland is very appealing. To keep it tight, you must enforce a "no exit to DOS" rule too. Otherwise, a tiny crack in the ointment could still leave a user knee-deep in mud puddles. For those users (say, MIS people) who you are more comfortable letting stray into DOS city unchaperoned, you can always allow a passworded menu choice.

Similarly, if you were in a Windows 3.X environment, you would want to limit most users' access to commands that they could blithely use without you knowing exactly what steps they were dancing. Very simplistically, within Windows' Program Manager itself, you can limit the use of the File menu to disallow the File Run command for example. Many of the third-party menuing systems provide further sophisticated ways of either eliminating various commands or limiting their application to a particular situation.

The overriding philosophy of a centralized network menuing system should be "monkey doesn't see so monkey won't do." In other words, if at all possible, present a menu of just those items the user really needs. Don't let him even see the "forbidden city" of items he can't possibly execute because you haven't given him the security clearance to do so.

Certain network menu systems (McAfee's Saber System for one) make it particularly easy to do this by enabling you to display menu items, or not, dependent on a user's membership in a group. Thus, you could have the graphics programs available only for members of the research department. Other factors that can control the appearance of a menu item (or even an entire submenu) include user name (if group membership is too sweeping) and hardware restrictions (e.g., only users possessing VGA color monitors, or at least an 80486 CPU processor).

Did They Touch It or See It?

No matter how carefully you set up your network workstations, file-servers, file system structure, trustee rights, and network menu structure, nothing in life is perfect, right? Situations may still arise that either slip through your carefully concocted cocoon of security, or that you just need to document or track. For that you need an organized way of knowing who *can* access what and when, as well as who *is* accessing what and when.

What's the big deal? Doesn't the network operating system let you set, and thus see, which users and groups have access to what file areas? Sure it does, but not exactly in the most compact, organized fashion. That is because of the difference between *assigned rights* and *equivalent rights*. Thus, you might assign the sales group the *read* and *filescan* rights to a directory (call it \DATA\SALES) that the group needs to access on a read-only basis.

A user's access to any particular subdirectory or file is based on the net sum of several factors, including a user's rights to higher subdirectories in the file tree as well as the rights of any groups of which the user is a member. So, if two members of the sales group also happen to be members of the administration group who just happen to have write access to files in \DATA\SALES, they can obviously change data in files within that subdirectory. With the complicated treelike hierarchy of many networks and the intricate web of security rights, you cannot get a real idea of any user's particular rights to a specific directory without some way of netting out these rights (to what is commonly called *equivalent* rights).

Although Netware V3.1X offers no tool to do this, there are a number of third-party products that automatically do. Thus, you can choose a subdirectory and a group of users, and the program will run through all the relevant rights rules and generate a list of equivalent rights for you to view. This makes it a snap and is an indispensable tool to determine if a particular user could possibly have any kind of access to a particular file or subdirectory. It saves you from the tedium of investigating every right associated with the user, the user's groups, and the subdirectories up and down the directory tree.

That takes care of knowing who can possibly access what subdirectories and files. If you also use a network menu structure as suggested earlier, you also have that second entranceway as a means of controlling access.

How do you find out who *did* actually access certain files or subdirectories, either as a spot check of how complete your network security structure is or as evidence to support the suspicion of a particular violation? Again, native Netware V3.1x does not offer a way to do this. And, again, third-party utilities have sprung up to fill the void.

Every network manager should have such an "auditing" program in place. The big plus of an auditing program is that it can track an extremely wide range of user actions on the network— file reads, file writes, file creations, directory creates, directory removals, print-job creations, new-user creation, and so on, for any action that is documented in the network bindery—and it does so fairly transparently. The major drawback of an auditing program is that it can track an extremely wide range of user actions on the network.

Extremely is the key word here. You can go nuts with a good network auditing program, tracking every single wisp of network activity, creating gobs and gobs of report files at which you eventually stare blankly, trying to spot some significant needle in the reporting haystack before the volume of report files climbs to the point that they are beginning to clog up the network. This is not the way to manage a network. As is often the case in most management situations, *more* data do not equal *more* information.

Rather, you want to reduce the amount of information you need to look at in order to actually look at it. To help you maintain your sanity, a flexible network auditing program should offer the ability to *filter* the auditing function. In other works, you specifically control what network activity is audited, against what subdirectories and files, and for which users or groups. You obviously need to play with this to zero in on the ideal combination of simplicity and comprehensiveness. For starters, you might audit just the open file access to a specific subdirectory or collection of files (e.g., spreadsheets), monitor how readable the resultant audit report is, gauge how fast the audit files grow, and adjust accordingly.

Surely, a network auditing program can flush out evidence of network hacking, too. One simple trick is to set up a very secure (no one but the network supervisor has access) but dummy subdirectory with a particularly tempting name such as \DATA\ PRIVATE or XFILES. These contain some dummy files with equally seductive names to attract any lurking hackers in your midst. Then, focus an auditing filter very tightly on that subdirectory; use as detailed a filter as you can, trapping any kind of network activity possible against that subdirectory and its files. Under normal circumstances you should see no activity whatsoever showing up in the auditing program for this subdirectory. Anything that does pop up, in this classic example of an exception report, warrants focused investigation because it implies a serious breach of security.

REMOTE ACCESS
CAN THEY SEE IT FROM JERSEY CITY?

In this day and age of the telecommuter and the road warrior, remote access to your network offers more than convenience. It also extends the risk exposure. Now you have to worry about the possible violation of your network security by anyone able to dial into it—just another few million computer users out there.

To keep your network the walled city you want it to be, the software you use to remotely access your network should have included within it password protection. Yes, this is in addition to whatever network security (including IDs, passwords, trustee rights, etc.) you already have in place. If you ever begin to think this is just going too far, remember that remote access is potentially opening up your network to a large new audience—the world out there. The remote access software should also offer encryption to help prevent interlopers from listening in on your conversations with your network.

Some remote access programs let you set up a predetermined list of allowed callers as another way of intercepting invaders. A further desirable extension of this is automatic callback, in which the software receives your incoming call, validates your ID against a preset list, hangs up on you (with no remorse whatsoever), dials up your modem number from the preset list, and reconnects at that point. In this way, a stranger who tries to call in and manages to divine a valid ID and password will be cut off at the pass (assuming he hasn't broken into your home and attempted the act of sabotage from there).

Assuming you are using remote control software (that takes over control of a host PC sitting at your company's headquarters), the software often allows you to blank the screen and lock the keyboard at the host end. This prevents anyone who might be passing by or sitting at your company desk from looking over your shoulder at your remote-controlled screen, or from confusing you by hitting keys at the host keyboard end.

Nowadays, the explosion of interest in the Internet has led to droves of companies exploring the many ways of connecting to the information superhighway. At the same time, it has begun to drive network managers wacky with nightmares involving Internet hackers, viruses, stacks of E-mail messages clogging up a network, and so on. Even at this point the subject could warrant a book all its own and we cannot go into great detail here. Suffice it to say that no matter to what extent you wind up connecting, there are ways of protecting access to your data and your network.

The arena of Internet access works both ways. Once you give your users access to the Internet (or Compuserve, America OnLine, Prodigy, etc.), you may want to explore ways of limiting such access. This is not so much an issue of security but actually more one of productivity. Are there valid reasons to be using the Internet? Are there opportunities to get distracted on the Internet? Software to control and limit the areas that on-line users access is beginning to make its way into the marketplace—initially aimed at parents needing to control their children's access, interestingly enough. As the concern swells in the business environment, this software may no doubt find an even more applicable niche.

It would appear that Internet E-mail access is a minimum requirement these days. This can indeed be set up with very few security complications. After all, you are not opening up your network to direct access by any outsider, merely their E-mail messages. You do have to worry about two issues: First, the pure volume of messages that might be incoming and clogging up a network; and second, the possibility of incoming file attachments that your network user could receive and subsequently execute on your network.

The first issue is a small subset of a network manager's responsibilities—file space—that the manager always needs to monitor on an ongoing basis. The second issue can be controlled by other network management techniques that you already have in place. One example is a network menu system that simply doesn't allow the user to execute programs at whim nor to move such programs to public areas on the network from which anyone could execute them.

BACKUP
IF THEY DID TOUCH IT, DID THEY STEAL IT
OR BREAK IT AND CAN I GET IT BACK?

Backup is very simple. Your networking hardware will not function perfectly forever; some link in the chain will fail. The remedy is simple enough—backup. And the underlying philosophy of backup can be summed up in three simple words—*do it often!*

Okay, now that I've got you onboard and nodding wildly in agreement, tell us truthfully—do you? If not, you might as well skip the rest of this chapter and pack it up. Plain and simple, it is worth it to spend the time and money to assure that you have an effective backup plan. Don't *not* do it!

Indeed, whether or not the backup plan is effective is quite dependent on your environment. Where a weekly backup regimen might be sufficient for one, it might not feel comfortable for another. The obvious trade-off you must consider is how many hours' or days' worth of lost work is "okay" to deal with, versus the time and money spent to administer the backup of data. What we can do here is at least consider the variables involved in such a decision.

When to Do It
Particularly if you are going after a daily backup routine, the usual time picked is overnight, when most users are not on the network. Even here, though, you may need to pick your time carefully because of the increased use of after-hours capacity to run batch jobs (a chunk of work that can be set up to run at a later time). Your choice of particular backup device and media may also be a factor here, because a fast device requires a smaller idle-time window within which to work.

Why worry about the time of day (or night) you are running a backup? In general, a backup operation will burp if it encounters an open file (e.g., one being used by some user, or another job running on the network at the same time); most backup software can attempt to retry and digest the file later on but again the file must be available.

What if your network is constantly running things, 24 hours a day? You will have to make some accommodation and, for example, before running some time-consuming overnight job, copy *its* files to another location on the network. Then, when backup runs, it will still hiccup over the running application's files but will still go ahead and back up the previously copied files.

What Kind of Backup?

Trade-off time again: What combinations of backup type—full, differential, incremental—should you be setting up and how often? Let's first get some definitions straight:

Full backup: the whole shebang. *Incremental backup:* backs up only those files that have changed, or new files since the last backup of any kind. *Differential:* backs up only those files that have changed, or new files since the last *full* backup.

Some people get confused about the difference between the incremental and the differential. Let's say you run a full backup every Sunday night and, for each day (Monday through Saturday) of the upcoming week, you run an incremental backup. The result is that Monday night's tape will contain only those files that have changed or were new on Monday, Tuesday night's tape will contain only those files that have changed or were new on Tuesday, and so on.

On the other hand, if you kept the full backup every Sunday night but ran differential backups for each upcoming day, Monday night's tape would look exactly like the prior example, but Tuesday night's tape would contain files that changed or were new on Tuesday *and* Monday both; Wednesday night's tape would contain files that changed or were new on Wednesday, Tuesday, *and* Monday; and so on. It is a cumulative thing. Each day during the week, the differential backup would take longer than the previous day's differential tape.

If—heaven forbid, knock wood, clutch that rabbit's foot—the network crashed on Thursday morning, the first scenario would require you to restore Sunday night's full backup and each of Monday, Tuesday, and Wednesday night's backup, in order to get you back in business. The second scenario would take less time and only require Sunday night's backup and Wednesday night's differential (because it already contains Monday, Tuesday, and Wednesday's file changes). Get the difference? What it comes down to is this—the fuller you make the backup regimen, the longer it'll take but the easier it'll be to restore if you have to.

Most backup software lets you password encrypt the backup. Take advantage of this feature. It can help you sleep better at night knowing that, should the tape fall into the wrong hands, it would be unreadable and thus unusable. The backup media should also be stored in a secure area, at the very least a locked desk, room, or off-site locked facility.

Beauty Is in the Eyes of the Restorer
No matter how careful you are in setting up a logically organized backup regimen and diligent in maintaining the schedule and doing it right, "it don't have no style if you can't find that file." In other words, the proof is in the restoring. It is crucial to periodically test your backups by doing a restore on a sampling of files; otherwise, how will you know you can count on them when a problem with your network occurs? It also keeps you on speaking terms with the restore process, in case you need it. Less often, you may also want to test out a *FULL* restore, including the crucial network operating files, again to confirm the backup is working properly and to stay familiar with the process of completely restoring a fileserver.

Depending on the never-ending trade-off of time/money versus peace of mind, there are deeper layers you can add to the backup process. Some companies maintain a backup server, on and/or off the premises, that replicates the operating servers' files on a minute-by-minute or once-a-day basis, ready to be pumped into action if a file-server problem occurs. Depending on exactly how this is set up, a side benefit is that it can also ease the burden of the occasional restoration of files that a user mistakenly clobbers; you can just bring over the backup copy sitting on the backup server.

In other variations on the theme, you can hire third-parties to have a *hot site* available in case of disaster; that is, a loss of or major damage to your company premises. The hot site can be equipped with backup servers, workstations, printers, modems, and so on. This would be set up in conjunction with some sort of offsite network backup or other way of getting your operational data to the site (e.g., a direct high-speed communications link between your site and the hot site).

To summarize—*do it*. Problems of some sort will happen. And you want to be prepared. The planning and the preparation pay off in peace of mind when things are running smoothly, and in rapid recovery when the occasional problem occurs.

Test it. The best-laid plans of mice and men won't cut it unless you know they work in practice.

Review it. Periodically, look over the procedures, plans, and protocols you've got in place to make sure they are best in synch with your organization and its operations as they change.

Redo it, if necessary. And then go have a good night's sleep.

INDEX

Abbaei, Mike, 61
Average monthly return, 199–200
Axelrod, C. Warren, 95

Barr, Dean S., 327
Berliner, Don, 337
Business process reengineering (BPR), 3
    approaches to managing, 8–11
    case studies of, 6–8, 26–33
    definition and key characteristics of,
        11–13
    in financial services companies, 22–26,
        33–37
    introduction to, 4–5
    role of information technology in, 20–22
    role of organizational culture in, 18–20
    successes and failures of, 13–18
Buy-versus-build analysis, 62–63, 178–179;
    see also Vendors
    costs and, 64–65
    importance of management expertise
        and, 65–66
    resources and, 63–64

Church, Elizabeth C., 181
Client/Server
    applications best performed on, 50–57
    downsizing from a mainframe to, 57–59
    how, differs from a mainframe, 43–50
    rightsizing and, 41–43
Compounded annual return, 202

Data/computer security
    backup and, 351–354
    for hardware, 337–339
    remote access and, 349–350
    for software, 340–349
Data warehouses, 274–276
Desktop publishing, 266–268
Document imaging, 276–278
Drawdown analysis, 209–211

Electronic mail, 261–262
Electronic market mechanisms, 143–144
    institutional broker research and,
        144–145
    integration of trade management
        through, 151–154
    liquidity indicators and, 145–147
    order delivery through, 147–151
    post–trade processes and, 154–158
Electronic messaging standards
    industry standards groups and, 228–231
    the Internet and, 234, 238
    introduction to, 227–228
    outlook for, 233–234
    Swift message layout sample, 237
    Swift message types, 235–236
    the trading cycle and, 232–233

Financial computational intelligence, 327
    neural networks and genetic algorithms,
        332–336
    nonlinear complex systems, 330–331
    time-series forecasting using, 328–330
Frank, Michael, 285
Frankel, Claire, 227
Frankel, Ralph, 299

Gartland, Robert F., 239
Global technology management (GTM),
    77–78; see also Integrated order manage-
    ment systems
    drivers of, 78–81
    and emphasis on organizational devel-
        opment, 91–93
    financial management as a component
        of, 87–91
    product management and, 84–87
    technology teams and; see Technology
        team
Goodman, Esther Eckerling, 195
Groupware, 262–264

IBM, 4
Integrated order management systems;
  see also Global technology management
  (GTM)
  benefits of, 164–166
  broker links and, 171–172
  build-versus-buy decision and, 178–179
  implementation process for, 173–178
  overview of, 159–164
  portfolio modeling and, 166–169
  post-trade linkages and, 172–173
  trade blotter and, 169–171
Internet, 59, 234, 238, 268–270, 293–294
Intranets, 59, 265–266
ISDN, 281–283

Keim, Armand, 41

Legal considerations
  acceptance, 124–126
  confidentiality, 120–122
  deliverables, 109–111
  delivery, 122–123
  documentation, 115–118
  general provisions, 137–140
  installation, 123
  intellectual property rights indemnity,
    131–133
  ownership, 120
  price protection, 119–120
  pricing and payment terms, 118–119
  remedies, 133–135
  site preparation, 122
  software license, 111–115
  termination, 135–136
  training, 126–127
  warranty and maintenance, 127–131
Lewis, Russell D., 77

Mainframe, see Client/Server
MAR Ratio, 202
Measurement of risk, 199–202; see also Risk,
  management of
  graphical, 203–209
  qualitative, 217–219
  through ongoing monitoring of
    traders, 215

Measurement of risk—Cont.
  through portfolio monitoring, 215
Merrill Lynch & Company, 5
Monassebian, Jeff, 109
Multimedia, 280–281

Naber, Lance J., 257

Object technology
  analysis and design, 309–314
  introduction to, 299–306
  key success factors in, 314–317
  need for, 307–309
  planning software development process
    for, 319–322
  preparing for reuse of, 318
  risk factors in, 322–324
Organizational development, 91–93

Payment, clearance, and settlement
  systems, 239
  future outlook for, 248–252
  participants in, 241–245
  process of, 253–254
  reducing risk in, 245–248
  role of technology in, 240–241
Poplawski, Caroline, 195
Portfolio management and accounting, 181
  determining investment technology
    needs for, 185–191
  evaluating vendors and products for,
    191–194
  overview of, 182–184
  technological change and, 184–185

Request for proposal (RFP) process; see also
  Vendors
potential benefits of, 67
steps in, 66–67
Risk, management of, 195, 196–198; see also
  Measures of risk
  in a portfolio of traders, 219–223
Rightsizing; see also Client/Server
  overview of, 41–43
Rosen, Joseph, 195
Rovenpor, Janet L., 3

Sharpe Ratio, 201
Standard deviation, 200–201
    replacing, 211–212
Sterling Ratio, 201–202
Strategic systems technology
    introduction to, 257–258
    risks of implementing, 258–261

Technology team
    assessment centers and, 83–84
    staffing a, 81–83
Telecommunications, 285–286
    implentation of, 289–291
    the Internet and, 293–294
    management issues concerning, 291–293
    and the strategic plan, 286–287
    technical background on, 295–298
Telephony, 278–280

Transition technologies, 95–96
    costs and benefits of, 101–107
    financial evaluation of, 96–101, 107–108

Vendors;
    buy-versus-build analysis and; *see*
        Buy-versus-build analysis
    evaluating and contracting with, 61–62,
        67–76
    legal issues relating to; *see* Legal
        considerations
    RFP process and; *see* Request for
        proposal (RFP) process
Videoconferencing, 270–271
Voice recognition, 272–274
Voice synthesis, 272

Walsh, Vincent A., 159

Other books of interest to you from Irwin Professional Publishing . . .

THE POWER OF IT
Maximizing Your Technology Investments

Timothy Braithwaite

Using familiar examples and easily understood models to illustrate complex issues, author Timothy Braithwaite gives non-technical business managers the means to communicate confidently with individuals and companies regarding information technology. In addition, *The Power of IT* enables business managers to better evaluate the quality awareness and practices of potential providers of information technology. (200 pages)
ISBN: 0-87389-349-2

THE INFORMATION TECHNOLOGY REVOLUTION IN FINANCIAL SERVICES
Using IT to Create, Manage, and Market Financial Products

William S. Sachs & Frank Elston

The Information Technology Revolution in Financial Services gives every banker insight to innovative and powerful tools for using customer information. Readers now have the ability to easily and effectively develop solid customer leads, identify cross-selling prospects and custom-design products to meet customer's needs. This book takes banking technology from the back room to the front-line. (300 pages)
ISBN: 1-55738-385-5

THE IRWIN HANDBOOK OF TELECOMMUNICATIONS MANAGEMENT
Second Edition

James Harry Green

This practical, hands-on guide details the techniques and skills necessary to manage a complete telecommunications system efficiently and effectively. Using numerous case studies as well as on-the-job problems and solutions, Green has thoroughly updated and expanded this comprehensive source for:
  • Forecasting telecommunications service needs.
  • Selecting data communications equipment and services.
  • Planning effective telecommunications security.
(675 pages)
ISBN: 0-7863-0480-4

Available at fine bookstores everywhere.